Project Management
in Construction

Other McGraw-Hill Titles of Interest

Project Management in Construction

Sidney M. Levy

Second Edition

McGraw-Hill, Inc.

New York   San Francisco   Washington, D.C.   Auckland   Bogotá
Caracas   Lisbon   London   Madrid   Mexico City   Milan
Montreal   New Delhi   San Juan   Singapore
Sydney   Tokyo   Toronto

Library of Congress Cataloging-in-Publication Data

Levy, Sidney M.
    Project management in construction / Sidney M. Levy—2nd ed.
       p.   cm.
    Includes index.
    ISBN 0-07-037590-9
    1. Construction industry—Management. 2. Industrial project
management. I. Title.
HD9715.A2L44 1994
624'.068'4—dc20   93-21585
                                        CIP

1 2 3 4 5 6 7 8 9 0 DOC/DOC 9 9 8 7 6 5 4 3

ISBN 0-07-037590-9

The sponsoring editor for this book was Larry Hager, the editing supervisor was Caroline Levine, and the production supervisor was Pamela A. Pelton. It was set in Century Schoolbook by Judith N. Olenick.

Printed and bound by R. R. Donnelley & Sons Company.

This book is printed on recycled, acid-free paper containing a minimum of 50% recycled de-inked fiber.

Contents

Chapter 12. Design-Build   225

Chapter 13. Safety in Construction   249

Chapter 14. OSHA Safety and Health Standards   263

x   Contents

Preface

Project management is one of the most important aspects within the entire construction process. Without it, the best planned project risks failure, but on the other hand, a faltering project may be saved from disaster if strong project management skills and techniques are brought to bear in time.

Just like a ship that cannot function with more than one skipper, so must there be one central figure to guide the construction project through perilous waters that lie ahead. This central figure needs to have sufficient knowledge of the entire construction process and act as the focal point for the many activities that must be united into one synchronized effort.

The project manager will be largely responsible for converting the two-dimensional construction drawings and the pages upon pages of written instructions into a three-dimensional structure that will house people and their machines.

The role of project management does not necessarily require the skills normally associated with a graduate engineer. The construction industry is a business, albeit a technically oriented one, and the qualities required of a top-flight project manager depend as much on good business judgment and the ability to work with people as on familiarity with sound engineering practices.

Project Management in Construction has been written to identify, define, address, explain, and illuminate the nonengineering skills that are so essential to the pursuit of a successful career in the building business.

I have been associated with the industry for more than 35 years. From summer jobs in high school to labor foreman, time clerk, superintendent, project manager, and senior vice president of a major general contracting firm in Connecticut, I can relate to the field and office activities that make this industry so interesting, so frustrating, and so rewarding.

Project Management in Construction contains many of the experiences culled out of a career in building the full range of residential, commercial, and industrial projects including high-rise apartments and office buildings, hotels and motels, manufacturing and research facilities, and various institutional structures in the private and public sectors.

There is an old saying, "Smart men learn from experience; wise men learn from the experience of others." Hopefully *Project Management in Construction* will fortify that proverb.

Sidney M. Levy

Project Management
in Construction

Introduction to the Construction Industry

The construction industry in this country is a microcosm of the American economic system. Where else can be found so many small, family-owned businesses, entrepreneurial to the core, seeking to carve out a niche in a hotly competitive marketplace, where hard work and a little luck can reap such big rewards? Of the more than 400,000 construction companies in the United States, more than 99 percent are small-business enterprises.

Construction Industry—Trends and Statistics

The construction industry in the United States is big business. The industry as a whole employs in excess of $4\frac{1}{2}$ million on-site workers and accounts for about 4.7 percent of the entire country's gross national product (GNP). When the value of building supplies and equipment used in construction is added such as structural steel, lumber, and concrete, construction's contribution of the GNP approximates 10 percent. But that's only part of the story, according to statistics published by the Associated General Contractors of America (AGC). For each dollar spent on new construction, a total of $3.61 in economic activity is generated across all industries and other services. And according to AGC, for each dollar of new construction, the earnings of households in the state in which it was spent is increased by $1.09.

The construction industry employs 33 percent more people than food stores and twice as many workers as the automobile industry and service stations combined.

In 1991 the volume of all construction in the United States amounted to $358.5 billion (in constant 1987 dollars), continuing a downward trend that began in 1986 when construction volume was valued at $421.4

billion. The recession that gripped the country in 1989 and continued through 1993 has had a devastating effect on the industry. While it is estimated that the industry will increase its volume to $378 billion in 1992, it is still well off the $400 billion marketplace that characterized the mid-to-late 1980s. Fewer projects on which to bid has created even more competition in an already fiercely competitive marketplace. Low profit margins have gone even lower, and costly mistakes have caused dramatic increases in business failures. Construction company failures in New England rose 106.8 percent between 1989 and 1990. In the middle Atlantic states 54.6 percent of the contractors in that area closed their doors during that same period of time, while in the southern Atlantic and central southeastern states, construction company failures rose by slightly more than 30 percent. And this trend seemed to continue in 1991, when Dun and Bradstreet reported a 47.8 percent increase in construction failures during the first quarter of that year. The excesses of the 1970s and 1980s and the euphoria that surrounded the real estate and banking businesses in those two decades are now taking their toll in the 1990s, and the seemingly loose and uncontrolled flow of investment funds and the ragtag development of projects may never be repeated.

Contractors will have to think and act smarter in the 1990s and beyond to survive, and management skills will need to be honed even sharper.

Former Assistant Secretary of the Army Robert W. Paige stated the case for better management clearly when he addressed an industry group several years ago:

> Every time this industry has failed, it's because of bad management. Every company that failed was managed badly. I don't know why we don't emphasize that, it's extremely important. You've got to start training people in college to at least begin thinking about management. And when they get out they have to understand that there's a bigger deal out there than just engineering or building. They must understand that they are going to a business. They will be part of the largest damn private sector business in the United States. Somebody has to manage it.

The Changing Role of the General Contractor

The character and role of the general contractor (GC) have changed over the past several decades. There was a time when the GC would construct almost every phase of the work with his own tradespeople.* As buildings became more complicated and business in general became more sophisticated, the special trade contractor, better known as a *subcontractor*, gained prevalence in the industry. In 1991, these special

---

*For the reason that the parties to a construction contract may be of either gender and may be singular or plural (individuals, partnerships, or corporations), singular, masculine pronouns are used throughout this book. That is the practice of the American Institute of Architects also.

trade contractors represented about 75 percent of all construction company establishments. General contractors increasingly assumed the role of broker, performing less and less work with their own work crews and relying more and more on a strong nucleus of subcontractors. The role of the construction superintendent also changed during this period of time, as he became a manager of peers rather than lord and master of the company's own work crews.

Changing to survive in the 1990s and beyond

Change is nothing new to contractors. When new construction activity is down, renovation and retrofit work is pursued. When private work is scarce, bids are prepared for public work. There are trends in the industry that are becoming more pronounced and will require changes in the way many contractors have been conducting business, if they want to even the odds on survival. And in the future contractors will have to devote more time and effort to basic business fundamentals.

Cost control

Although cost control has always been a critical part of the contractor's portfolio, the "tight" bidding market that developed in the early 1990s has created a need to control costs with even more diligence. More contractors pursuing diminishing markets resulted in still lower profit margins in the competitive bid market, and even negotiated work saw downward pressure being exerted on builder's profits.

Volume versus profits

Rapid growth without corresponding controls and capable personnel is another killer. Contractors are becoming more aware of the need to increase profits rather than increase volume and hope for the best. Bloated organizations are downsizing back to a critical mass.

Marketing and strategic planning

Well-thought-out and professionally executed marketing plans began to take shape in the construction industry in the past few years, and, coupled with strategic planning, many contractors have now mapped out the markets they wish to tap and have set plans in motion to reach those markets. More and more contractors are "specializing," becoming more proficient in interiors fitup, medical and pharmaceutical work, cleanroom construction, and so forth. They find that competition in these markets is somewhat limited and profit margins may be more stable.

Financial management

No longer can Aunt Sophie come in twice a week to work on the "books." With bankers and bonding companies requiring more sophisticated financial audits before agreeing to provide working capital and bonds, the bookkeeper of yesterday is giving way to the comptroller or financial professional. Tight profit margins require close scrutiny of the business' cash flow, and credit and collection policies take on added importance.

Human resources

Construction is a people business, and the job becomes more difficult if qualified, dedicated managers are lacking in the organization. Creating and maintaining a dynamic company may make it somewhat easier to attract the right people, but developing the proper compensation package has also taken on new dimensions in order to keep these valued employees and reward them properly. An increasing number of companies are looking at compensation packages tied to performance instead of automatic yearly salary increases supplemented by year-end bonuses. Performers are rewarded, while laggards are not.

Risk and the Contractor

All businesses have associated risks, but the construction industry seems to have more than its fair share, as reflected in the following chart of U.S. business failures in 1990:

Mining	0.6%
Agriculture	2.9%
Transportation and utilities	4.3%
Finance and real estate	6.4%
Nonclassifiable	6.9%
Wholesale trade	7.2%
Manufacturing	7.9%
Construction	13.4%
Retail trade	21.2%
Service	29.2%

SOURCE: Dun and Bradstreet, AGC.

All the facts and figures cited support the following thumbnail sketch of the construction business:

> The U.S. construction industry in overall physical size and volume of business conducted, is a major force in the economy. It is characterized by a large number of independently owned and operated small companies that work close to their home base. To survive and prosper, these companies must be able to shift into whichever segment of construction activity is prospering.

Because of any number of outside forces, and by its very nature—building a one-off product subject to the vagaries of the market in an outdoor factory—it is much more risky than the average industrial business establishment.

The risk factor lies at the heart of the construction industry, and it is possibly the main reason for this book. The potential for risk taking and the various uncertainties unique to the construction process make the need for competent, capable managers even more critical than in other industries. Along with the normal economic cycles and the effect of interest rates on construction activity, risk emanates from the very foundation of the industry: the construction estimate.

The construction estimate is just that—an estimate. The basis for a multi-million-dollar contract is the amalgamation of educated guesses obtained from a number of sources. These guesses include an interpretation of the work required, gleaned from a set of drawings and specifications; estimation of what the exact cost of labor and materials will be at some point in the future; a prediction of weather conditions during the construction cycle; and the anticipated cost to complete a specific unit of work that has never been exactly performed before.

The Project Manager's Role

Control over the work process and control over the costs associated with the work process are overwhelmingly important in the construction business. But it doesn't stop there. Management of a construction project can be divided into four major components:

Construction engineering.   The proper technique of assembling materials and components and selecting the best construction technology for a given project.

Project management.   How best to implement the construction process which would include proper scheduling, coordination, and controlled flow of materials and equipment to the job site.

Human resources management.   Since labor productivity and a harmonious working environment are critical to an effective construction process, control over these factors becomes important.

Financial management.   Construction is a business, and control over costs, cash flow, and project funding is an essential part of any successful endeavor.

All these tasks, to some degree, will fall to the most visible member of the construction team: the project manager.

The project manager's role in the construction process may vary from company to company. Depending on the size and sophistication of the individual firm, the project manager will have more, or less, support staff. Some companies will have the project manager prepare and assemble the construction estimate, and when a contract award is made, negotiate all the subcontracted work, purchase all the materials required, and administer the construction process. Other companies divorce the estimating function from project management, and still others maintain separate purchasing departments to negotiate subcontracts and issue purchase for materials and equipment.

In smaller companies the project manager will probably assume more functions. He may log in, review, and process shop drawings; prepare monthly requisitions; update schedules and various reports; and even follow up on delinquent payments from owners.

The one responsibility which remains constant in the role of project manager is that of administering the construction process. Project management means managing projects, and that is what this book is all about.

2

The Start of the Construction Process

The construction contract, in its many forms, is usually the trigger to the construction process. If there is a delay in the preparation of a formal contract agreement, the letter of intent is often used as an interim measure. Let's take a closer look at these documents.

The Letter of Intent

The letter of intent is usually a temporary measure to authorize the commencement of construction. Limits are often placed on the extent of construction to be performed and the dollar value of liability that will be assumed by the issuer of the letter of intent.

This document may authorize the general contractor, for instance, to perform specific tasks such as sitework or site preparation up to a certain agreed-on sum, or a letter of intent may be issued by an owner prior to the actual start of construction to permit the preparation of reinforcing-steel shop drawings or even structural-steel shop drawings with a specific dollar cap on these costs. There are several reasons for using a letter of intent. An owner may have received a verbal commitment for construction funding from a lending institution but wants to await a formal, written commitment before assuming all the financial obligations that a construction contract would effect. The owner may decide to assume some degree of risk in order to get a much-needed construction project under way and could decide on the letter of intent to do so. The letter of intent should be rather specific as to the limits of the work to be performed with respect to scope and reimbursable costs and associated fees. If there are plans and specifications available at the time, the letter of intent can reference those drawings and define the scope of work that is to be performed. If no plans or specifications are available, then the scope of work can be spelled out in the body of the letter of intent. A typical letter of intent might be worded as follows:

> Pursuant to the issuance of a formal contract for construction, the undersigned authorizes the J. J. Batter Construction Company to proceed with tree removal in the area designated on Drawing L-100, prepared by ABC Engineers, dated October 21, 1993. All debris including tree stumps are to be removed from the job site and erosion control measures indicated on Drawing L-101, ABC Engineers, dated October 21, 1993, are to be installed. All the above work is not to exceed $75,000, including the contractor's overhead and profit.
>
> *signed*: J. J. Impatient
> President
> Hurryup Corporation

Scope, tasks, and reimbursables included in these letters of intent may extend to shop drawing preparation; cancellation charges for any materials orders; and in-house costs incurred by the general contractor for estimating, accounting, or interim project management expenses. All costs incurred during work under a letter of intent should be segregated in such a manner that if the work does not proceed beyond the letter-of-intent stage, all associated costs and fees can be identified and invoiced. If and when a formal contract is issued for the complete job, it may contain all the work performed under the letter of intent, and all payments made by the owner will be credited to the contract amount.

While operating under the limits of a letter of intent from the project owner, the general contractor may have to make certain commitments to various suppliers and subcontractors, and any purchase orders or contracts issued to these vendors or subcontractors should contain the same basic language as the letter of intent.

For example, if the owner's letter of intent contains provisions for the preparation of structural-steel shop drawings and the placing of a mill order for structural steel, the restrictions placed on the general contractor must also be placed on the structural-steel subcontractor in the letter of intent prepared for that subcontractor.

There could be times when a contractor may be tempted to proceed with construction without a contract, letter of authorization, or letter of intent because a very favorable relation exists between contractor and client; however, this can be risky business for any number of reasons, such as changes in executives in one or both organizations, misinterpretation of what was actually agreed on, or a desire to back out of a previously issued verbal commitment. Requesting a letter of intent while awaiting a formal contract is not only the proper business approach but is also a way of preserving a previously established good relationship since misunderstandings will probably be lessened or avoided altogether.

Prevalent Types of Construction Contracts

Most construction contracts today will take one of the following forms:

1. Cost of the work plus a fee

2. Cost of the work plus a fee with a *guaranteed maximum price* (GMP)

3. Stipulated or lump sum

4. Construction management (CM)

Cost of the work plus a fee

Although this form of contract may appear to need no explanation, a definition of what constitutes "cost" may not be so clear. A cost-plus-fee contract is as the name implies; the contractor will perform a certain scope of work and will be reimbursed for the cost of that work plus a fee usually calculated on a percentage basis. Cost-plus contracts are seldom used, but when they are there must be good communication between contractor and owner to avoid misunderstandings and possible disputes.

This form of contract is often used when severe time restrictions are imposed on the owner and it becomes necessary to begin construction as quickly as possible—often without the benefit of well-defined plans and specifications.

For instance, the owner of an office building may have an opportunity to lease space to a tenant that requires occupancy in short order and demolition of existing work must begin immediately in order to facilitate the implementation of the new configuration. If a well defined scope of work can be established in a narrative form, even without plans and specifications, the contractor can create budget estimates for various phases or components of the cost-plus work so that the owner can have some idea of the order of magnitude of costs that ought to be committed to the project.

It is not uncommon for plans and specifications to be developed as these cost-plus projects are under way, and it becomes essential for the general contractor to promptly review these documents and report back to the owner if the scope of work changed drastically and will therefore alter the original concept, scope, and corresponding estimate.

Hopefully, the cost-plus-fee contract will be used only as a temporary measure until enough contract documents can be produced to support a more finite form of contractual arrangement. If that is not the case, and the cost-plus-fee contract will be used throughout the project, the project manager may look forward to a "learning experience." For example, in the initial discussions with an owner a clear understanding of what a "cost" is must be established. The standard American Institute of Architects (AIA) Document A111, Cost of the Work Plus a Fee, defines costs to be reimbursed and those which are not to be reimbursed. These "costs" can be summarized as follows:

Costs to be reimbursed:

1. Wages paid for labor, including all fringe benefits

2. Salaries of contractor's personnel stationed at the job site. (If project management is stationed in the office and these costs are to be reimbursed, this should be clarified with the owner.)

3. Cost of insurance, taxes, assessments, unemployment compensation, and other remuneration paid to employees working on the project

4. Portion of reasonable travel and subsistence expenses incurred by contractor while administering the cost-plus work

5. Cost of all materials, equipment, and supplies used, including freight, delivery, and unloading charges

6. Payments made by general contractor to subcontractors

7. Cost of hand tools and other consumables used in performance of the work and not salvageable at the end of the project. (When power tools are purchased for the cost-plus work, sometimes the owner will request that they be turned over to him at the end of the job since he has paid for them!)

8. Rental charges on all equipment and machinery, exclusive of hand tools, and the repair costs associated with the equipment and machinery

9. Bond and insurance premiums

10. Sales and use taxes associated with the project

11. Permits, fees, and deposits lost for causes other than contractor's negligence

12. Losses and expenses not compensated by insurance if they result from causes other than the fault or negligence of the contractor

13. Minor expenses such as faxes, telephone calls, express mail, and petty-cash items associated with the work

14. Debris removal

15. Costs associated with an emergency affecting the safety of personnel

16. Other costs specifically agreed on and approved in writing in advance

Costs not to be reimbursed:

1. Salaries or other compensation for contractor's personnel in contractor's principal or branch offices

2. Expenses of contractor's principal and branch offices

3. Any part of contractor's capital expenses

4. Overhead or general expenses except as expressly included in costs-to-be-reimbursed contract

5. Costs due to negligence of the contractor

Changes to, additions to, or subtractions from these standard "costs" need to be clearly stated when the agreement is formulated and the segregation of these costs during construction will be an important part of the project manager's administrative duties.

The author had an experience with one cost-plus-fee contract that illustrates the dangers facing the project manager who is working with an owner under that type of contract. The owner of a vacant 80,000-ft^2 one-story building had been trying to lease all or a portion of it for several years with no luck. The building had once been a supermarket and consisted largely of open space. Heating and cooling was accomplished through rooftop units with little or no distribution ductwork. The floors were covered with vinyl-composition tile, and because moisture had been present in the building since it had not been heated or cooled for years, many of these floor tiles were loose and badly cupped. The ceilings were 2×4 acoustical tiles which were also badly warped and discolored. Recessed fluorescent lighting fixtures in the ceiling grid were discolored, and many had broken or missing acrylic lenses. The building's structural system was composed of bar joists bearing on interior steel columns and exterior block walls. The building was far from being in serviceable shape.

The building owner suddenly had an opportunity to lease about 30,000 ft^2 to a major retail lumber and home improvement company. The lease that was negotiated contained improvements to be made by the owner that would include a major exterior face-lift, new fascia and canopy, and new aluminum storefront work complete with aluminum entrances. The tenant's architectural design department would also be submitting drawings to show the interior improvements to be incorporated.

Oh, yes, the lease contained a provision that if all the improvements were not completed within 60 days, the tenant could cancel the lease and would not be responsible for any costs incurred by the owner to date. Needless to say, work had to be started immediately, and structural and architectural drawings began to flow within a few days. Since it was known that new entrances would have to be created, a crew of masons and carpenters were put to work preparing the front loading-bearing masonry wall so that portions of it could be demolished.

After a 2- to 3-hour discussion with the owner and his architect, it was decided that a cost-plus-fee contract would be awarded to the author's company. On the basis of the scope of work discussed and agreed on by all parties, budget estimates were given to the owner the following morning, and he requested that work begin as quickly as possible. While the openings for the new entrances were being created, sketches of the canopy construction across the front of the leased space were made. The owner was so pleased with the appearance that he decided to extend the canopy the full length of the building, some 400 ft as opposed to the 120 ft initially budgeted. That additional work proceeded while the owner waited for the tenant to deliver drawings for interior layouts which would have an impact on the heating and cooling design as well as electric power and lighting systems.

To ensure that a sufficient number of carpenters would be available for the interior work, it was decided to extend the workday for the canopy construction. The owner authorized overtime of 2 hours/day per worker, and that was quickly changed to 3 hours/day per worker to obtain more production. With a 15-worker carpentry crew, the cost for the premium time work would be significant. Job meetings were held every 2 or 3 days to review newly prepared drawings and to keep the owner apprised of approximate costs to date.

Meanwhile attention was turned to interior work, and although the existing lighting fixtures were initially budgeted to be cleaned, reballasted, and relocated, when work began, the electrical subcontractor said that significantly more funds would be needed to replace all these fixtures. The owner agreed, and new fixtures were immediately ordered and the owner was presented with a cost differential for this change.

Time was ticking away. The tenant's interior design drawings were late in coming and therefore the design of the ductwork and electrical systems would be delayed. When drawings finally arrived and the new mechanical and electrical design developed, all trades had to work overtime to meet the construction deadline.

The floor was a mess. The owner insisted that it was to be patched by using tiles from other sections of the building even though he was advised that a new floor could be installed for a specified sum whereas patching could be performed only on a time-and-material basis and therefore final costs could not be ascertained until the work was completed. At the last minute (4:00 P.M. the day before the grand opening scheduled for 8:30 A.M. the next day) the district manager for the tenant informed the owner that unless a new floor was installed in his 30,000-ft^2 area, he would cancel the lease. The flooring contractor drove to his supply house and picked up the necessary materials while his laborers set to work removing the old floor. It required an around-the-clock effort to complete this new flooring installation.

As the red, white, and blue buntings were being hung over the front entrance at 8:00 A.M. on opening day, the floors were just being waxed and buffed.

The deadline was met; the tenant had begun to move in during the night; and opening day was a smashing success.

During all the hectic work in the last 2 weeks of construction, costs were discussed and reviewed by the owner, although many costs were not well defined. All these discussions were verbal, and just a few written memos, letters of authorization, and cost estimates had been prepared and sent to the owner. When the final costs and scope changes were assembled and presented to the owner, there was funereal silence. These final costs were 30 percent higher than the initial budget that had been prepared primarily on discussions between contractor, architect, and owner and two sheets of sketchy drawings. Many of the increased scope items discussed and implemented at the numerous job meetings were suddenly not "remembered" by the owner.

It took about 2 to 3 weeks to assemble all the detailed labor, material, and subcontractor cost sheets together along with a detailed history of how the scope of work had changed so drastically. Meeting after meeting was held with the owner in an attempt to review all the project changes, scope increase, and related costs. Most of these meetings ended with a glazed look in the owner's eyes. Unfortunately, written documentation of all the events contained in the history was rather scanty and the owner's memory remained conveniently vague. It took about 3 months to receive the final payment, and the author had the distinct impression that the owner felt he'd been abused when in fact he'd had the work completed on time and at a reasonable cost, given the circumstances. The experience certainly made painfully evident the importance of proper and timely documentation when cost-plus-fee projects are being administered.

Four critical elements in a cost-plus-fee contract must be addressed by the project manager:

1. Identify all scope changes as soon as they occur.

2. Establish approximate or firm costs for these changes.

3. Notify the owner of the changes and related costs as soon as they are identified. *Confirm in writing.*

4. Hope for the best!

Stipulated or lump sum

A stipulated or lump-sum contract is most frequently used in competitively bid work, either private or public. Contractors are required to estimate the cost of work contained in a specific set of instructions: the plans and specifications, no more, no less. Since the stipulated-sum contract price has been assembled by estimating the scope of work represented by a set of drawings and specifications, any deviation from these documents will result in a change of scope, and the associated costs will be dealt with by a change order once a contract has been signed.

Although this may appear to be a rather straightforward approach, it is not always as simple as it looks. The intent of the plans and specifications can be interpreted in different ways by all participants to the contract: the owner, the architect, the general contractor, and, when subcontracts are awarded, the subcontractor. This subject is discussed more fully in subsequent chapters on change orders and claims and disputes.

In the case of renovation or rehabilitation work, the stipulated-sum contract may include a contingency allowance to cover the costs of unanticipated problems that generally occur in this type of construction. If no such contingency is requested, it is wise to ask the owner if additional funds have been allocated to cover the cost of unexpected work that may be required when existing conditions are actually known and when unforeseen problems arise while uncovering work to be altered.

The contractor's fee in the stipulated- or lump-sum contract will depend on how costs tally up at the end of the job. If everything goes well, the contractor will achieve his anticipated fee, and possibly more. If, inadvertently, costly items have been omitted from the estimate, costs have been miscalculated, or adverse job conditions for which there is no reimbursement have been encountered, the contractor's fee may diminish or disappear. This is what is known as a *high-risk business.*

Guaranteed maximum price

The guaranteed-maximum-price (GMP or "GMAX") construction contract is frequently used because it allows the owner to gain the protection of a maximum cost of construction while retaining the potential for cost savings. It is basically a cost-plus-fee contract with a cap on it.

The GMP contract is often used for a fast-track project when incomplete or sketchy construction documents are available at the time of contract preparation. The GMP contract is also quite often used when design-build work is being considered.

The contractor's fee is usually prenegotiated, based upon a percentage of cost but not entirely dependent on final costs since there generally is a provision containing a minimum fee with overrides for work above and beyond the initial scope.

The GMP contract usually contains a clause that specifies how savings will be shared by owner and contractor. Some owners prefer to have the contractor receive a greater portion of the savings, which should create more incentive for the builder to seek out potential cost reductions. At other times the savings are shared on a 50-50 basis, which provides the owner with incentives to look more favorably on value engineering suggestions proposed by the contractor.

A standard feature of the GMP contract is a requirement for cost certification once the project has been completed. This audit is required to determine the extent and nature of the savings or verify that no savings have accrued.

If the audit is to be conducted by an independent accounting firm, payment for this cost should be included in the contract as either a contractor-excluded cost or a specific sum set aside for the audit. Proper identification and isolation of all costs as they are incurred and as they relate to the particular GMP job will save countless hours and tempers at the end of the project when it may be difficult or impossible to accurately reconstruct all the job-related costs. If a project manager's time spent administering the GMP job in the office or in the field is to be included in the reimbursable costs and the project manager is managing several jobs at the same time, a daily log can be set up and maintained. The log should include the number of hours the project manager spends on the particular GMP project and his specific activities during that time, such as negotiating a contract with a particular subcontractor, purchasing materials for the job, and discussing construction details with the superintendent or possibly the project architect. All this information may prove to be invaluable if the project manager is called on to account for all of his billable hours and related activities.

Prior to the issuance of a subcontract, some GMP contracts require the project manager to submit all subcontractor proposals to the owner, together with recommendations for an award. Some contracts include a provision requiring the owner to approve a subcontract agreement before it is issued. This adds another burden to the project manager's job.

First, the owner's review must be done in a timely fashion so that critical subcontractors can be brought on board as the schedule demands. Second, the qualifications of the bidding subcontractors must be known prior to submission to an owner, and if any are unqualified for the job, they should be struck from the bidder's list. If an unrealistically low bid is received, unsolicited, from a subcontractor who has a past record of poor performance or poor quality levels, the bid should be forwarded to the owner with a comment stating that this was an unsolicited bid and is not to be considered. The reasons for the bid rejection should be included. In the absence of such a procedure, an owner may feel that he is not being afforded the most competitive prices and a feeling of distrust may be created that will be difficult to dispel throughout the entire procurement process.

To be safe, the project manager should forward all unsolicited bids to the owner, if in fact the GMP contract calls for the owner to review these bids, with comments and recommendations. In most cases the owner will follow the contractor's advice.

On the other hand, if a contractor does not pre-qualify subcontractors and receives an unrealistically low bid from one of them, forwarding it to the owner with a comment that the bid should be rejected, the client's response may be, "Why was an unqualified contractor permitted to submit a bid on my job?"

With the GMP contract, any change in scope which has been requested by either the owner or the architect-engineer will be cause for issuing a change order. Since the GMP contract is based on a specific scope of work, any change in that scope should theoretically increase or decrease the guaranteed maximum price.

Particularly when the scope of work increases, if the added costs for this work are folded into the original GMP, costs will be higher and the contractor's fee will be lowered by a proportionate amount.

One of the many functions of a project manager administering a GMP contract will be to look for potential savings. All subcontractors should be requested to review their work with an eye toward developing possible cost savings. As these suggestions are received, the project manager must review and analyze them to determine whether a savings in one trade may result in an increase in another trade, in effect resulting in no savings at all.

After these potential costs savings are reviewed by the project manager, they should be submitted to the appropriate design consultant for review and comments before they are formally submitted to the owner.

The more adept a contractor becomes at suggesting meaningful cost savings, the easier it will be to build a solid reputation as an effective administrator of GMP contracts.

Construction Management Contracts

The following question remains unanswered by many contractors, owners, and design consultants: What is the actual definition and function of a construction manager (CM)?

Some experts state that the concept of a CM was created when the Wicks Law was enacted in New York state in 1921. This law mandated that four prime contracts—one for heating, ventilation, and air conditioning (HVAC); one for electrical; one for plumbing; and one for general construction—were to be awarded for all contracts with public agencies in the state when the value of the work exceeded $50,000. All these "primes" had responsibility for their own work, but none had overall project responsibility, so another supervisory level was added in the form of a CM. By the 1960s the role of the CM expanded far beyond the concept created by the Wicks Law and became a method whereby an owner purchased the professional services of a construction expert who would act as his agent in administering the construction process.

This owner-agent relationship was meant to provide construction advice to an owner on a fee basis without any involvement in the profit (or loss) resulting from the actual construction process.

The CM could be hired during the design stage to work directly with the design consultants, lending his construction expertise to ensure that the project design tracked with the owner's budgetary requirements. The CM could also be engaged to work with the owner after design had been completed, and would then recommend how the project was to be made ready to bid. The CM would prepare bid packages, develop a bidder's list, receive bids, review them, and send recommendations to the owner, who would issue the subcontract agreements and purchase orders.

The CM would supervise the project's quality levels and schedule adherence and would review and approve monthly subcontractor requisitions. In return for these services, the CM would be paid a fee and in addition be paid for certain preestablished reimbursable expenses. Since the CM had no risk exposure and his project administration costs would be reimbursed, his fee would be low, in the range of 1.5 to 2.5 percent on large projects. This method of CM contracting might be called "pure" CM work inasmuch as the construction manager is performing supervisory and "consulting" work. Today there are CMs "at risk" who, in addition to receiving a fee plus reimbursement for expenses such as project management and project superintendent salaries and field office and accounting costs relating to the project, also guarantee the final cost of the project. Critics of this system claim that by adding the "risk" factor the CM is no longer a disinterested construction professional but now must look to make a profit on the work in order to obtain a "cushion" to offset any possible project cost overruns.

Participation of the Construction Manager in the Design and Construction Stages

One advantage of engaging a construction manager is that the owner can obtain the services of a construction expert during the design stage of a project. The construction manager will evaluate the cost-effectiveness of structural systems, the building envelope, and mechanical and electrical systems as well as other building components. A truly effective CM will have these kinds of engineers on staff and will not have to rely on subcontractors for advice.

When CM services are being solicited, the proposal will generally indicate whether the CM will be required to participate in the design stage, the construction stage, or both. Normally a separate fee structure is established for each phase, and a schedule of reimbursable expenses will be included with each fee structure.

The CM proposals will often include the number and type of staff to be utilized in the project, the hourly rate for each staff member, and the approximate number of hours or weeks their assignments will last. This gives the owner a guide to the extent and cost of construction management services.

A term frequently used by construction managers during the design stage is *value engineering*. As it applies to design analysis, this term means not only weighing capital costs in the design decision-making process but considering operating costs as well. Sometimes a more expensive piece of equipment will more than pay for itself quickly through less expensive operating costs and longer operational life. For example, fluorescent light fixtures may be more expensive to purchase than incandescent fixtures, but their longer lamp life and lower power requirements will return savings to the owner in a relatively short period of time. And fluorescent fixtures with electronic ballasts are more expensive yet, but offer even more savings in utility costs and less frequently required repairs.

Specific contract forms must be used whenever construction management services are to be provided, and whenever possible these forms should be used rather than attempting to modify a standard contract. The CM contracts contain specific language relating to services to be preformed and costs to be reimbursed.

Services during design stage:

1. Consultation during project development

2. Scheduling

3. Preparation of a construction budget

4. Coordination of contract documents

5. Developing a bidding strategy

Construction phase:

1. Preparing bid packages, soliciting bids, evaluating bids, selecting subcontractors

2. Providing project supervision during physical construction

3. Providing cost-control and scheduling services

4. Assisting the owner in obtaining permits required for the project

5. Establishing change-order procedures and monitoring change orders

6. Consulting with the owner on selection of any consultants required

7. Inspecting the work in place and accepting or rejecting it

8. Acting as a conduit between subcontractors and owner for contract interpretation

9. In collaboration with architect-engineer, establishing a shop drawing processing procedure

10. Recording and processing all reports and site documents

11. Determining substantial completion dates and preparing a list of incomplete and unacceptable items

12. Monitoring start-up of all equipment and assignment to owner

13. Obtaining, reviewing, and approving all closeout documents

14. Assisting in assuring that warranty work is being performed properly and in accordance with warranty or guarantee provisions.

Some CM contracts do not prohibit the construction manager from performing portions of the work with his own forces if he has exhibited previous experience in those kinds of work and can prove that his involvement will be cost-effective. In that event, the construction manager is usually allowed to include a certain percentage for administrative costs to be added to raw costs. The construction manager would then be permitted to add the amount of overhead and profit normally associated with this work.

Contracts with Governmental Agencies

Many local, state, and federal government agencies have their own contract forms. Although these forms may borrow heavily from many standard AIA or AGC contracts, they will also include pages of various types of compliance requirements such as Equal Opportunity (EO), Disadvantaged Business Enterprises (DBE), Women-Owned Business Enterprises (WBE), Minority Business Enterprises (MBE), war veteran provisions, handicapped employment, and ordinances and laws printed with such fine print that they are virtually unreadable—but still require compliance. It is not uncommon for these kinds of contracts to include liquidated-damage provisions to be enforced if there are undocumented delays in completing the project.

Cost certification is generally required, and weekly payroll costs will need to be documented on special forms provided by the government agency. These forms are to be distributed to all subcontractors working on the project. When certified, they will include the name, hourly wage rate, and total weekly wages of each worker employed on the project. These forms are required so that adherence to wage rates, primarily Davis-Bacon compliance (more fully discussed in Chapter 9), is verified. At times, a government inspector may ask selected workers on the site to produce a payroll check stub to verify that wages as reported on the certified payroll form were actually being paid.

Monthly requisitions submitted to the government agency will not be paid if these certified payroll forms do not accompany the request for payment, so compliance with the law and prompt payments dictate that proper attention be paid to certified payroll reporting. For the project manager embarking on his first government project, a thorough review of the specifications "boilerplate" is a must. In these special conditions, general conditions, and supplementary conditions sections there are stipulations that will affect the way negotiations are to be conducted with subcontractors and various provisions that should be included in their contracts, methods by which minority participation is to be solicited, how the site logistics plan is to be established, and the various closeout requirements that must be addressed even before the job begins.

The notice to proceed

This document, sent to the contractor by the government agency, in most cases starts the contract time clock, the date from which the contract time will be charged. In some cases there are two notices to proceed: the first one issued for the installation of the contractor's field offices only (the contract time clock does not start with this notice) and the second one stipulating when the contractor is to commence construction, and this one does start the clock.

Provisions affecting subcontractor negotiations

Prompt payment provisions are being included in an increasing number of government contracts. These provisions typically state that the general contractor must pay their subcontractors within 30 days of receipt of payment and these subcontractors must pay their subcontractors within 30 days of receipt of payment.

These Special Conditions sections often contain provisions for fees that will be allowed on change order work and need to be discussed during subcontractor negotiations. A typical requirement may be as follows:

> On work performed by a subcontractor, his allowance for overhead and profit will be as follows: for changes up to and including $5000, 10 percent overhead and 10 percent profit; for change orders from $5001 to $15,000, 10 percent overhead, 7 percent profit; for change orders from $15,001 to $25,000, 10 percent overhead and 5 percent profit.

Requirements to be met for off-site storage of material and equipment is frequently spelled out in these government contracts, and the methods by which payment is allowed is an important consideration to all concerned. Along with the documentation required in order to requisition for payment of off-site stored materials, there could also be a provision that the inspecting engineer's time required to verify the existence of these materials, and equipment will be charged to the general contractor's account.

Subcontractors should be made aware of these provisions at the time of contract negotiations to avoid misunderstandings at a later date. These kinds of limitations on overhead and profit extend to the general contractor as well and set the limit on how much overhead and profit he can place on work performed with his own forces and on work performed by his subcontractors.

Change-order clauses in government contracts

Some contracts may contain clauses that state that no changes other than those for project "enrichment" or extra work ordered by the owner or architect will be approved. The term *enrichment* can have one meaning for the owner but a different one for the contractor.

For example, in the beginning stages of a contract, plans and specifications are presented to and reviewed by the local building officials and usually, the fire marshal. On the basis of these plans and specifications meeting all local and state requirements, a building permit is issued and construction begins.

More often than not, as the building is nearing completion, local building officials and fire department personnel will visit the site and begin their final inspections. And, more often than not, these officials may point out the need to install more exit lights or relocate ones already installed, add smoke or heat detectors, install a few more emergency lights as necessary, and so forth. Typically this means that the subcontractor will request additional money to perform this work and the general contractor will feel justified in preparing a change order to the owner—who will be reluctant to recognize these costs as "extra" to contract. Their arguments will be based on these additional costs not representing enrichments to the contract but merely compliance with local and state building codes.

The project manager can argue strongly for the inclusion of these enrichments because if these additional items have not been installed, the certificate of occupancy will not be issued, and without the certificate of occupancy the building cannot be occupied and is therefore worthless. This argument can also be used when meeting resistance from owners in the private sector even though there was no enrichment clause in their contract.

Administering contracts with local, state, and federal authorities can be a demanding task. The project manager should be thoroughly familiar with all phases of the contract because they probably will be enforced to the letter.

Partnering—a New Name for an Old Concept?

While "partnering" is not a definitive contract form, it may be best described as a method of contract administration where productive working relationships between owner, designer, contractor, and subcontractor are developed to create cooperation among all parties instead of adversarial ones. By getting to know each participant in the construction process better and working together on the problems that inevitably occur on all construction projects, a more cost-effective, higher-quality project will be created.

The partnering concept is relatively new, having been developed, according to some sources, by the Mobile, Alabama District of the U.S. Army Corps of Engineers in 1988 during the construction of the William Bacon Oliver Lock and Dam in that state. The Corps, eager to avoid the large amount of claims endemic to government projects, met with representatives from each group that would be working on the project before work began. Officials from the Corps of Engineers hoped to iron out any unclear or ambiguous scope of work early on so that once work began, the potential for disputes and claims would be eliminated or at least substantially reduced. Their *Guide to Partnering for Construction Projects* is still available if inquiries are addressed to the Federal Regulatory Affairs Department of the U.S. Corps of Engineers.

The Associated General Contractors of America are strong advocates of the partnering process and state in their booklet on partnering that the key elements of the process are:

- *Commitment.*   Commitment to the process must come from top management.

- *Equity.*   All participants to the process have a stake in the project, and this stake is recognized as mutual goals are developed.

- *Trust.*   The development of personal relationships will dispel the cynicism that often creeps into the process. With trust, a synergistic relationship will enfold.

- *Development of mutual goals.*   Jointly developed and mutually agreed-on goals will include value engineering savings, meeting the financial goals of each party, timely completion of the project, minimizing paperwork (which can become mountainous in an adversarial relationship), and the absence of litigation.

- *Implementation.*   Together, all parties to the process develop strategies and methods to implement their mutual goals.

- *Continuous evaluation.*   Periodic evaluation of the mutually agreed-on goals is necessary to ensure that everyone is carrying their share of the load.

- *Timely responsiveness.*   Timely communication and timely response to these communications will keep problems to a minimum and keep these problems from growing into disputes. Unresolved problems are not set aside but are moved up to the next level of management for resolution.

Advocates of partnering today recommend that the following guidelines be implemented:

1. Involve subcontractors, suppliers, local authorities, and even testing and inspection services. The partnering process should include everyone who will become involved in the project.

2. Successful partnering projects should be advertised. Nothing succeeds more than success. Public awareness of the process and the advantages to be gained will make subsequent attempts at partnering easier to implement.

3. Without competent people the partnering process will be difficult to achieve.

4. Some advocates of the process recommend a 2-day retreat to get to know each partner better, but it doesn't end there. Follow-up and periodic meetings throughout the project are an absolute necessity.

5. The use of a formalized decision-making process will result in the creation of documents that memorialize the joint effort of the team.

6. Backup team members should be selected so that momentum is not lost if one or more members of the original team are transferred to other projects or leave the company.

Partnering is not a panacea for many of the ills that face the construction industry, but it does work. It will reduce exposure to litigation, open the lines of communication between all parties, and create a more rapid flow of information. Partnering can result in an increase in quality because energies are focused on the ultimate goal, not on warding off litigation or building a paper trail to cover one's gluteus maximus.

Partnering involves risk sharing and a desire to attain goals common to all parties to the process. Through a cooperative effort, confrontation is minimized, litigation is eliminated, and all partners finish the job as winners both individually and collectively.

Bonds

The high-risk nature that characterizes the construction industry, coupled with the ever-changing financial stability of individual subcontractors and general contractors, has created the need to provide a layer of assurance or insurance to protect owners against the possibility of default by the builder prior to completion of the project. This can be accomplished by the issuance of bonds, the most prevalent types of which are

1. Bid bonds

2. Payment bonds

3. Performance bonds

Bid bonds

Requirements for bid bonds will be clearly indicated in the bid documents. There will be a statement to the effect that each bid is to be accompanied by a bid security in an amount ordinarily not less than 10 percent of the bid amount. The American Institute of Architects has a bid bond form, AIA Document A310, which is often used in private work, but government contracts often include their own format for bid bonds. In lieu of a bid bond, a contractor usually has the option of submitting a certified check payable to the owner, in the amount stipulated in the bid bond specifications.

The purpose of the bid bond is to ensure the owner that if the apparent low bidder is awarded the contract for construction, he will be able and willing to commence work. The bid bond gives an owner added protection in that if, for some reason, the selected contractor declines to accept the contract, there is assurance that any losses which the owner might incur because of the contractor's nonacceptance will be covered. The bond amount, in that case, would be payable to the owner as compensation for those losses. Total compensation, however, will be limited to the amount of the bond.

Some bid bonds contain a stipulation that if it becomes necessary for the obligee (the project owner) to accept a higher bid because the principal (the general contractor) declines to enter into a contract, the principal (general contractor) shall pay the obligee (owner) the difference between his bid and the next-highest bid, said amount not to exceed the penal sum (the maximum amount of the bond).

Other bid bond requirements can include contractor liability for liquidated damages if the contractor declines to accept a contract when designated as apparent low bidder. Making the contractor responsible for liquidated damages as opposed to "actual" damages is significant. Actual damages can be interpreted as the difference in dollar value between low bidder and next-highest bidder, whereas liquidated damages can be interpreted as being those that approach the "reasonable expectation" of what these costs might be over and above the difference between bids.

Payment bonds

The payment bond is sometimes referred to as a *labor and material payment bond* because its purpose is to ensure that the general contractor will pay his subcontractors and material suppliers who have provided labor and/or materials to the project. The penal sum of this bond is usually the amount of the construction contract. The payment bond requires that the principal (the contractor) pay the subcontractor or supplier promptly and that if these parties are not paid within 90 days after the last day they worked on the project or delivered materials to the job site, the claimants may "sue on the bond." This means that they can notify the issuer of the bond of their nonpayment status and the bond issuer may elect to "call the bond" and pay these claimants.

Performance bonds

The performance bond ensures the owner that the contractor (the principal) is to promptly and faithfully perform in accordance with the terms of the construction contract. If the contractor does not perform, the owner (the obligee) may elect to have another builder fulfill the contractual obligations and hold the principal (contractor) liable for all costs to complete performance up to the specific dollar amount of liability stipulated in the performance bond. The existence of a performance bond means that a financially responsible entity stands behind the general contractor and will be responsible to furnish the funds necessary to complete the project up to the penal sum of the bond. The "penal sum" is construed to mean the amount of the contract for construction.

Dual-obligee riders to bonds

A dual-obligee rider may be attached to either the performance bond or the payment bond. When an owner is arranging construction financing, the lender may wish to be named in the bond as an "interested party." The owner is known as the *obligee,* and if the lender has an interest in the project similar to that of the owner, the dual-obligee rider will name both owner and lender as interested parties in case of default by the contractor.

3

The General Conditions to the Construction Contract

Most construction contracts are supplemented by general conditions. These general conditions can be incorporated into the project specifications or be contained in a separate document attached to the construction contract.

AIA Document A201

The most prevalent form of general conditions document is AIA Document A210, General Conditions of the Contract for Construction. On the face of this document is printed, "This document has important legal consequences; consultation with an attorney is encouraged."

Too often, this document is not even reviewed, or, when it is, is given only a cursory examination. As the warning on the cover sheet states, it does contain some very important points.

The latest edition of AIA Document A201 is the 1987 issue, which supersedes the 1976 version.

This chapter will review each section of the AIA document, commenting on its salient provisions, but because this document should be read and understood by all project managers, it is suggested that a complete review of the entire document be made at least once.

Article 1. The contract documents. Beside defining the components of the contract documents, this article contains a provision in paragraph 1.2.2 that, on signing or executing the contract, the contractor stipulates that he has visited the job site and has become familiar with the work to be performed. This last statement has important implications. Let's say the job has just begun and a site condition not shown on the drawings has been discovered. If this condition could have easily been discerned by a job-site visit, it might be very difficult to initiate a claim for extra work.

For example, if an abandoned well were found in the area of a proposed footing and the well cap or well cover were clearly visible, the architect could invoke the provisions of Article 1 as the reason for disallowing a contractor's claim for additional costs for footing work in that area.

Article 2. Owner. A provision in this article requires the owner to furnish to the contractor reasonable evidence that sufficient financial arrangements have been made to pay for the work under contract. Although hardly ever invoked by the contractor, there have been cases where an owner has not had financing in place at the time of contract signing and the contractor's first request for payment has been stalled while the owner scrambles to obtain financing. Just as the owner is concerned with a contractor's ability to pay his subcontractors and suppliers, so should a contractor be assured that the owner has the necessary funds in place to honor his monthly requests for payment.

This article also charges the owner with the responsibility to furnish all surveys describing the physical characteristics of the job site and also stipulates that the owner obtain all necessary approvals, easements, and other charges required for construction. The question of building permits is covered in a subsequent article.

Paragraph 2.2.5 states that the contractor shall be furnished, free of charge, enough copies of the plans and specifications that are reasonably required for the project. The term "reasonable" may be up for discussion, but the contractor is entitled to more free drawings beyond the bid set, unless the contract states otherwise.

The last paragraph in this article deals with the owner's right to carry out work if the contractor fails to carry out, or correct deficiencies in, the work. After giving the contractor two 7-day notices, the owner can have the work performed and deduct the costs from the contract sum via change order.

Article 3. Contractor. There are 18 paragraphs in this section, all of which should be read, but some should be read more carefully than others.

Paragraph 3.2.1 requires the contractor to study and compare the contract documents, but he shall not be liable for damage "resulting from errors, inconsistencies, or omissions in the contract documents unless the contractor recognized such error, inconsistency, or omission and knowingly failed to report it to the architect." This is easy to say, but hard to prove. How can a contractor prove that he did or did not "knowingly" fail to report a mistake in the documents? But at least this opens the door to discussion about a contractor's responsibilities for the designer's errors.

The next paragraph, 3.2.2, requires the contractor to take field measurements and compare with those in the plans before starting work. Any errors, omissions, and inconsistencies are to be reported to the architect.

There have been times when, at the end of the project, during partial occupancy by the owner, various mechanical systems are turned over to him for operation, and by not maintaining them properly, a failure could occur and the contractor will be looked to for replacement. Article 3.8.1 excludes the contractor's responsibility for damage due to improper or insufficient maintenance under normal usage.

One of the most important provisions of this article rests in paragraph 3.7.3, which states that a contractor is not responsible to ascertain that the contract documents are in accordance with applicable laws, statutes, building codes, and ordinances. When these deficiencies are discovered, the contractor is to notify the architect and owner in writing. This may settle that old argument as to who is responsible to furnish and install those extra fire alarm devices or exit signs required when the fire marshal makes his last tour through the building prior to sign-off.

What constitutes an allowance? Is it to include labor and materials? Paragraph 3.8.2 states that allowances are to include the cost of materials and equipment delivered to the site, all taxes, and any discounts. It is important to note that costs to unload and install and the contractor's overhead, profit, and any other expenses *shall be included in the contract sum and not in the allowance item.* Shop drawings are discussed in this section of the general conditions, and the contractor is to verify that materials and field measurements have been confirmed. The contractor is not relieved of responsibility for errors, omissions, and inconsistencies in the shop drawing submission as they relate to contract requirements. A contractor cannot state that once the architect has approved the drawing, but it is later found that the approval was not consistent with the contract requirements, the contractor's responsibility for nonconformance ends.

This article places the responsibility for cutting and patching on the general contractor. If a subcontract agreement does not include cutting and patching for their trade and the AIA A201 document is attached to the subcontract agreement, the general contractor may have to assume all costs for cut and patch. Finally, Article 3 requires the contractor to keep the construction site clean and free of debris, and if not done, the owner may perform the necessary cleaning and charge the contractor for all costs.

Article 4.   Administration of the contract.   The architect may not dictate means and methods of construction to the contractor.

Review of shop drawings, product data, and samples required of the architect shall be performed with reasonable promptness so as to cause no delay in the work. No specific time frame is indicated; however, in a subsequent paragraph, the architect is permitted 15 days after receipt of a written request from the owner or contractor in which to respond to queries. Delays will begin to accrue after this 15-day period. Bearing in mind that this document was written by architects, it should come as no surprise that the architect's decision in response to a contractor's claim relating to errors and omissions in the plans and specs is to be reviewed and judged by the designers. This is somewhat analogous to the fox watching the chicken coup.

A decision rendered by the architect is necessary before a claim can be processed for arbitration or legal action. Claims by any party to the contract are to be made within 21 days after occurrence of the disputed event.

Paragraphs 4.3.4, 4.3.6, and 4.3.8 warrant particular attention because they deal with how claims are to be handled, and several of these changes differ significantly from the 1976 edition of A201.

Pending resolution of a claim, the contractor must forge ahead with the project, rather than wait for the claim to be settled.

Claims for concealed conditions are clearly delineated, and if they differ materially from "those ordinarily found to exist and generally recognized as inherent in construction activities," notice should be given not later than 21 days after being discovered or uncovered. Claims for adverse weather conditions are also discussed, and the contractor is directed to document the claim with data substantiating that weather conditions were abnormal and could not have been reasonably anticipated. Possibly copies of local weather bureau reports from previous years may satisfy that requirement.

Arbitration and the methods by which it is initiated is also reviewed in this section of the general conditions.

Article 5.   Subcontractors.   The owner or architect can reject a contractor's subcontractor selection if they submit reasonable and timely objections. If that is the case and the contractor submits another candidate that meets with the approval of the owner or architect, the contract sum may be increased or decreased on the basis of this new selection.

Subcontractors are to be bound to their contract in accordance with the terms of the contract between owner and contractor, which, in effect, means that subcontractors are to receive a copy of the owner's agreement.

This provision takes on added importance if the contractor agrees to certain terms that are not industry standards. For instance, a 1-year warranty is standard in the industry, but if the owner has negotiated a 2-year guarantee on mechanical equipment and the general contractor has not negotiated a similar guarantee from the mechanical subcontractor, the general contractor will be responsible for that two-year warranty.

Article 5.3.1 goes even further. On the request of a subcontractor, the general contractor is to identify the terms and conditions of the proposed subcontract agreement and how these terms and conditions vary from the contract between owner and general contractor.

A new requirement in the 1987 edition of the A201 document requires the general contractor to insert an "assignment" clause in each subcontract agreement. In case of the termination of contract between owner and builder, these subcontracts would be assigned, or taken over, by the owner.

Article 6. Construction by owner or by separate contracts. The owner reserves the right to perform certain construction work with his own forces or other subcontractors. Even though the owner has a right to perform work in his building under construction, his right should not go unchallenged. A union contractor may experience problems if the owner selects a nonunion subcontractor to work alongside union workers. Although job actions may not be legally defensible, they could create temporary work stoppages or slowdowns and have a serious effect on a tight schedule. Coordination is another concern, and although the owner is to provide coordination for forces he employs, if he is not a sophisticated purchaser of construction work, other problems can, and probably will, arise. Who will cut and patch for these owner's subcontractors? Will they severely damage finished surfaces and then state that their contract with the owner precludes repair? The contractor should attempt to assist an owner in reviewing the scope of work being considered prior to the owner's award of contract in such cases. Expert advice at this time will make for good public relations and lessen the chances of arguments later on.

The owner's right to keep the premises clean permits him to award a contract for cleaning per paragraph 6.3.1 of this article, if a dispute arises with his general contractor, these costs will be backcharged to the contractor in an amount determined by the architect.

Article 7. Changes in the work. A new term is introduced into the 1987 version of Article 7, *construction change directive,* which is defined as "agreement by the owner and architect that may or may not be agreed to by the contractor." This construction change directive is a written order prepared by the architect and signed by the owner directing the contractor to perform certain items of work in the absence of total agreement with the contractor as to cost. If a change in contract sum is anticipated, a price adjustment will be made using one of the four methods:

1. Mutual agreement on a lump-sum basis
2. In accordance with units prices contained in the contract
3. Costs determined in a manner agreed on by all parties
4. Documented cost of the work, which will include
   a. Cost of labor to include all fringe benefits
   b. Cost of materials, supplies, and equipment
   c. Rental costs of machinery and equipment exclusive of hand tools
   d. Cost of bond premiums, insurance, permits, fees, and taxes
   e. Cost of supervision and field office personnel directly attributable to this change
   f. A reasonable fee for contractor overhead and profit

It appears that in most cases where a contractor's cost proposal is not accepted because of what is perceived to be too high a price, the construction change directive presents a fair alternative.

This article dictates how a change order containing both adds and deducts is to be totaled. Any deducts are to be applied to adds before contractor overhead and profit are calculated.

Article 8.   Time.   Contract time is measured in calendar days, not working days, unless otherwise noted in the contract.

If the contractor's progress is delayed by actions or inactions of the owner or architect, the provisions of this article are invoked in order to request an extension of contract time. Since the architect is the one to determine what will be a reasonable time extension, he may have difficulty remaining objective if he has been the cause of the delay.

Article 9.   Payments and completion.   Applications for payment are to be submitted by the contractor at least 10 days prior to the date established for progress payments. Payments for off-site storage of materials and equipment are to be approved in advance, and in writing.

This latest edition of A201 contains a definition of *substantial completion,* a term that was not well defined previously. Substantial completion is determined to be reached when the work or a portion of the work is sufficiently complete so that the owner can occupy the building and use it as intended. When substantial completion has been attained, the architect is to prepare a certification to include the date of substantial completion and contain statements as to division of responsibility for security, maintenance, and payment of utility costs. Warranties will generally commence on this date, and the architect usually prepares a list of items to be completed by the contractor. If partial occupancy is mutually acceptable to all parties, Article 9 sets forth the terms and conditions for building use. Partial occupancy carries with it the potential for damage to surfaces with any or all parties disclaiming knowledge. Movers hired by the owner, furniture, and management information system (MIS) installers employed by the owner can each create damage, and a walk-through with the architect who signs off on areas to be occupied will assist the contractor in establishing accountability for damage.

Article 10. Protection of persons and property. A new provision in this article addresses asbestos and polychlorinated biphenyls (PCBs) that may be encountered on a construction site. The contractor shall cease work in these areas immediately and shall be held harmless against any claims, damages, losses, and expenses until presence or absence of these substances has been verified and these substances have been subsequently rendered harmless.

This article requires that the contractor maintain safe work practices and maintain a safe working environment.

Article 11. Insurance and bonds. Insurance and bonding procedures are included in this article. A new provision in paragraph 11.4.1 allows the owner the right to request a bond if stipulated in the bidding documents or specifically required in the contract. When agreeing to partial occupancy, the insurance company providing property insurance must also agree to the partial occupancy.

Article 12. Uncovering and correction of work. When requested to correct rejected work, a contractor must also bear the costs of additional testing and inspections as well as added compensation for the architect's services and related expenses. If work is found to be defective or not in accordance with the contract documents, the warranty period for these items is to be extended for a period of 1 year from the date after they have been corrected.

If the owner elects to accept defective or nonconforming work, the contract sum may be reduced in an appropriate and equitable manner.

Article 13. Miscellaneous provisions. This article contains statements about testing and inspections and stipulates that unless otherwise indicated, the contractor shall make arrangements for all tests and inspections by an independent testing laboratory. The owner is to bear the costs of these tests until such time as bids are received and negotiations concluded.

Article 14.   Termination or suspension of the contract.   This final article in A201 sets forth reasons for contract termination. The contractor may terminate the contract if work is stopped for 30 days, if that comes about through no act or fault on his part. The contractor may terminate the contract if the architect has not issued a certificate for payment within the time frame specified in the contract or has not notified the contractor for reasons why no certification has been issued.

If, within a reasonable period of time, the owner fails to furnish the contractor with evidence of ability to pay for the work, the contractor may cancel the contract.

AIA Document A201CM

A separate edition of AIA Document A201, designated as A201CM (General Conditions of the Contract for Construction—CM version), has been prepared for construction management work. In 1992, a revised edition of A201CM was issued, designated A201CMa, and is to be used when the construction manager is not a constructor but is hired only as a manager-adviser.

The construction manager's role and responsibilities and relationship with both the architect-owner and the contractor are defined. A review of a few of the articles in the A201CM general conditions document will illustrate some of the ways in which this form differs from AIA Document 201.

Article 2.   Administration of the contract.   In the standard A201 version, this article is entitled "Owner." Administration of a construction management contract is basically a team effort by the architect and the construction manager, both acting as the owner's representatives. This article in the CM document states that the construction manager will determine whether the contractor is performing the work in compliance with the contract documents. The construction manager will review applications for payment and after the review will forward the contractor's request for payment to the architect with his recommendations. The architect remains the interpreter of the plans and specifications if a dispute arises, and if the architect's decision is not agreeable to the contractor, arbitration can be requested. The architect retains the right to reject work that does not appear to conform to the contract drawings and specifications, but only after consultation with the construction manager. Change orders are issued only after the architect consults with the construction manager.

Article 3. Owner. Article 3 of A201CM is entitled "owner," whereas Article 3 of A201 is captioned "contractor." The CM version states that all instructions to the contractor will pass through the construction manager and not the architect. Under Section 3.45, the owner may carry out the work if the contractor does not perform in accordance with the contract documents. However, any additional fees for architectural services may be billed to the contractor, as in A201, but now any additional fees incurred by the construction manager will also be included in the owner's backcharge.

Throughout the balance of A201CM, the construction manager's interaction with the architect and contractor is called forth in such a fashion that any project manager embarking on a construction management form of construction contract should read these articles carefully.

AIA Document A201SC

Still another version of the general conditions document may be used when a federally funded construction contract is involved. AIA Document A201SC is officially known as the Federal Supplementary Conditions of the Contract for Construction. This document includes provisions for many conditions unique to contracts involving federal funds. A portion calls for a labor and material performance bond equal to 100 percent of the contract sum. It also references the various federal safety and health regulations and executive orders pertaining to equal opportunity and nonsegregated facilities. The matter of wages to be paid to all workers participating in the project is fully detailed. Usually a minimum-wage scale is attached to this form or included in a separate document. This wage scale approximates the local union wage scale and is officially known as the "prevailing wage" for all trades employed in the project. This prevailing wage requirement is also known as Davis Bacon, after the federal act mandating that specific wage guidelines are to be followed on federally funded construction projects.

There is a section in these supplementary conditions that provides for the payment to apprentices and trainees that allows for payment to these workers at less than Davis-Bacon wages as long as proof is submitted indicating that these apprentices or trainees are properly enrolled in a federally recognized apprenticeship program.

In the section on wages, there is a stipulation that those who work in excess of 40 hours weekly be paid time and one-half. A requirement for certified payroll is included requiring that all subcontractor and general contractor weekly payrolls be certified and identify workers by name, trade classification, hours worked daily and weekly, and their corresponding rate of pay.

Federal inspectors assigned to federally funded projects may, from time to time, interview workers at random to verify their last week's pay record with respect to hours worked, hourly rate of pay, and gross pay. These inspectors will usually ask to see a worker's payroll check stub to verify this information. The data collected will be compared to the certified payroll. If these wages and hours do not agree, a federal law has been violated, monthly requisitions will be withheld until these disparities are corrected, and other legal action may be pursued by the concerned government agency.

The General Conditions—Engineers Joint Contract Documents Committee

In 1990 a joint committee composed of the National Society of Professional Engineers, the Consulting Engineers Council, the American Society of Civil Engineers, and the Construction Specifications Institute prepared several contract documents for use by engineers. In cases where roadwork and several forms of infrastructure are concerned, engineers are the designers, and it was felt that these designers should have their own contract and general conditions format.

The Standard General Conditions of the Construction Contract, prepared by the joint committee, contains a rather definitive index which takes up a full 12 pages. This document contains several unique features. Article 2, entitled "Preliminary Matters," requires that a preconstruction conference be arranged within 20 days after contract signing. The purpose of the conference is to establish a working understanding of the project and discuss schedules and procedures for handling shop drawings and other submittals. Article 3, "contract documents, intent, amending, reuse," states that although it is the intent of the contract documents to describe a "functionally complete project," the "intended result will be furnished and performed whether or not specifically called for." This phrase puts the contractor on notice that "intent" of the documents is of equal importance to the definitive plans and specifications. Although several articles prohibit the engineer from dictating means, methods, techniques, sequences, or procedures of construction, the contractor is not allowed to work overtime on Saturdays, Sundays, or any legal holidays without written consent of the engineer.

Throughout this document the term *engineer* is substituted for the word *architect,* which appears in the AIA version, and all communications between owner and contractor must pass through the engineer.

Change orders, rejection of work, and approval of progress payments are somewhat similar to the AIA document, but Article 16, "dispute resolution," is rather unique. The Engineers Joint Committee requires that a dispute resolution method and procedure be spelled out in a separate document, entitled "Exhibit GC—a dispute resolution agreement." If no such agreement has been created, the owner and contractor may use whatever remedy at their disposal as long as it does not conflict with any contract language.

Take time to become familiar with the general conditions to the contract in whichever form they may occur. These documents will contain many conditions required for intelligent administration of the basic construction contract, and as the warning printed on the front page of AIA201 indicates, "This document has important legal consequences."

4

Estimating

With the advent of digitizers and computerized estimating, it is easy to overlook the basics. Light pencils and sonic beams now provide a company's estimating department with more rapid and more accurate takeoffs. When a solid data base of historical cost information is used in conjunction with electronic takeoff and a computer's ability to store, sort, and retrieve, the keen competitive edge required in today's business climate can be achieved and maintained.

Acquiring a Data Base

A data base can be acquired by purchasing a data-base program and modifying it to meet one's individual needs or by developing field-generated cost data and combining it with acquired cost data. A number of companies have been publishing unit-price data obtained by averaging construction unit costs from all parts of the country. The R. S. Means Company, Inc., of Kingston, Massachusetts has been publishing these costs for years and advertises that it has more than 20,000 thoroughly researched unit prices for various labor and material construction components. Means also publishes cost data-base information for electrical and mechanical work. McGraw-Hill also publishes some construction cost data in their *Engineering News-Record* magazine. Of course, the general contractor can build an individualized data base in any manner that is compatible with his estimation of hardware and software.

With the drastically reduced price of personal computers over the years, most general contractors will be using electronic data processing equipment in their estimating department, but it can also be quite easily accumulated and processed manually.

The weekly field labor report

In order to build a data base, a method of field reporting has to be established. This is accomplished by creating a weekly field labor summary which will

1. Report the actual costs of work performed by the contractor's own field forces.

2. Report the actual costs and compare them with the estimated costs for these operations.

3. Report the actual quantities of work in place versus the estimated quantities.

4. Report the amount of weekly work performed to reflect job progress.

5. Provide a basis for projecting completed costs for each task.

A page from a typical field labor report is shown in Fig. 4.1. This report lists all the operations that the general contractor is working on in the field, and each task is assigned a cost code and a unit of measure. The estimated quantity and the total cost of each task are listed along with the unit cost for the item of work. As the weekly costs are reported each week, generally when the payroll is being prepared, they are displayed opposite their corresponding estimated value. Therefore, on a weekly basis, the project manager can monitor how a specific operation is performing compared to the dollar amount estimated. Also, actual quantities can be compared with the quantities estimated for each work task.

The field labor report can be one of the most effective means of establishing a data base and monitoring costs for those tasks usually performed by the general contractor with his own work crews. In order to establish such a report, the daily time sheet will have to be modified and coded in accordance with a very specific cost-coding system. First let's consider the prime document, the daily field labor report, which up to now may have been used solely to report hours for payroll purposes.

The prime data-base document

The acquisition of a sound data base within the organization has as its foundation the daily time sheet on which is recorded the worker by name, trade classification, and hours worked during a particular pay period. By the addition of one more category, *daily activity,* the time sheet will be able to contain sufficient information to establish the number of hours spent on specific job tasks. Since it is unwieldy to write these tasks in longhand on the time sheet, numbers will be assigned and will be known as *cost codes.*

CONSTRUCTION CONSULTANTS
WEEKLY LABOR REPORT

JOB # 354-79   NAME: PERIOD ENDING:

| | ESTIMATED | | | ACTUAL TO DATE | | | THIS WEEK | | | % | EST COST | EST | GAIN |
	QTY	UCOST	TOTAL	QTY	UCOST	TOTAL	QTY	UCOST	TOTAL	CMP	TO COMP	FIN PROJ	/LOSS
12100 ROOF BLOCKING-1 MEMBER - LF	0	0.00 / 0.00	0 / 0	0	0.00 / 0.00	0 / 0	0	0.00 / 0.00	0 / 0	0 / 0	0	0	0
12110 MISC. BLOCKING - LF	0	0.00 / 0.00	1,200 / 0	0	0.00 / 0.00	0 / 0	0	0.00 / 0.00	0 / 0	0 / 0	1,200	1,200	0
12210 ROOF CURBS - LF	0	0.00 / 0.00	0 / 0	0	0.00 / 0.00	0 / 0	0	0.00 / 0.00	0 / 0	0 / 0	0	0	0
12300 WINDOW BLKG - 1 MEMBER - LF	0	0.00 / 0.00	0 / 0	0	0.00 / 0.00	0 / 0	0	0.00 / 0.00	0 / 0	0 / 0	0	0	0
12312 BLOCKING @ CEILING - LF	1,450	1.00 / 0.00	1,450 / 0	150	0.54 / 0.00	81 / 0	0	0.00 / 0.00	0 / 0	10 / 0	702	783	667
12313 BLKG @ TOILET ACCESSORIES-LF	2,300	1.45 / 0.00	3,340 / 0	0	0.00 / 0.00	0 / 0	0	0.00 / 0.00	0 / 0	0 / 0	3,340	3,340	0
12314 RAMP FRAMING - LS	250	0.82 / 0.00	205 / 0	0	0.00 / 0.00	0 / 0	0	0.00 / 0.00	0 / 0	0 / 0	205	205	0
12606 BASE CABINET BLOCKING - LF	4,700	0.60 / 0.00	2,820 / 0	0	0.00 / 0.00	0 / 0	0	0.00 / 0.00	0 / 0	0 / 0	2,820	2,820	0
13100 WOOD DOORS - EA	200	23.00 / 0.00	4,600 / 0	0	0.00 / 0.00	0 / 0	0	0.00 / 0.00	0 / 0	0 / 0	4,600	4,600	0
13103 BIFOLD DOORS-2 LEAF - EA	161	8.07 / 0.00	1,300 / 0	0	0.00 / 0.00	0 / 0	0	0.00 / 0.00	0 / 0	0 / 0	1,300	1,300	0
13104 BIFOLD DOORS-4 LEAF - EA	309	11.97 / 0.00	3,700 / 0	0	0.00 / 0.00	0 / 0	0	0.00 / 0.00	0 / 0	0 / 0	3,700	3,700	0
13200 BASE CABINETS - LF	202	54.95 / 0.00	11,100 / 0	0	0.00 / 0.00	0 / 0	0	0.00 / 0.00	0 / 0	0 / 0	11,100	11,100	0
13220 COUNTERTOPS - LF	0	0.00 / 0.00	0 / 0	0	0.00 / 0.00	0 / 0	0	0.00 / 0.00	0 / 0	0 / 0	0	0	0
13320 WOOD HANDRAIL - LF	1,100	3.00 / 0.00	3,300 / 0	0	0.00 / 0.00	0 / 0	0	0.00 / 0.00	0 / 0	0 / 0	3,300	3,300	0
13507 WINDOW STOOLS - EA	0	0.00 / 0.00	3,480 / 0	0	0.00 / 0.00	0 / 0	0	0.00 / 0.00	0 / 0	0 / 0	3,480	3,480	0

Figure 4.1 Page from a typical field labor report.

Along with the correlation of time and task, the *quantity* of work performed is all that is required to complete the data-base picture. Once all three criteria—time, task, and quantity—can be determined, the data base will begin to take shape and emerge. The end result of all these figures will be a dollar cost per unit of work.

Preparing the Cost Code System

In order to segregate and compartmentalize the information received from the field reports, a system of cost coding for all reportable operations or tasks must be established. A master list will be set up to include all categories of work the general contractor performs with his own forces. This master list will establish major divisions along the lines of the Uniform Construction Industry (UCI) codings or the more popular MASTERFORMAT system established by the Construction Specifications Industry (CSI): Division 1—General Conditions, Division 2—Sitework, Division 3—Concrete, Division 4—Masonry, and so on to Division 17—Control Systems.

Once the major divisions are established, subdivisions will be set up. Finally, the most elementary tasks, which are sometimes called "items," will reflect a further breakdown of the division. For example, Figs. 4.2 to 4.4 show typical task breakdowns for general conditions, sitework, concrete, drywall, carpentry, and related items. The concrete cost codes illustrate the major division, subdivision, and item breakdown.

03	Identifies the major division—Concrete
03<u>200</u>	Identifies the subdivision—Forming and Stripping
03<u>258</u>	Identifies the base item—Forming and Stripping Piers

It just so happens that cost code 03200 is to be used for both forming and stripping. If it is desirable to separate these tasks, a subdivision code for stripping can be established, leaving Subdivision 2 for forming operations only.

Figure 4.5 represents a data-base report item list format from one software company. Division 1 is designated for general conditions. Subdivision 1.0 is reserved for project coordination; Subdivision 1.1 is for field supervision, and this is followed by other categories for the remainder of the general conditions work. The cost-coding system can be expanded or contracted as required. However, the more complex it is, the more supervision will be required to implement and maintain it. As each operation is performed in the field, worker hours will be recorded and applied against a specific task code number. On either the same time sheet or on a separate quantity sheet, the quantity of work tabulated for

TYPICAL COST CODE DESIGNATED FOR:

General Conditions and Sitework

Cost Code	Description	Unit	Cost Code	Description	Unit
	GENERAL CONDITIONS			**SITEWORK**	
01002	As Built Drawings	LS	02002	Clear & Grubb	LS
01004	Field Eng./Survey	WK	02004	Plantings	LS
01006	Drawings	LS	02006	Seeding	LS
01008	Field Off. Utilities	MO	02007	Irrigation Systems	LS
01010	Field Off. Supplies	LS	02010	Bitum. Paving/Curbs	LS
01011	Dumpsters	EA	02012	Line Painting	LS
01012	General Cleaning	MH	02022	Disp. Excess Mat.	CY
01013	Final Cleaning	LS	02024	Site Cuts/Fills	CY
01014	Misc. Small Items	LS	02026	Excav. Ftgs & Walls	CY
01016	Project Sign	EA	02020	Trench for Trades	CY
01018	Safety-OSHA	LS	02032	Strip & Pile Topsoil	CY
01019	Scaffolding	LS	02036	Backfill Footings	CY
01020	Sanitary Facilities	MO	02040	B.F. Trench for Trades	CY
01022	Snow Remov/Dust Cont.	LS	02042	Spread & Compact Fill	CY
01023	Pickup/Del. Materials	LS	02044	Rough Grade Inside	SF
01024	Storage Sheds	MO	02046	Rough Grade Outside	SF
01026	Superintendent	WK	02048	Fine Grade Inside	SF
01027	Assist. Supervision	WK	02050	Fine Grade Outside	SF
01028	Job Trailer	MO	02052	Furn. & Del. Borrow	CY
01030	Telephone	MO	02054	Furn. & Del. B.R.Grav.	CY
01032	Temp. Enclosures	SF	02056	F & D Process Gravel	CY
01034	Temp. Heat	WK	02058	F & D Stone	CY
01036	Temp. Light & Power	WK	02060	F & D Sand	CY
01038	Temp. Water	WK	02061	Respread Loam	CY
01039	Equipment Fuel	LS	02062	Hand Grade for Ftgs.	SF
			02064	Hand B.F. & Compact	CY
			02065	Equipment Moving	EA

Figure 4.2 Typical cost-code designations for general conditions and sitework.

each corresponding task will also be reported. The unit of measure for each work task should correspond to the generally accepted practice in the industry, for example, forming—square-foot basis; reinforcing-steel placement—per-pound or per-ton basis; concrete placement—cubic yard basis.

At the end of the work week, when time sheets and quantity sheets are sent to the head office for payroll preparation, the unit costs will be

ESTIMATING COST CODES FOR:

Concrete and Carpentry Divisions

Cost Code	Description	Unit	Cost Code	Description	Unit
	CONCRETE			**SLAB-ON-GRADE**	
03258	F/S Piers	SF	03410	Fine Grade for Slab	SF
03260	F/S Int. Wall Ftgs	SF	03420	Bulkheads/Set Dowels	LF
03262	F/S Foundation Walls	SF	03430	Bondbreaker/Exp Joint	LF
03264	F/S Keyways	LF	03440	Mesh for Slab-on-Grade	SF
03266	F/S Grade Beams	SF	03450	Rebar for Slab-on-Grade	TN
03268	F/S Ret. Wall Ftgs	SF	03455	Conc. for Slab/3000 psi	CY
03270	F/S Retaining Walls	SF	03456	Conc. for Slab/4000 psi	CY
03272	F/S Concrete Stairs	SET	03457	Conc. for Slab/Others	CY
03273	F/S Dock Leveler Pits	EA	03458	Vapor Barrier	SF
03274	Form Brick Shelves	SF	03460	PL & Fin S.O.G. 4"	SF
03275	Mud Sills	LF	03462	PL & Fin S.O.G. 5"	SF
03298	Repair/Rework Forms	LS	03464	PL & Fin S.O.G. 6"	SF
03299	Shoring	LS	03466	PL & Fin S.O.G. Other	SF
03302	PL & Fin. Col. Ftgs	CY	03470	Apply Curing Compound	SF
03304	PL & Fin. Con. Ftgs	CY	03480	Saw Cut Control Jnts.	LF
03308	PL & Fin. Piers	CY	03490	Diamonds	EA
03310	PL & Fin Int Wall Ftgs	CY	03498	Misc. S.O.G. Items	LS
03312	PL & Fin. Found. Walls	CY	03499	S.O.G. Subcontractor	LS
03316	PL & Fin. Ret Wall Ftgs	CY			
03318	PL & Fin Ret. Walls	Cy		**SUPPORTED SLAB**	
03320	PL & Fin Conc. Stair	SET			
03322	PL & Fin Leveler Pits	EA	03505	Form Supported Slab	SF
03352	Set Anchor Bolts	EA	03510	Bulkheads/Set Dowels	LF
03354	Set/Grout Base Plates	EA	03520	Bondbreaker/Exp Joint	LF
03356	Rub Walls	SF	03530	Rebar for Supp. Slab	TN
03358	Perimeter Insulation	SF	03535	Mesh for Supp. Slab	SF
03360	Waterstop	LF	03450	PL & Fin Supp. Slab 2½"	SF
			03542	PL & Fin Supp. Slab 3"	SF
			03544	PL & Fin Supp. Slab 4"	SF
			03545	Conc. for S.S./3000 psi	CY
			03546	Conc. for S.S./4000 psi	CY
			03457	Conc. for S.S./Others	CY
			03550	Apply Curing Compound	SF
			03560	Mtl. Pan Stairs	LS
			03570	Supp. Slab Subcontr.	LS
			03575	Misc. Supp. Slab Items	LS

KEY

SF = Square Feet
LF = Lineal Feet
EA = Each
LS = Lump Sum
CY = Cubic Yard
TN = Ton
SET = Set

Figure 4.3 Estimating cost codes for concrete and carpentry divisions

calculated either manually or electronically.

For example, Mr. John Doe, carpenter, was working on concrete wall forming last week and the hours spent on this operation, combined with the quantities reported on another sheet, will be computed as follows, assuming that Doe worked 40 hours on forming and reported it on cost code 03278 (forming 8-ft-high foundation walls). The quantity of walls formed and reported was 283 ft^2 of *surface area* (forms installed on both sides of the wall).

TYPICAL COST CODE DESIGNATED FOR:					
Drywall, Carpentry, Hollow Metal and Hardware					

Cost Code	Description	Unit	Cost Code	Description	Unit
	DRYWALL			**CARPENTRY**	
06027	Sht.Rock Walls 10' & und	SF	06102	Column & Pipe Surrounds	SF
06028	Sht.Rock Walls Over 10'	SF.	06104	Counters & Tops	LS
06029	Ext. Sheathing-Walls	SF	06106	Handrails	LF
06030	Sht.Rock-All Others	SF	06108	Jambs & Door Trim	LF
06031	Tape & Spackel Sht.Rock	SF	06109	Misc. Wood Trim	LS
06032	Wd. Stud Part.-10' & Und.	SF	06110	Paneling with Trim	SF
06033	Wd. Stud Part-Over 10"	SF	06111	Cabinets	LS
06034	Mtl. Stud Partitions- 25ga. 10' & Under	SF	06112	Closet Poles & Shelves	LF
06035	Mtl. Stud Partitions- 25ga. Over 10'	SF	06113	Finish Wood Trimming- Borr. Lites & Windows	LF
06036	Mtl. Stud Partitions- 3-5/8" 20ga. 10' & Und.	SF	06114	Window Sills	LF
06037	Mtl. Stud Partions- 3-5/8" 20ga Over 10'	SF			
06038	Mtl. Stud Partitions- 6" 20gal. 10' under	SF	06116	Wood Doors	EA
06039	Mtl. Stud Partitions- 6" 20ga. Over 10'	SF	06118	Wood Doors-Bifold	EA
06040	Mtl. Stud Partitions- All Others	SF	06120	Wood Doors-Sliding	EA
06041	Wood Framed Ceilings	SF	06121	Millwork-Unload & Dist.	MH
06045	Frame Overhang	SF			
06046	Ext.Sheathing-Overhand	SF		**HOLLOW METAL**	
06047	Cedar Facia	SF	08011	Hollow Mtl.-Furn & Del.	LS
06048	Metal Facia	SF	08012	HM Unload & Distribute	MH
06049	Duraply for Soffit	SF	06014	HM Intall Doors	EA
06050	Cedar Soffit	SF	08016	HM Install Borr.Lites	EA
06051	Soffit-All Others	SF	08018	HM-Inst. Frames-Drywall	EA
06055	Clerestory Wind. Dtl.	LF	08020	HM-Inst. Frames-Masonry	EA
06060	Rough Carpentry-Misc.	LS	08022	HM-Install Transoms	EA
				HARDWARE	
			08051	Fin. Hardware-Furn & Del	LS
			08052	Install Fin. Hardware- Wood Doors	EA
			06053	Install Fin. Hardware- Metal Doors	EA
			08080	Fin. Hrdwre. Cabinets	LS
			08081	Misc. Hardware	LS

Figure 4.4 Typical cost-code designations for drywall, carpentry, hollow metal, and hardware.

DATA BASE REPORT ITEM LIST

Item # Description	Unit	Class	Conversion	Order Unit	Unit Cost	C/I#	C/I Amount

DIVISION 1 -- GENERAL CONDITIONS

SUBDIVISION   1.0 -- PROJECT COORINATION

1.000 PROJECT SUPERVISION	LS	3 LABOR	x1.00	LS	0.000	0	0.000
1.001 PRINCIPAL/EXEC.	WK	3 LABOR	x1.00	HR	37.000	0	0.000
1.002 SENIOR PROJECT MGR.	WK	3 LABOR	x32.00	HR	20.000	0	0.000
1.003 ASST. PROJECT MGR.	WK	3 LABOR	x16.00	HR	21.000	0	0.000
1.004 CLERICAL/ACCOUNTING	WK	3 LABOR	x8.00	HR	22.000	0	0.000
1.005 CONSTR'N MANAGEMENT FEE	LS	5 OTHER	x1.00	LS	72485.000	0	0.000
1.006 CONTINGENCIES	LS	5 OTHER	x1.00	LS	0.000	0	0.000
1.007 PROJ SUPER'N COMPUTER RM	LS	3 LABOR	x1.00	LS	7310.000	0	0.000
1.008 CM FEE- COMPUTER ROOM	LS	5 OTHER	x1.00	LS	14468.000	0	0.000

SUBDIVISION   1.1 -- FIELD SUPERVISION

| 1.101 GENERAL SUPER | WK | 3 LABOR | x8.00 | HR | 25.930 | 0 | 0.000 |
| 1.102 SUPER | WK | 3 LABOR | x40.00 | HR | 22.810 | 0 | 0.000 |

Figure 4.5   Electronic-data-processed (EDP) produced cost-code report.

John Doe, Carpenter Journeyman	Hourly wage rate	$18.50
	Fringe benefits per hour	5.50
	Total hourly cost	$24.00

Computation to arrive at unit cost will be

40 hours × $24.00 per hour	$960.00
Total area of wall formed	283 ft^2
Unit cost per square foot	$3.39

Unit costs may vary from week to week throughout the life of the operation. When a task is being started, there is a familiarization period in which construction details are worked out, a pattern of work is established, and worker crews formed, and a rhythm created for each repetitive operation. In the beginning, reported unit costs may be double their estimated value, but as the operation continues, costs should go down. When the operation has ended, the unit price, based on the completed costs and final quantities, will represent *one* cost per unit for a particular operation for a particular project. If this unit cost is used in the preparation of an estimate, it will represent a good cost model; however, not until several costs for similar operations from other projects are accumulated will a more accurate cost be presented.

Displaying and Analyzing the Unit Costs

Unit costs for the same operation will vary from job to job for a number of reasons. Weather conditions can have an appreciable effect on costs. Concrete-forming operations should be less costly in May than in December when working in the northern part of the country. Forming very high concrete walls will be more costly than forming lower ones because scaffolding may be required and material handling demands are more pronounced. Repetitive operations will produce lower costs than start-and-stop operations. More qualified workers, of course, will have an effect on costs. When unit prices are compared from one job to the next, not only the costs but also the similarity or dissimilarity of the operations must be taken into account. One way to view unit costs for the same operation or task is to prepare a spreadsheet, either electronically or manually.

Figure 4.6 shows such a spreadsheet in which a series of tasks or operations are listed along with their respective costs culled from four different projects.

Figure 4.6 contains cost code 03254 form and strip footings on a square-foot basis. Costs vary from $1.04/ft^2 for the Elcon project to $1.39/ft^2 for the

SPREAD SHEET ANALYSIS OF UNIT COSTS*						
DESCRIPTION	COST CODE	UNIT	JOB–537 APEX MAF.	JOB–486 B&G TOOL	JOB–502 ELCON	JOB–498 ONEX CORP
FORM AND STRIP FOOTINGS	03254	SF	$ 1.24	$ 1.39	$ 1.04	$ 1.17
FORM AND STRIP WALLS	03262	SF	2.21	2.75	2.01	2.34
FORM AND STRIP DOCK PITS	03273	EA	375.00	N/A	N/A	425.00
PLACE AND FINISH FOOTINGS	03304	CY	20.00	24.00	19.00	27.00
PLACE – FINISH FOUNDATION WALLS	03312	CY	65.00	72.00	84.00	69.00
SET ANCHOR BOLTS	03352	EA	2.35	1.95	2.70	2.10

*Note:Above unit costs are not actual but have been inserted for illustrative purposes only

Figure 4.6 Spreadsheet analysis of related unit costs from four projects.

B&G Tool Company building. A comparison can take several forms. By obtaining the average of all costs, it is reasonable to assume that $1.21/ft^2 can be used to estimate future projects. However, the cost from the B&G Tool job is 33 percent higher than the Elcon project. There may, of course, be a reason for this disparity, and a more accurate unit cost may be arrived at by averaging Apex, Elcon, and Onex, resulting in a unit cost of $1.15. If data processing equipment is available and each project is assigned a project number, by programing the software these costs may be able to be called up rather easily.

The accumulation, preparation, and refinement of cost-gathering activities is a complex and time-consuming exercise, but it is essential in these times of low-margin and fierce competition.

The Cost Code Orientation Process

Implementation of a good unit-cost data-base program will add more workload onto all players. The superintendent in the field will now have additional work to do at the end of a normally long and sometimes grueling day. The costs, if they are to be meaningful, depend on accurate information. Quite possibly, the accumulation of quantities of work put into place may fall to the carpenter or labor supervisor and the project superintendent must oversee their daily record keeping. There will be added work for the accounting department whose job it will be to sort out materials invoices and ascertain that they are cost-coded properly, and the payroll clerk will be responsible for typing the raw data on the time sheets into the computer.

This orientation period is a critical one, and the project manager, who is the liaison between field and office, becomes a key player and will probably take on the biggest role in seeing to it that the system succeeds. No matter how well a system is conceived, as it is put into practice, fine tuning will be required. It will be the project manager's responsibility to review the system and its procedures with the field people. As time sheets are being cost-coded at the job site and quantity reports are being prepared, the project manager will have to review all these documents when they come in from the field and before they are passed on to the accounting department.

The cost-code orientation process—what to look for

Are the proper codes being used? The project manager, who should be familiar with which operations are currently taking place on the job, can scrutinize the time sheets to determine whether the correct code numbers are being assigned to the work tasks. If he finds that rough carpentry cost code numbers are being applied to concrete formwork, the field should be notified of this error immediately.

Are the square-foot quantities being reported correctly? Does everyone understand how they *are* to be reported? Is the square-foot area of concrete formwork, or drywall work, to be based on the square footage of contact area or the total square-foot area of forms or wall board installed?

If a 4-ft-high foundation wall is being formed and its total length is 8 ft, does the superintendent report 64 ft^2 (32 ft^2 per side) or a total of 32 ft^2, which represents total contact area? It may not matter which method is used as long as the same unit costs are reported in a consistent manner.

Similar questions may arise when drywall work is being performed. Do the reported areas include the square feet of gypsum board installed on each side of the partition or the total square footage of contact area? Is steel stud framing to be reported on the basis of square feet of wall area or linear feet of full-height wall area? Questions of these types will probably arise when the cost-coding system is first put into effect, and it will be the project manager's duty to establish some kind of uniformity in reporting after consulting with all the reporting parties.

Once the cost-reporting system has been operating for a number of months and has been monitored to unearth inconsistencies and develop meaningful unit costs, the value of the report will become more apparent to many people. To anyone having pride in his job, cost reports will provide an added element of job satisfaction. The superintendent can see very graphically how a specific operation is performing in relation to the dollar amount estimated. The cost report provides a gauge by which performance can be measured. If, on the other hand, the field-generated unit costs substantially exceed the estimated costs and the superintendent feels that these operations are being performed efficiently, he and the project manager may determine that the problem lies with the way in which the job was estimated, requiring another look at the unit costs for those work tasks.

Instead of waiting until an operation is complete to determine whether the actual costs exceed or are less than the estimated costs, periodic monitoring should take place as the work progresses. If costs drastically exceed the estimate, maybe something can be done about it. At least the warning signs have been raised and closer scrutiny should be paid to this losing operation to see if there are ways to mitigate losses.

Manipulating the unit codes—pitfalls to avoid

The project manager must monitor the weekly cost reports to ensure that they are accurate because they can be manipulated by any number of reasons, creating inaccurate figures. The author was once the project manager on a 14-story apartment house project and the job superintendent was first-rate. His specialty was concrete work, and his concrete unit costs were always very good. He would plan ahead, and if there were complicated footing or foundation details, he would create his own form of shop drawings for that work, and he utilized manpower efficiently. One day while making an unexpected visit to the job site at about 4:30 P.M., the author saw some concrete foundation wall forms literally flying out of the excavation around the building. When he got closer to the building, he saw the superintendent stripping the foundation wall forms after all the other workers had gone home for the day. He was a big, strong guy and was able to throw these forms out of the foundation onto the ground. He said that he had caught up on his paperwork and needed some exercise and decided he needed to do something physical. A few days later, in the office, the author happened to check the time sheets for the current week for that job and in particular the activities that took place on the day of his visit. All the superintendent's time was charged against the cost code for "supervision." When asked why he did not apportion any of his time against the code for foundation wall form stripping, he replied with a smile, "Job security." Of course, his job would not have been in jeopardy if his concrete form stripping unit costs had been somewhat higher, but he certainly was creating optimistic unit costs which were not truly representative of actual form stripping.

Good systems can be conceived and initiated, but it is management's responsibility to ensure their success.

Extracting cost data from completed projects

Once projects are completed, they can supply a wealth of information for the future use. The individual building component costs, subcontracts, change orders to the subcontracts, and materials purchased should be reviewed with an eye to adding to the company's data base.

How did the final project costs compare with the initial estimate, taking into account any scope increases or decreases? It is just as important to analyze costs which were much lower than those estimated as well as those which were higher. If any of the final costs were substantially lower than estimated, the method by which these estimated costs were assembled might reveal why some previous bids were lost by a small margin when they should not have been noncompetitive.

The information gleaned from final job costs can be assembled into another type of data base which might be called a *project parameter data sheet*. In order to establish the project parameter costs, the recently completed project has to be broken down into basic components of construction in order to properly allocate final costs. The unit costs obtained in this manner will not be as well defined as those obtained from the field cost reporting system, but they will be more broad-based and are

PROJECT PARAMETER COST MODEL DATA SHEET

JOB: _____WOODBRIDGE PLAZA_____
START: May 1,1992 FINISH: April 30, 1993
SIZE: 14,400 each floor x 2 = 28,800 Square Feet
FLOOR TO FLOOR: _____12'-0"_____

EXCAVATION/SITE:		$	75,000
SITE UTILITIES		$	18,000
SITE IMPROVEMENTS/LANDSCAPING		$	15,000
PAVING		$	17,500
TOTAL SITE:		$	125,500

FOUNDATIONS–SLABS	Walls 4'-0" high,5" S.O.G.,3½" S.O.M.D.			$	105,000
STRUCTURE:	Strl.Steel cols.,joist,20 gauge metal deck			$	299,000
EXTERIOR:	TYPE: Brick,cavity wall	9408	SF	$	141,120
ROOF:	TYPE: EDPM	14,400	SF	$	61,200
DRYWALL:	EXTERIOR: 6"-20 ga.studs,gyp sheath	9,408	SF	$	70,560
	INTERIOR: 3 5/8" 25 ga.studs, 5/8FCSR		SF	$	22,500
CARPENTRY:	ROUGH			$	9,600
	FINISH			$	18,000
WINDOWS:	TYPE 4'-0"high alum strip,1"I.G.	4,704	SF	$	117,600
FINISHES:	ACT	26,000	SF	$	45,500
	PAINT		SF	$	9,000
	VCT	750	SF	$	1,500
	CERAMIC	300	SF	$	3,450
	CARPET	2,111	SFyd	$	31,665
ELEVATORS:	One hydraulic			$	25,000
PLUMBING:	20 fixtures-3 roof leaders @ $5000			$	65,000
HVAC:	Gas fired boiler,hot water baseboard perimeter roof top gas fire central cooling			$	302,500
SPRINKLER:	Throughout			$	43,200
ELECTRIC:	800 amp service,2x2 fluor.lights w/electronic ballasts, lobby chandelier			$	287,000
OTHER COSTS:	Permits,fees			$	13,800
GENERAL CONDITIONS:	4%			$	74,729
TOTAL COST:				$	1,942,924
OVERHEAD & PROFIT:	* 5% overhead,5% profit			$	199,149
CONTRACT AMOUNT:				$	2,142,073

COMMENTS: * Note: 5% overhead is applied to total cost and then added to it.
5% profit is then added to this total.

Figure 4.7   Project parameter cost model sheet.

to be used as such. Conceptual estimating depends on having this kind of broad-brush cost data readily at hand. And when a similar project is being estimated in-house, the project parameter data sheet obtained from a recently completed comparable job can be used to check against components for the new job.

A typical project parameter data sheet prepared for a hypothetical project called the Woodbridge Plaza Office Building is shown in Fig. 4.7.

The starting and completion dates are inserted at the top of the page and will be used in future comparisons to compensate for inflation factors and weather conditions. The size of the building, number of floors, total square footage, and floor-to-floor heights are also required for proper assessment of costs. More descriptive information can be included if necessary. Since data is relatively easy to extract when a project has been completed recently, the project manager might want to expand on the number and types of components used in the building.

Excavation and related sitework costs are kept separate inasmuch as they could vary so much from job to job that they can be used in only the most general way. By keeping these costs separate, the true building costs can be analyzed. It is helpful to obtain actual square-foot areas of certain components such as exterior wall construction, windows, and possibly some of the interior finish work such as partition area, areas of flooring, and special ceiling construction areas, so that square-foot prices for these areas rather than costs per square foot of building area can be obtained.

The square-foot measurements or calculations for the project parameter or cost model sheets do not have to be exact to be meaningful. Before filing the drawings away when the job is complete, a rather rapid series of measurements can be taken if the information was not developed during the construction period. If any unusual foundation conditions were encountered, such as a requirement for pile foundations, mud slabs, or subsurface drainage, these conditions should be noted and estimated costs assigned. When the building's structural system is described, bay spacings or unusual loading requirements should be noted. In the mechanical and electrical portions of the project parameter sheet there should be space to describe the systems very briefly. Plumbing fixture count can be used to establish unit costs; alternatively, plumbing cost as a function of the area of the building can also be used. If the cost per fixture will be the basis for comparison, the other significant plumbing costs, such as interior roof drains, can be separated. Heating, ventilating, and air-conditioning costs, as well as fire protection or sprinkler costs, are most effectively handled on the basis of cost per square foot of building. A brief description of the HVAC system is helpful in relating costs for a general type of system such as hot-water baseboard radiation with centrally located cooling equipment, hot-air heating and cooling from centrally located equipment, heat pumps, or variable-air-volume systems. Several factors may affect the electrical costs. One is the size of the incoming service; another is the number of metering devices inside the building, building equipment loads, or specialized equipment such as emergency generators or uninterrupted power sources (UPSs).

The cost model sheet contains a line item "other costs," which is just a catchall for the costs of miscellaneous or special components that are required to arrive at a total project cost, but are so unique in nature that they need to be separate for cost-comparison purposes. A separate category has been established to record the general conditions or general requirements. By segregating these costs, which can be substantial, and analyzing them from job to job, general condition costs, for estimating purposes, can be converted to an average percentage figure for future use. General conditions can range from 3 percent to as high as 10 percent, but once a range is established for your company, it can represent a key element in the conceptual estimating process. The overhead and profit final tabulations will be the difference between final costs and the contract sum and should prove interesting to see if profit goals as initially estimated have been met.

The cost information as set forth on the project parameter sheet will be used as an estimating tool and as a conceptual estimating guide. Let us first look at the project parameter as an aid in assisting in the preparation of an estimate for a competitively bid job. The next time a project is being competitively bid and is similar in nature to the Woodbridge Plaza office building, the costs developed in the project parameter cost sheet can be used to compare bids on the new project. A written or mental checklist can be prepared to determine compatibility of the two jobs.

1. Are bay spacings, floor-to-floor heights, and floor loadings about the same?

2. Are both buildings open office space with no tenant fitup included? If not, do both include tenant fitup?

3. Are the exterior walls and roof construction similar?

4. Are window installations similar? What about glass and frame materials of construction?

5. What about plumbing, HVAC, sprinkler, and electrical systems? Are they so alike as to merit comparison?

If all or most of the answers indicate that there are close similarities between the two projects, cost comparisons can be made. The objective will be to compare pricing and bid quotations received from subcontractors on the new project with the known costs of the older, similar one. This will give the estimating department a chance to compare some prices before the bid tabulation has been completed, if time permits.

Utilizing the cost model to check on pricing on new jobs

Let us assume that the estimating department is assembling a bid for a very similar office building and subcontractor prices are in process of being received. A look at the updated Woodbridge Plaza costs might be of some assistance in analyzing the new prices. It will be assumed that for accurate comparison purposes the Woodbridge Plaza costs will have to be escalated for a 12-month period during which inflation has been pegged at 4 percent, but first we need to establish some unit prices from the original project parameter sheet. When we use the word "cost" it is just that, and will not include their overhead or profit:

Structural steel total cost		$299,000
Cost per square foot of building	$10.38	
Brick veneer total cost		141,120
Cost per square foot of building	4.90	
Cost per square foot of surface area	15.00	
Drywall curtain wall total cost		70,560
Cost per square foot of building	2.45	
Cost per square foot of surface area	7.50	
Windows total cost		117,600
Cost per square foot of building	4.08	
Cost per square foot of surface area	25.00	
Roof and insulation total cost		61,200
Cost per square foot of building	2.13	
Cost per square foot of surface area	4.25	
Total cost of project, less sitework		$1,746,655
Cost per square foot without escalation	$60.65	

Plumbing can be analyzed as a function of building area or fixture count, if identifiable components such as roof leaders can be separated from the total plumbing costs. For example

Total plumbing costs,	$65,000	Cost per square foot of building, $2.26
Less roof drains,	$15,000	
Fixture cost,	$50,000	Cost per fixture, $2500
HVAC total cost, $302,500		Cost per square foot of building, $10.50
Sprinklers total cost, $43,200		Cost per square foot of building, $1.50
Electrical total cost, $287,000		Cost per square foot of building, $9.96

By taking one trade as an example, these unit prices can be used to check the quotations received for the new project being bid. The electrical cost of $9.96 updated for the 4 percent inflation factor for a one-year period established a new "cost" of $10.57. If prices for the new office building, which is 34,000 ft², range from $257,760 to $493,000, look at the following analysis:

	Cost per square foot
Woodbridge Plaza updated unit cost	$10.57
ABC Electric price, new job, $372,300	10.95
Star Electric Company, new job, $419,900	12.35
P&M Electric, new job, $257,760	8.95
Alcan Electric Company, new job, $493,000	14.50

It would appear that ABC Electric has the more competitive price. P&M's price of $257,700, or $8.95/ft^2, seems out of line on the low side and, conversely, Alcan Electric's $14.50/ft^2 is too high to consider. Although, in today's competitive bid marketplace, a general contractor may have no choice other than to use the P&M's unrealistically low price, these unit prices may be cause to generate a phone call to both high and low bidder to determine whether they understood the scope of work to be included in their bid.

Now let us see how the project parameter cost sheet can be used in the process known as *conceptual estimating*.

Conceptual Estimating

Conceptual estimating, quite literally, means preparing an estimate based on a concept. The concept can be represented on the back of a napkin, by the prospective client's verbal description of a building, or by a page or two of preliminary or progress drawings.

The general contractor will be asked to assemble an estimate without the strict guidelines represented by an architect's drawing and specifications, but must rely instead on experience and a knowledge of building systems and related costs.

Who uses conceptual estimates?

An architect will sometimes request or resort to conceptual estimating after being interviewed by a client who would like to know approximately how much the building they have just been discussing will cost. A general contractor will use his skill in conceptual estimating when he attempts to sell his services to a prospective client. The more adept a general contractor is at this sort of thing, the more effective his sales effort will be. A client may request conceptual estimates for use in determining project feasibility when starting discussions with a lending institution or with his capital projects or appropriations director. A delicate balance must be maintained during the process of developing conceptual estimates. If the initial estimate is unrealistically high, it may influence the client to abandon the project or seek the assistance of another general contractor to prepare budget figures. On the other hand, the general contractor will be accused of "low-balling" if a considerably higher estimate emerges after sufficient plans and specifications have been developed. The key to successful conceptual estimating is ready access to a solid and reliable data base of construction costs.

Source of conceptual estimating data

Conceptual estimating can be based on costs obtained from the following sources:

1. Costs developed in-house from previous projects

2. Cost index data published by companies that specialize in compiling and selling construction cost data on a national or regional basis

3. Component estimating with in-house or purchased cost data

4. Square-foot estimating

5. Order-of-magnitude estimates

Costs developed in-house.   Conceptual estimates can be prepared from the information in the project parameter cost sheets. Let us create a scenario to show how this can work.

A prospective client has seen the Woodbridge Plaza building and would like to discuss construction of a similar structure that would, however, be four floors with a total area of 48,000 ft^2. By referring to the Woodbridge Plaza costs and deducting all site-related costs, and working from costs which do not include overhead and profit, a square-foot price of $60.65 is established. Assuming the client would like to begin construction of the new project in 6 months, and since the Woodbridge Plaza job was completed one year ago, price escalation of 18 months must be factored in. If inflation has been estimated to be 4 percent per year, an updated Woodbridge Plaza square-foot price, based upon a construction start in 6 months, will be $64.34. By adding overhead and profit and multiplying by the square-foot area of the proposed building, a rather rapid conceptual estimate can be prepared, exclusive of sitework.

The prospective client, a somewhat knowledgeable building owner, would like to make certain changes in the building design and wishes to know how these changes would affect the budget price. He would like to use reflective glass in the exterior windows instead of the bronze-tinted glass at Woodbridge Plaza. Having had good experience with a certain PVC roofing membrane, he prefers that material instead of the EPDM. Also he would like to delete all carpeting in the building because he would structure his tenant leases to include building standards materials. To start the process at this time, it is wise to sketch an outline of the building's footprint and also one of a typical elevation. These sketches will help in establishing floor and roof areas as well as analyzing bay spacings to compare with the cost model. The elevation will provide a more exact exterior wall surface and window area. By using bay spacings of 28 ft, a footprint of 140 × 84 ft emerges. This equates to 11,760 ft^2 per floor and 47,040 ft^2 for the entire four-story building. On the basis of this configuration, the elevation sketch can be quickly drawn and will indicate that approximately 7168 ft² of ribbon or strip window will be required. A telephone call to a reliable glass and glazing subcontractor will reveal that this reflective glass in aluminum frames similar to Woodbridge Plaza should cost about $35.00/ft² installed.

As far as the single-ply PVC roofing membrane is concerned, the roofing subcontractor offered two prices: one for the unballasted roofing membrane, adhered with mechanical fasteners; and the other for PVC-ballasted roofing membrane, using 2-in river stone for ballast. The PVC-ballasted roof was quoted at $3.95/ft² and the unballasted, mechanically fastened roof would cost $4.39/ft². If the ballasted roof were to be used, the structural-steel price would have to be increased to accommodate this heavier load. The Woodbridge Plaza project used a mechanically fastened rubber roof. The client is made aware of this fact, and until more studies can be made to determine all costs involved, the higher-priced mechanically fastened roof price of $4.39 will be factored into the job.

With all that information in hand, the Woodbridge Plaza costs will now be adjusted to compensate for the changes proposed by the client. Going back to the cost model data, we look at the following.

Contract amount	$2,097,126
Less overhead and profit	194,971
Less sitework	155,500
Building cost	$1,746,655
Less client-requested changes	
Delete cost of EPDM roof	$ 61,200
Delete cost of windows with bronze-tint glass	117,600
Delete carpet	31,665
Total deducts from above building cost	$209,465

With these further deducts the cost model is now $1,537,190, divided by 28,800 ft², represents $53.37/ft². Updating this figure again for 18 months of cost escalation at 4 percent, the cost becomes $56.61/ft².

Now we will apply this square-foot value to the proposed square footage of the new building, add back the current prices for windows and roofing, and add our overhead and profit.

Proposed new office building 47,040 ft² × $56.61	$2,662,934
Add PVC unballasted roof 11,760 ft² × $4.39	51,626
Add reflective windows 7168 ft² × $35.00	250,880
Conceptually estimated cost without sitework	$3,087,744
Add 5% overhead	148,272
Subtotal	$3,113,712
Add 5% profit	155,686
New conceptual estimated project cost, $69.50/ft² (without sitework)	$3,269,398

The client can now be presented with a fairly accurate budget of $3,270,000 for the proposed new office building, exclusive of site costs, and hopefully, your company will be selected for the construction of the project.

Cost index data.   Companies that specialize in compiling and publishing cost index data provide another source of conceptual estimate preparation. The R. S. Means Company of Kingston, Massachusetts is one source that comes to mind. Figures 4.8 and 4.9 illustrate some of the square-foot and cubic-foot costs for various types of construction projects and selected components and systems. Figure 4.9 contains various costs for office buildings and by extracting costs for "OFFICES low-rise (1- to 4-story)," these costs can be used as a cross-check against cost estimates prepared from other sources such as in-house cost data. As an example, the hypothetical 47,000-ft^2 office building, which was assembled from cost model sheets, can be compared with published cost data indices. It is interesting to see how these square-foot prices compare with those published by R. S. Means for low-rise office buildings in 1993 (Table 4.1).

TABLE 4.1   Contractor's versus Published Cost Data

Cost Model data	Contractor's Cost Data		Published Cost Data		
	Price/ft^2	Escalated for 12 months	Low	Median	High
Total cost, less site	$60.65	$63.07	$49.60	$63.55	$83.55
Masonry	4.90	5.09	1.67	3.95	7.45
Plumbing	2.26	2.35	1.88	2.85	4.07
HVAC	10.50	10.92	4.02	5.65	8.25
Electrical	9.96	10.36	4.20	5.80	7.95

By this comparison, it appears that the overall square-foot costs derived from the cost model fall within the median range established by Means. Masonry square-foot costs seem to fall somewhat on the high side, but the cost of the masonry units, complexity of design, and production rates of the local masons may all be contributory. Plumbing costs per square foot also seem to be within the median range established by the published cost data. Only HVAC and electrical costs seem to vary beyond the high-side parameters reported by Means, exceeding the top three-fourths by 32 percent. If these in-house costs were derived via competitive bidding received from electrical and mechanical contractors, it may well be that the individual components of these systems or the complexity of installation and/or control have contributed to their higher-than-normal costs.

Component estimating.   Component estimating involves breaking the proposed budget down into the various building components such as

171	S.F., C.F. and % of Total Costs								
**171 000	S.F. & C.F. Costs**			**UNIT COSTS**			**% OF TOTAL**			
		UNIT	1/4	MEDIAN	3/4	1/4	MEDIAN	3/4	
650	2900	Electrical	S.F.	5.25	7.40	8.80	7.40%	9.40%	11%	650
	3100	Total: Mechanical & Electrical	↓	11.55	15.90	22.10	16.50%	21.40%	26.30%	
660	0010	POWER PLANTS	S.F.	452	596	895				660
	0020	Total project costs	C.F.	10.75	19.85	54.95				
	2900	Electrical	S.F.	23.20	60.75	98.80	9.20%	12.30%	18.40%	
	8100	Total: Mechanical & Electrical	*	70.05	151	339	28.80%	32.50%	52.60%	
670	0010	RELIGIOUS EDUCATION	S.F.	50.10	59.70	73.65				670
	0020	Total project costs	C.F.	2.92	4.18	5.50				
	2720	Plumbing	S.F.	2.14	3.10	4.25	4.30%	4.90%	7.10%	
	2770	Heating, ventilating, air conditioning		4.83	5.55	7.90	7.20%	9.70%	11.40%	
	2900	Electrical		3.81	5.15	7	7.30%	8.90%	10.30%	
	3100	Total: Mechanical & Electrical	↓	7.50	10.55	16.20	13.80%	18.70%	22.40%	
690	0010	RESEARCH Laboratories and facilities	S.F.	71.80	106	158				690
	0020	Total project costs	C.F.	4.94	9.05	12.70				
	1800	Equipment	S.F.	2.67	6	14.15	1.20%	4.90%	9.30%	
	2720	Plumbing		7.30	10.05	14.30	6.10%	8.50%	12.80%	
	2770	Heating, ventilating, air conditioning		7.10	23.45	31.40	10.70%	17%	22.70%	
	2900	Electrical		8.70	14.10	24.75	9.40%	12%	15.80%	
	3100	Total: Mechanical & Electrical	↓	18.40	36.10	65.60	20.30%	31.90%	41.90%	
700	0010	RESTAURANTS	S.F.	71.80	94.55	122				700
	0020	Total project costs	C.F.	6.35	8.30	10.45				
	1800	Equipment	S.F.	4.38	11.80	18.50	5.50%	13.40%	16.60%	
	2720	Plumbing		5.95	7.45	10.20	6%	8.40%	9.30%	
	2770	Heating, ventilating, air conditioning		8.10	10.55	13.80	9.60%	12.30%	13%	
	2900	Electrical		7.85	9.75	13.15	8.30%	10.60%	12%	
	3100	Total: Mechanical & Electrical	↓	16.95	23	30.60	18.10%	22.50%	31.10%	
	5000									
	9000	Per seat unit, total cost	Seat	2,400	3,600	4,400				
	9500	Total: Mechanical & Electrical	*	515	670	1,050				
720	0010	RETAIL STORES	S.F.	33.30	45.55	60				720
	0020	Total project costs	C.F.	2.32	3.29	4.58				
	2720	Plumbing	S.F.	1.21	2.08	3.66	3.10%	4.50%	6.80%	
	2770	Heating, ventilating, air conditioning		2.72	3.75	5.60	6.70%	8.70%	10.20%	
	2900	Electrical		3.11	4.21	6.15	7.30%	10%	11.80%	
	3100	Total: Mechanical & Electrical	↓	5.75	8.75	12.35	14.80%	18.70%	24.10%	
740	0010	SCHOOLS Elementary	S.F.	55.90	68.15	81.60				740
	0020	Total project costs	C.F.	3.75	4.77	6.10				
	0500	Masonry	S.F.	4.91	7.60	10.05	7.50%	9.60%	15.30%	
	1800	Equipment		1.42	2.91	5.50	2.20%	4.10%	7.90%	
	2720	Plumbing		3.25	4.65	6.05	5.60%	7.10%	9.30%	
	2730	Heating, ventilating, air conditioning		4.85	7.85	10.85	8%	10.80%	15.10%	
	2900	Electrical		5.10	6.45	8.15	8.30%	10%	11.60%	
	3100	Total: Mechanical & Electrical	↓	11.45	17.05	21.25	19.80%	25.60%	31.30%	
	9000	Per pupil, total cost	Ea.	5,000	9,500	11,400				
	9500	Total: Mechanical & Electrical	*	1,525	2,235	5,050				
760	0010	SCHOOLS Junior High & Middle	S.F.	58.05	68.05	81.65				760
	0020	Total project costs	C.F.	3.59	4.63	5.30				
	0500	Masonry	S.F.	4.63	7.95	10.55	7.90%	9.10%	14.30%	
	1800	Equipment		1.83	3.34	5.45	2.60%	4.70%	6.20%	
	2720	Plumbing		3.47	4.20	5.45	5.40%	6.90%	8.10%	
	2770	Heating, ventilating, air conditioning		4.27	8.15	11.50	8.70%	11.50%	17.40%	
	2900	Electrical		5.30	6.70	7.90	7.60%	9.20%	10.60%	
	3100	Total: Mechanical & Electrical	↓	12.55	16.80	24.05	19.30%	26.80%	31.90%	
	9000	Per pupil, total cost	Ea.	5,200	7,135	9,785				

See the Reference Section for reference number information, Crew Listings and City Cost Indexes.

Figure 4.8 Published square-foot cost data for various types of structures. (*Courtesy of R. S. Means Company Inc., Kingston, MA.*)

171 | S.F., C.F. and % of Total Costs

171 000 | S.F. & C.F. Costs

				UNIT	UNIT COSTS			% OF TOTAL			
					1/4	MEDIAN	3/4	1/4	MEDIAN	3/4	
010	0010	APARTMENTS Low Rise (1 to 3 story)	R171 -100	S.F.	37.05	46.60	61.60				010
	0020	Total project cost		C.F.	3.34	4.39	5.40				
	0100	Sitework	R171 -200	S.F.	3.10	4.48	7.15	6.40%	10.60%	14%	
	0500	Masonry			.67	1.75	2.95	1.40%	4%	6.50%	
	1500	Finishes			3.92	5	6.60	8.90%	10.60%	12.90%	
	1800	Equipment			1.22	1.84	2.68	2.80%	4%	6.20%	
	2720	Plumbing			2.90	3.79	4.74	6.70%	9%	10.10%	
	2770	Heating, ventilating, air conditioning			1.85	2.28	3.31	4.20%	5.80%	7.70%	
	2900	Electrical			2.15	2.87	3.96	5.20%	6.70%	8.60%	
	3100	Total: Mechanical & Electrical		↓	6.45	7.90	10.25	15.90%	18.30%	22.20%	
	9000	Per apartment unit, total cost		Apt.	29,100	43,100	64,900				
	9500	Total: Mechanical & Electrical		*	5,350	7,850	11,200				
020	0010	APARTMENTS Mid Rise (4 to 7 story)		S.F.	47.45	58.35	71.80				020
	0020	Total project costs		C.F.	3.84	5.25	7.30				
	0100	Sitework		S.F.	1.91	3.74	6.95	5.20%	6.70%	9.20%	
	0500	Masonry			2.99	4.20	6.20	5.20%	7.50%	10.50%	
	1500	Finishes			6.10	7.70	9.80	10.40%	11.90%	16.90%	
	1800	Equipment			1.62	2.21	2.95	2.80%	3.50%	4.50%	
	2500	Conveying equipment			1.12	1.37	1.64	2.10%	2.20%	2.60%	
	2720	Plumbing			2.90	4.57	5	6.20%	7.40%	8.90%	
	2900	Electrical			3.30	4.43	5.45	6.60%	7.20%	8.90%	
	3100	Total: Mechanical & Electrical		↓	9.10	11.45	14.15	17.90%	20.10%	22.30%	
	9000	Per apartment unit, total cost		Apt.	36,600	55,600	65,100				
	9500	Total: Mechanical & Electrical		*	10,900	12,700	18,700				
030	0010	APARTMENTS High Rise (8 to 24 story)		S.F.	55.95	67.80	79.15				030
	0020	Total project costs		C.F.	4.63	6.45	7.85				
	0100	Sitework		S.F.	1.72	3.29	4.61	2.50%	4.80%	6.10%	
	0500	Masonry			3.18	5.75	7.25	4.70%	9.60%	10.70%	
	1500	Finishes			6.10	7.80	8.90	9.30%	11.70%	13.50%	
	1800	Equipment			1.75	2.20	2.85	2.50%	3.30%	4.20%	
	2500	Conveying equipment			1.14	1.87	2.67	2.20%	2.70%	3.30%	
	2720	Plumbing			3.59	4.87	6.15	6.70%	9.10%	10.60%	
	2900	Electrical			3.86	4.95	6.60	6.40%	7.60%	8.80%	
	3100	Total: Mechanical & Electrical		↓	11.40	13.95	17.35	18.20%	22%	24.40%	
	9000	Per apartment unit, total cost		Apt.	51,700	61,000	66,700				
	9500	Total: Mechanical & Electrical		*	12,600	14,400	15,600				
040	0010	AUDITORIUMS		S.F.	56.10	79.15	104				040
	0020	Total project costs		C.F.	3.72	5.20	7.45				
	2720	Plumbing		S.F.	3.61	4.80	6.20	5.80%	6.90%	8.40%	
	2770	Heating, ventilating, air conditioning			7.50	18.20	21.10	6.90%	16%	19.80%	
	2900	Electrical			4.60	6.55	8.50	6.70%	8.80%	11%	
	3100	Total: Mechanical & Electrical		↓	9.55	12.65	22.10	14.70%	18.50%	23.80%	
050	0010	AUTOMOTIVE SALES		S.F.	39.40	48.40	66.05				050
	0020	Total project costs		C.F.	2.90	3.31	4.42				
	2720	Plumbing		S.F.	1.96	3.41	3.80	2.80%	6.20%	6.90%	
	2770	Heating, ventilating, air conditioning			3.02	4.71	6.75	6.30%	10%	10.70%	
	2900	Electrical			3.35	5.20	7.25	7.30%	8.70%	12.30%	
	3100	Total: Mechanical & Electrical		↓	7.10	10.70	14.35	15.40%	19.10%	27%	
060	0010	BANKS		S.F.	85.15	106	138				060
	0020	Total project costs		C.F.	6.05	8.20	10.85				
	0100	Sitework		S.F.	8.40	14.55	22.90	7%	13.40%	16.90%	
	0500	Masonry			4.27	7.20	14.50	2.90%	6.10%	10%	
	1500	Finishes			6.95	9.55	12.60	5.40%	7.60%	9.90%	
	1800	Equipment			2.49	7	16.95	2.50%	7.90%	13.60%	
	2720	Plumbing			2.75	3.92	5.80	2.80%	4%	4.90%	
	2770	Heating, ventilating, air conditioning			5.25	7.05	9.40	5%	7.20%	8.60%	

See the Reference Section for reference number information, Crew Listings and City Cost Indexes.

Figure 4.9 Published cost data for apartment buildings. (Courtesy of R. S. Means Company, Inc., Kingston, MA.)

Foundations

Superstructure, including slab on grade and suspended slabs

Building envelope, including exterior walls, windows, exterior entrances, and doors

Roofing, moisture protection, insulation

Interior partitions and finish work

Elevators and conveyance devices

Plumbing, HVAC, sprinklers, electrical and possibly control work

General conditions, overhead and profit

In this type of conceptual estimating, design information, even though it is sketchy, must be developed at an early stage. A building footprint and an elevation drawing are required, even if they are rudimentary. For instance, the concrete foundation work can be priced out after a simple structural drawing is prepared to reflect building dimensions, column spacing, and some assumed footing and foundation dimensions. Figure 4.10 is an example of a simple foundation drawing. By multiplying a few dimensions, the following concrete quantities can be obtained:

Structural element	Dimensions, ft	Concrete quantity, yd³
Continuous footings	$336 \times 2 \times 1$	24.9
Exterior column footings	$12 \times 3 \times 3 \times 2$	8.0
Exterior column piers	$12 \times 1.5 \times 1.5 \times 3$	3.0
Interior column footings	$4 \times 5 \times 5 \times 2$	7.4
Foundation walls	$336 \times 3 \times 1$	37.3

A common basis for rapid concrete pricing is *cubic yards in place,* which should include forming costs; reinforcing steel, labor and materials; and ready-mix concrete in place. Assuming that the data base reveals the cost of continuous footings to be \$175/yd³, spread footings to be \$225/yd³, foundation walls at \$300/yd³ and pier concrete at \$350/yd³, the concrete foundation portion of this component conceptual estimate will be \$59,250.

By proceeding down the list of components, pricing can be put together by using a combination of subcontractor pricing input and one's own database information. The superstructure cost can be such a combination. The steel structure, columns, beams, metal deck, interior stairs, and miscellaneous metal costs can be obtained from a knowledgeable structural-steel subcontractor.

Continuing to the building envelope, the component costs can also be derived from subcontractors and suppliers along with data-base informa-

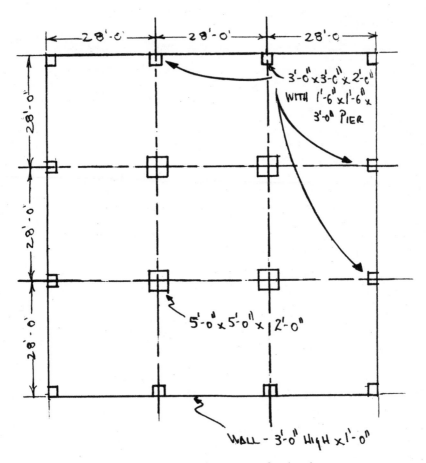

Figure 4.10 Simple foundation plan used for conceptual estimating.

tion. Wall areas of the various components will be needed, and they can be calculated from the simple footprint and elevation drawing prepared at the inception of the estimating process.

Note: When estimating drywall, many drywall subcontractors ignore wall openings for doors, windows, louvers, and such and their "takeoff" is based on total wall area exclusive of these openings. Their justification is that the additional framing, cutting, and trimming required to create these openings compensates for treating these areas with the same unit costs as regular wall construction.

Roofing and insulation work is treated in a similar manner. Current prices should include smoke and vent hatches, and any skylights that are required. Elevator quotes, with the cab finish assumed to be standard or a cab "allowance" can also be solicited from subcontractors. The elevator enclosure must not be overlooked. Is it to be masonry-laminated with gypsum board on the exterior surface, or can it be constructed of a fire-rate drywall assembly such as coreboard?

Mechanical and electrical systems are estimated on the basis of a review of a design scope with the appropriate subcontractors who will base their budget prices on the definitions of systems to be installed. General contractor input in all of these exercises is important. Costs obtained from suppliers and subcontractors in this fashion need to be compared with component costs derived from in-house comparative data. Once all the "costs" are assembled and totaled, both general conditions and overhead and profit, as percentages of tabulated construction costs, will be added. The question of site and site-related costs can be addressed either as an exclusion, an allowance, or a term known as "cost per disturbed acre." By that term we mean the costs associated with the square-foot area, or acreage, that was actually stripped of its topsoil so that other site operations could take place. The total site and site-related costs divided by the number of acres which are disturbed provides a guideline for site costs. The Woodbridge Plaza project on the project parameter cost sheet had site-related costs of $155,500. If the total area of the project was 7 acres but only 3 were "disturbed," a cost per disturbed acre would be $51,833/acre. To this cost must be added general conditions and overhead and profit, if these costs will be reported separately from general construction costs.

Order-of-magnitude estimating.   The order-of-magnitude method of establishing preliminary budgets or estimates is commonly used for motels, hotels, apartment buildings, hospital work, and parking garages. This system involves establishing unit costs based on a per-room, per-apartment, per-hospital-bed, or per-car basis.

Owners who have had prior experience with such structures will quite often ask, "How much do you think it will cost per room for this 200-room motel I'm planning?" or "this 600-car garage I am considering?" or "a 125-bed nursing home addition?"

The term "per room" or "per bed" or "per car" does not literally mean the cost of the room, bed, or car but will include all portions of the entire project reduced to these terms.

A general contractor who has built a number of elevated parking garage structures will have the necessary data base to establish a "per car" cost, for example. Order-of-magnitude estimates are obtained through experience and project this experience in not only construction costs but construction techniques as well.

The general contractor who has built a number of parking garages for both public and private owners is in an advantageous position to respond to a client's request for information relating to such a proposed project.

Various costs related to various types of parking garage structures ranging from structural steel, metal deck, and cast-in-place concrete to precast concrete and prestressed, precast concrete decks, and with "per car" costs, range from $8000 to $11,000, or so.

At times, order-of-magnitude estimates are linked to similar projects with similar space requirements. For example, the federally subsidized Section 8 Elderly Housing Program dictates certain Minimum Property Standards (MPS) for these apartment buildings, one of which is size of each one-bedroom apartment (approximately 650 ft^2). However, when the corridors, lobby areas, community rooms, stairwells, and elevator areas are included, the overall project size divided by the number of apartments may actually compute to 800 ft^2 per unit, which will include all non-rent-producing areas.

Therefore, when costs for subsidized elderly housing is being discussed on the basis of order-of-magnitude budgeting, a per-apartment cost of, say, $60,000 for a 100-unit building will result in a total project cost of approximately $6,000,000. Each apartment will be about 650 ft^2, but the total size of the building may be 80,000 to 90,000 ft^2, based on the size of areas historically dictated by this program, which will include common or public areas.

Order-of-magnitude costs are derived from historical costs, but because of industry practice, they are expressed as per-room, per-bed, per-car, per-apartment costs. When dealing with order-of-magnitude estimates, recognize the following adjustments and limitations:

1. Price escalation must be considered.

2. When one cost per room is compared with a proposed cost per room, exact duplication of an existing facility is implied.

3. As in other types of conceptual estimating, site costs must be defined, treated as an allowance, or excluded.

4. When submitting an order-of-magnitude proposal, include a brief narrative which will include scope definition.

Peculiarities Associated With Office Building Estimating

Whenever a general contractor is discussing the cost of an office building, an important aspect of the budget has to do with tenant improvements, if all or a portion of the building is to be constructed with an eye to leasing space.

Since costs of these improvements can amount to as much as 20 to 25 percent of base building costs, it is important to obtain a clear understanding of how the owner plans to handle the cost of items classified as "tenant improvements." Landlord leases are often structured on the basis of allowing the tenant X number of dollars per square foot of rentable space to be applied against the total cost of their improvements. For example, if 10,000-ft^2 office space is being rented at $25.00/ft^2 and the landlord includes a "fitup" allowance of $7.50/ft^2, the tenant will be "credited" $75,000 against the total cost of the fitup.

In most cases, estimates for office buildings incorporating leased areas will be accompanied by a rather complete list of unit prices ranging from painting and door and hardware costs to electrical outlets and electric water coolers.

The electrical system can be estimated so as not to include lighting fixtures in the proposed tenant areas, but installing service to the area via a separate panel and excluding any branch wiring, lighting fixture costs, and installation. The owner may require a separate unit price for the furnishing and installation of the tenant fixtures, after determining the exact type of fixture, or establishing a quality level for these fixtures.

If the HVAC system includes perimeter baseboard heat as a base building component and includes a variable-air-volume (VAV) system for air distribution and cooling purposes, it is standard practice to exclude the installation of VAV boxes and associated distribution ductwork, leaving those costs separate from base building costs and generally included in the unit-cost schedule that will form the basis of the tenant improvement package.

The sprinkler and fire protection systems, as required, can be estimated in several different ways: either a completed system with sprinkler heads or one with only risers and mains, with branch piping and heads estimated separately.

Depending on the fire code regulations, an entire building, or just the floor above and below the occupied floors, must be fitted with sprinkler heads before occupancy can be effected. But in any case, repositioning or adding sprinkler heads will probably be required, and estimated costs for this work will also be included in the list of unit costs requested by the owner.

The entire question of tenant work and its relation to the conceptual budget price will depend on how the prospective owner is planning to structure the lease. Rental rates may be based on having the tenant pay for all improvements including lighting fixtures, ceilings, partition work, doors, frames and hardware, heating and cooling distribution, and sprinkler installation or relocation costs.

A more-or-less standard package of improvements included in tenant rental rates, generally called the "tenant work letter," is as follows:

1. *Interior partitions.* These may be $3^1/_2$" metal studs with one layer of $^5/_8$" gypsum board on each side extending to ceiling height, taped, ready

for paint. Included in the rental rate will be a quantity of this partition work, usually expressed as a quantity per square footage of space rented, i.e., 75 ft of this partition per 100 ft² of space rented.

2. *Interior doors and frames.*   One solid-core stain grade oak door 3' 0" × 7' 0" in a hollow metal frame, for example. Hardware type and quality is included and it is usual to include one such door and frame per X linear feet of partition, say, for every 30 ft of partition.

3. *Painting.*   Prime coat plus two finish coats of an alkyd or latex paint is included. Sometimes an allowance is included for wall coverings. Areas to be painted are pegged on partition footage, and the number of doors and frames is included in the work letter.

4. *Flooring.*   The landlord may allow the tenant a specific dollar value per square yard for carpet, to include installation cost.

5. *Lighting.*   The lease rate may include a building standard fixture for a specified square footage of rented space.

6. *Light switches and electrical outlets.*   Light switches are included, one per room, and electric outlets, usually 15- to 20-A capacity, are furnished on a square foot of leased space basis.

7. *Telephone and MIS.*   At times an owner will provide one or two empty conduits per linear foot of partition and at other times, will provide a centrally located telephone room with a riser conduit but no branch conduits emanating from that room.

8. *HVAC.*   It is standard to allow a VAV terminal with flex connection and one control device based on amount of leased perimeter wall area and interior square-foot area.

Any tenant requirements over and above these improvements, when the tenant's design documents have been completed, will be paid for by the tenant.

When the conceptual or budget estimates for base building costs are presented to the client, the cost of each of the above improvements will more than likely be discussed. If a written proposal is requested, the hypothetical unit costs will be included as follows:

Partitions 10' 0" height	$38.00/ lineal ft
Doors, frames hardware	$510.00 each
Painting	$0.65/ft²
Acoustical ceilings 2 × 4	$2.25/ft²
VAV boxes with 14' flex duct	$1000 each
Light fixtures, 2 × 4 fluorescent	$225.00 each
Electrical switches	$65.00 each
Electrical outlets, 20 A	$65.00 each
Sprinkler heads, new	$200.00 each
Sprinkler heads, relocated	$90.00 each

The only other concern to address is the time span in which the tenant improvements may be required. If subcontractors have to return to the site to do tenant fitup work after they have completed the base building work, their unit costs will probably be somewhat higher. When unit-cost prices from subcontractors are being addressed, it will be necessary to establish differing prices for each unit based on the time frame in which it is anticipated they may be required. This chapter has been devoted to developing a system or systems to establish a data base and to refine and expand it. Using the data-base information, a conceptual estimating capability can be achieved. With the acquisition of data-base information and the experience obtained from conceptual estimating, the general contractor might wish to explore design-build opportunities, and Chapter 12 is devoted to that subject.

Project Organization

After a contract has been signed and prior to the start of construction, there usually is a lull period during which there is time to properly organize all of the project documents accumulated to date. All telephone bids, confirming subcontractor and supplier quotes, along with the architect's bidding instructions, must be sorted out. Once construction is under way, information storage and retrieval must be made easy.

Correspondence from the various consultants as well as the owner will be incoming, and responses to all their questions and comments will be outgoing. Shop drawings and reports of various types must be logged in and sorted as well as distributed. This process must be made simple and understandable. Individual idiosyncrasies must give way to a standard office filing procedure to ensure that everyone in the office follows the same method of document storage. Far too often a project manager has had to take over a job in midstream from a recently departed project manager only to find that the documentation was so poor, improperly filed, or even nonexistent that it was extremely difficult to pick up the threads of continuity. Of course, there are other compelling reasons for proper job organization, and the time to start that organization process is now.

Organizing the Job in the Office

When the construction contract is received and properly executed, and before it is filed, it should be reviewed to see if it contains any provisions, restrictions, or instructions that may be at variance with the plans and specifications. This contract language, if at variance with the plans and specifications, will take precedence in case a dispute or disagreement arises, and the project manager must clearly understand the terms and conditions of the prime construction directive.

Coping with Addenda

If during the bidding process the architect or engineer has issued a number of addenda to the plans, specifications, or both, it is now important that these addenda be properly categorized and identified for future use in the job administration and when negotiating contracts with subcontractors and suppliers.

There may be confusion, at times, between the terms *addendum* and *bulletin*. Generally *addenda* are changes or clarifications issued by the designers prior to the issuance of a contract to a general contractor. Changes made to the plans and/or specifications after contract signing are usually referred to as *bulletins*.

When addenda have been issued as changes to the specifications, they can be incorporated into the specifications book in one of several ways. One method involves cutting out the line item changes and pasting them directly over the lines which they supersede. To identify the addenda from which they were extracted, the addendum number can be written alongside or in the margin of the specifications book where the change took place. If these cutout portions are taped on one end only, they can be lifted for comparison with the original document and the revised one.

These changes can also be handwritten above or below the affected lines in the specifications book, if they are not too wordy. When addenda add full pages or even full sections to the specifications book, it will be difficult to insert the pages into the already bound volume, and if that is the case, remove the binding and put the specifications into a large-capacity loose-leaf binder. The binder will also allow the project manager to put either separators or tabs on the various sections, making it easier to find a specific section when needed.

When addenda to the specifications book have been incorporated into a binder with the proper sections identified, a duplicate book should be prepared for the job superintendent to maintain in the field office. Addenda will also take the form of sketches, details, or drawing clarifications printed on $8^{1}/_{2} \times 11$-in paper, and these addenda can be taped directly to the construction drawing. If this is not done, these sketches may languish unnoticed in the specifications book.

Job Files

All the written materials coming into and going out of the construction office will end up in files, and it is important that, when they do end up in files, it will be easy to retrieve them. Although this sounds so simplistic as to not warrant discussion, there are times when improper filing techniques can lead to frustration and fury. Of course, letters to and from the architect, engineers, and the owner will be filed in folders entitled "Correspondence with architect," "Correspondence with engineer," and "Correspondence with owner." Some project managers handle their filing under the theory of job security, "They can't fire me because I am the only one who knows where all the documents are hidden." But what if that project manager is on vacation and the office calls with an irate boss on the other end wanting to know where in the blazes is that letter to Client J. Whimple?

The central file

One central filing system in one central filing area must be established. A master list of all files can be prepared, and when a job is just starting, the project manager can check off the file folders to be prepared for the current job. At the same time, a more abbreviated list of file folders can be prepared for the field office to assist the project superintendent in getting organized in the field. The whole purpose of filing is to be able to retrieve a document that is needed, and usually needed rather quickly. When a project manager is on vacation, home sick, or tied up in a meeting out of the office, someone else should be able to retrieve a document if a standardized filing method has been established and everyone is familiar with it.

The chronological file

In addition to the central file for a particular project, another filing system can be used to supplement the central file and is very useful in document retrieval. It is called a *chronological file* because a duplicate copy of each letter sent out of the office by a project manager will be filed in this file according to the date on which it was typed. Letters in this file will be filed without regard for subject matter but only with respect to date typed. There will be many times when a project manager will remember the date, exact or approximate, when a letter was sent, but cannot remember whether it was filed in one folder or another because it may have been applicable to several files. If a chronological file is kept, a quick flip through the time period when it was supposedly sent will retrieve the document in a hurry. Now that the contract has been reviewed, all addenda accounted for and properly posted, and the project files set up, the project manager can try to get the project administration started.

Rereading the Specifications

The specifications section related to project start-up and also project closeout should be reread thoroughly at the beginning of the job and before subcontractor negotiations begin inasmuch as some of the provisions in these sections may affect these negotiations. Certain conditions may have to be met before actual construction can start, and certain guidelines may have to be followed during construction to comply with closeout procedures.

If project closeout requirements include as-built drawings to be submitted by the mechanical and electrical trades, these conditions will have to be included in the contract negotiations with the electrical and mechanical subcontractors. If lien waivers are to be submitted with each subcontractor request for payment and a final lien waiver is required from each subcontractor at the end of the project, that information is also needed in the preparation of subcontractor contracts.

Getting back to the start-up of a new project, a quick review of the specifications might reveal that the following conditions need immediate attention:

1. Insurance requirements and insurance certificates for both general contractor and any subcontractor prior to starting work will probably be required.

2. Requirements for field offices and temporary utilities, possibly including new telephone service for contractor, architect, and clerk of the works will require some lead time to obtain. Some architects require the filing of a site logistics plan prior to placement of field offices. Will architect and clerk of the works require separate field offices?

3. Job identification signs may be required. Some federal projects require elaborate signs to be made and placed on the site before any requests for payment can be honored. Are there zoning requirements with respect to size and location of signs? Remember that the site will have to be identified for future deliveries of materials, so a company sign takes on added importance.

4. If the project is a rehabilitation project, are there any restrictions on the use of the existing facilities for office and/or materials storage use? Can the existing telephone and electrical services be reactivated for use by the general contractor and subcontractor? Is there sufficient power available? Is the owner's permission required to activate these services?

Being aware of all conditions, requirements, and restrictions outlined in the specifications and making certain that they are being complied with at the inception of the project will project an image of "getting off on the right foot" with the owner, architect, and engineer, who will begin to feel that they are dealing with a professional who will probably exhibit the same degree of thoroughness throughout the job that has been exhibited in the early stages.

Organizing the Estimate

During the period when a project is being either competitively bid or negotiated, the estimate will probably have been modified many times and in many different ways. Once a contract has been awarded, all additions, deductions, and corrections made to the estimate during the bid process or negotiations must be properly allocated to the sections of the estimate to which they belong. For instance, the apparent low-bidding electrical subcontractor may have taken exception to the inclusion of temporary power when he submitted his bid, so the estimating department added X dollars to the electrical price; however, a late-breaking price from a competitor included this work, so a deduct adjustment was made to the bid. All these last-minute adds and deducts should be inserted into the estimate in an organized manner so that it will be relatively easy to determine at a later date how these final numbers were obtained. When all the line items have been adjusted to reflect the correct budget amounts, the correct guidelines for purchasing and contract awards will be established. This updated and corrected estimate will also serve as the basis for a schedule of values which will probably be required as part of the monthly requisition form. Since the requisition format and the schedule of values will need approval by the architect or government agency, if one is involved, it is best to submit a proposed form well enough in advance of the first requisition so that any necessary changes can be made in time.

The estimate will also be used in the formulation of a job cost code report so that materials, labor, and subcontracts, when issued can be cost-coded against the proper category for future cost code budget analysis. Once all the changes in, or modifications to, the initial estimate have been placed in their proper places, it is wise to make up a new estimate sheet that incorporates all these changes. Do not, however, throw away the original estimate or any of the worksheets with information on them that shows how all the changes to this estimate had been made.

In addition to getting the estimate in shape, the entire job file needs some attention. It will be bulging with all the letters, inquiries, and telephoned and written bids received during the bidding process. These papers require organization. If a written confirmation of a previously telephoned bid has been received, staple it and the memo together. Collate all the bids of a similar trade. At some future date each of these bids will be analyzed for scope and price, but for now just put them together; any letters of inquiry or product data sheets can be put in their respective files. *Don't throw anything away until a contract is awarded and properly executed!* Keep all those scraps of paper, notes, and records of telephone calls. In some states courts have ruled that if a general contractor can prove that by using a telephone bid received from a subcontractor they were selected as low bidder, the subcontractor cannot later withdraw that bid without incurring damages.

Investigating Allowance and Alternates

A review should be made of any specification sections having to do with allowances and/or alternates. First, allowance items should be segregated on the schedule of values and monthly requisition forms, noted as allowance items with their corresponding values assigned. While looking through the allowance section, determine how the allowances are to be handled; do they include materials only, or do they include materials and the labor to install these materials? Were the allowance items to include the contractor's overhead and profit or listed as costs without any markups? Are the allowance items to be bid competitively and such bids forwarded to the architect for review and approval before an award is made? Do the allowances have definable scope, or will more information be required from the architect at a later date?

For example, if the finish hardware for the project is an allowance item, how is the hardware schedule to be handled? Will it be prepared by the architect, the hardware subcontractor, or a combination of the two? Is the architect planning to select a hardware supplier to work with them to develop a schedule within the price range of the allowance? Although this might not seem like an immediate problem when the construction trailer is being set up, it could be. Hollow metal doors and frames may be needed for the project, and they may be custom-designed.

Hollow metal door and frame suppliers will require an approved hardware schedule, and possibly templates of the various hardware items that are to be installed in these doors and frames. Special hollow metal doors and frames can take quite a while to progress from the shop drawing stage to production and delivery, and without the required information for all cutouts, this entire process may come to a halt early on. This is one reason why finish hardware must be awarded early in the project. The same might be true of wood doors that are to be premachined and prefinished. The manufacturer will require an approved hardware schedule well in advance of the manufacture and machining of these doors.

Many times it is preferable to order the doors as "blanks" so that the doors can be prepared in the field, if it appears that an approved hardware schedule will be a long time coming.

There are many other reasons why it is important to look at the allowance items early on. It might be advantageous to incorporate some allowance work in contract negotiations with subcontractors rather than negotiate at a later date. When awarding a contract to a drywall subcontractor, for example, it may be advisable to include installation of hollow metal and hardware installation at that time when the general contractor's buying power is greatest. The point is to look at them promptly to see if they might have implications for immediate concern. If alternates are to be selected or elected at some future date, are any of the selections of a critical or immediate nature? If an alternate has to do with the installation of carpet or vinyl-composition tile in a certain area, there is no immediate need to have the selection made shortly after contract signing. However, if there is an alternate for quarry tile set in a mortar bed, in lieu of carpet in a specific area, the decision must be made well in advance of the concrete slab installation in the affected area. The project manager, after reviewing the alternates section, should decide when each alternate must be selected and send a letter to the architect requesting that these selections be made in advance of the critical dates.

Shop Drawings and the Shop Drawing Log

A review of the specifications may establish the procedures for shop drawing submissions. Is there a special stamp required with the project name and other identifying data that must be used on each shop drawing submission? If so, the stamp will have to be ordered. How many copies of shop drawings are required for submission? How many sepias or other reproducibles are needed? How many copies of product data or equipment catalog sheets are required for submission? How are samples to be handled? Are all the types of shop drawings to be sent to the architect, or will structural drawings be sent directly to the engineer with an informational copy only to the architect? All these procedures should be worked out and clarified as the job is just beginning.

A shop drawing log should be started so that when the shop drawings start arriving from subcontractors and suppliers, each drawing can be properly logged into the register. Not only will a log of shop drawing activity allow a project manager to keep tract of what drawings have been received; it will also show where the drawings have been sent and how long they have been there. The project manager needs to prod each subcontractor and product supplier to submit their drawings promptly. At the first job meeting, the major subcontractors and/or material suppliers should be requested to submit a preliminary shop drawing submission schedule. The schedule should include the major pieces of equipment for which shop drawings are required and the anticipated date when each drawing will be submitted. The subcontractor and/or supplier should also include the approximate delivery date of equipment after the approved shop drawings have been returned to them. The sample shop drawing schedule shown in Fig. 5.1 for the Woodbridge Plaza office building project pertains to submissions by an electrical subcontractor. Once shop drawings have been received, the next hurdle is getting them approved in a timely fashion. The project manager should review the incoming shop drawings to determine whether they conform to the project specifications and requirements. If compliance is questionable, contact the party that submitted the drawings to discuss compliance. If there are deviations, it might be best to note them before submitting the drawings to the architect. It is at this point that the project manager must establish a degree of credibility with the architect and engineer and must show that shop drawings are being reviewed for compliance with the plans and specifications and not merely passed through without any scrutiny whatsoever.

When the shop drawings are sent to the architect or engineer, a note should be entered on the accompanying transmittals indicating whether any are to be expedited or if there is an order of importance. The project manager must monitor the shop drawing log from time to time to make sure that the drawings are being cycled in a timely fashion. The shop drawing log should show what action has been taken on each drawing when the drawing is returned. Although the transmittals forwarding the copies and the transmittals that accompany the returned drawings will be the documents of record, the shop drawing log will highlight the activity. The log should contain a column showing the disposition of the drawings after they have been reviewed by the designers. If any drawings are disapproved, they will probably be returned to their originator. If approved, they will be distributed to their originator, with copies to any concerned subcontractors, a copy to the field, and one for the office file.

Care must be taken to discern which subcontractors should receive informational copies of shop drawings. For instance, when a mechanical subcontractor is being sent an approved copy of their boiler shop drawing, the electrical contractor should have an informational copy in order to confirm the line voltage requirements. All too often a piece of equipment is ordered with electrical characteristics at variance with the voltage requirements shown in the drawings. If an error such as this can be caught in the shop drawing stage, there may be little or no additional cost involved to make the equipment compatible with the building's electrical system.

PRELIMINARY DWG. SUBMISSION & EQUIPMENT DELIVERY SCHEDULE			SUBMITTED BY ABC ELECTRIC CO., INC. PROJECT: WOODBRIDGE OFFICE BUILDING
	10/09/92 ********		
EQUIPMENT (DESCRIPTION)	DWGS SUBMITTED	DELIVERY AFTER APPROVAL	DELIVERY DATE
1. Wiring devices 16140	11/19/92	04 Weeks	01/06/93
2. Panelboards 16160	10/26/92	04 Weeks	12/14/92
3. Safety switches 16170	10/26/92	04 Weeks	12/14/92
4. Switchboard 16440	10/26/92	10 Weeks	01/25/93
5. Motor control center 16480	10/26/92	10 Weeks	01/25/93
6. Lighting fixtures 16500	11/19/92	10 Weeks	02/18/93
7. Lighting protection system 16601	11/19/92	06 Weeks	01/21/93
8. Emergency lighting system 16610	11/19/92	10 Weeks	02/18/93
9. Fire alarm system 16721	11/19/92	10 Weeks	02/18/93
10. Time switch 16930	11/19/92	06 Weeks	01/21/93

Figure 5.1 Preliminary drawing submission and equipment delivery schedule (submitted 10/09/92 by ABC Electric Co., Inc.; Woodbridge Plaza office building project).

A typical shop drawing log is shown in Fig. 5.2. Generally when this form of log is used, a separate page should be kept for trades that will be submitting large numbers of drawings such as structural steel, plumbing, HVAC, sprinkler system, and electrical work.

There are several computer software programs on the market today that allow the project manager to create a transmittal forwarding the shop drawing to the architect or engineer and transfer this information automatically onto a shop drawing log.

Figure 5.3 reveals a transmittal for electrical equipment, fire alarm, and sound equipment. The information inserted at the time of preparation will be stored and transferred to the shop drawing log (Fig. 5.4). Although the shop drawing log in this case contains material from various subcontractors, separate pages can be created for individual trades.

Abbreviations and Acronyms Referred to in the Specifications

As the specifications are reviewed, there will be repeated references to certain alphabetical and numerical combinations in connection with design and performance criteria. Some examples are

Precast manholes	Conform to ANSI/ASTM C-478
Concrete quality	To meet American Concrete Institute (ACI) specifications
Wood doors	Per Architectural Woodwork Institute (AWI) quality guidelines

Listed in the Appendix are some of the organizations frequently referred to in the written specifications; organizations which have set standards for their respective industries. Some of these organizations and various trade associations can supply a wealth of information about their products or services.

For instance, the National Electrical Contractors Association publishes an easy-to-understand explanation of Occupational Safety and Health Administration (OSHA) ground fault protection guidelines. The Steel Door Institute (SDI) has a wealth of information on the manufacture and installation of hollow metal doors and frames. The names, addresses, and telephone numbers of these organizations and trade groups are listed in the Appendix.

SHOP DRAWING LOG

SUBCONTRACTOR _____

CONTACT & PHONE NO. _____

PROJECT _____

TRADE _____

Date Received	Shop Drawing Number & Title	No. of Copies	Sent To	Date sent to Arch./Eng.					Action				Distribution		No. of Copies			Remarks
				Initial Submission	Resubmission	Final Submission	Date Returned	No. of Copies Returned	No Exceptions Taken	Note Corrections	Resubmit	Rejected	Distribution Date	Subcontractor	Jobsite	File	

Figure 5.2   A typical shop drawing log.

SUBMITTAL ITEM

Project: UT/P&W oper.Fl. Plan Bldg 450   Job: 1075

December 18, 1992   Page: 1

Package:16000	Submittal: 16160SWITCHGEAR	Title: Switchgear advance copy	
Number :00013	From : CWPOND	To :	Req'd Start :01DEC92
Drawing:		Days Overdue: 0	Req'd Finish:
Status :AAN	BIC :	Days Held : 0	Days Elapsed: 14

Rev No.	Description/Remarks	Received from CWPOND JP	Sent to MAGUIR DN	Returned by MAGUIR DN	Forwarded to CWPOND JP	Sta tus	Copy S P	Drawing Date	No. Name	Reviewer Status Set	Cycle Days/ Held
0	Advance copy/ no deviation	30NOV92	01DEC92	14DEC92	14DEC92	AAN	0 1				14
										N	13

Approved FMS	JB :01DEC92	Source Vendor: CWPOND JP	
Approved MAGUIR	DN :14DEC92	Code:	Items in Submittal: 1

Rev No.	Distribute To	Date	DISTRIBUTION Copies	Remarks	Transmit Y/N

	Submit	Approve	SCHEDULE Release	Fab Start	Ship Date	Delivery Date
Date :	30NOV92	14DEC92	01DEC92			
Act ID:						
Filed:	by	Fab Time	Ship Time			

Figure 5.3   Computer-generated transmittal used in preparation of shop drawing log.

Inspections and Testing

Another section of the specifications book that requires reviewing prior to the start of the job concerns inspections, testing, and quality control procedures. The responsibility for providing and paying for these services is usually assigned in the specifications. The section will also include the type and number of tests required during excavation and sitework operations, the tests required when concrete is being placed, and the number of concrete test cylinders that are to be taken. If a structural-steel frame is being constructed, the schedule of testing or inspections will also be set forth in the quality control or testing section of the specifications. It may even include a visit to the steel fabricator's plant by the engineer.

If testing is to be performed by the general contractor, the specifications might require architect or engineer approval of the testing laboratory before it can be engaged. As for the reports generated by the tests, how are they to be distributed? Some testing procedures require that a copy of each test report be sent directly to the architect or engineer. If that is not the case, all reports should be sent to the office for distribution by the project engineer. Many local building departments or building officials will require that a copy of all compaction or concrete cylinder test reports be sent directly to their office. The project manager can establish the distribution list at the beginning of the project so that all interested parties will receive the reports they require.

Job Scheduling

A job progress schedule was probably prepared when the job was being estimated. Its purpose at that time was primarily to determine the duration of construction so that an estimate of the general conditions or general requirements containing time-related costs could be prepared. Now that the project has become a reality, the job progress schedule needs to be reviewed and refined for other purposes. The specifications might require that a job progress schedule be submitted to the architect within a specified time after the contract has been signed. Even if there is no such requirement, a job schedule must be assembled so that an initial set of construction landmarks can be set for planning purposes. There will be many revisions to this initial schedule as subcontracts are awarded and more information is obtained as construction proceeds.

The bar chart

If a bar chart was initially prepared and is to be used throughout the life of the job, it can now be reanalyzed. Instead of a bar chart with one month as the unit of time, a chart with a week as a unit might be considered. That will allow for more detailed planning and show the interrelations of concurrent operations more clearly. As contracts are awarded, subcontractors should be requested to submit their own work or progress schedule to see how they fit into the overall schedule. Subcontractors should be given the complete project schedule containing their portion of work, and they should be asked to comment on the length of time and sequences allotted to them. With their input initially and updates from time to time the schedule will not only be more accurate; it will reinforce their feelings that they are an integral part of the construction team.

As discussed previously, subcontractors should be requested to submit a list of proposed shop drawing submittals and delivery dates of the equipment after receipt of approved drawings. When these schedules are received, the project manager must review them to ascertain that these

UT/P&W oper.Fl. Plan Bldg 450
RW-SBTR

Submittal/Transmittal Log

SUBMITTAL	TITLE	DRAWING	REQUIRED START	REQUIRED FINISH	DAYS HELD	BIC	STATUS	TRANSMITTAL DATE	ITEM DATE	TRANS NO.
05000-MANIS	Roof Ladder Details	4254M-3	18NOV92	28NOV92	0		APP	08DEC92	08DEC92	00049
05000-SHORING	Shoring detail	AS NOTED	18NOV92	28NOV92	0		APP	08DEC92	08DEC92	00049
05000-SHORING	Shoring detail	AS NOTED	18NOV92	28NOV92	0		APP	08DEC92	08DEC92	00049
05000 ROOF DECK	Vulcraft Roof Deck Submittal	43-2-485 DWG JD10F1	22OCT92	30OCT92	36	BERLIN	REJ	12NOV92	12NOV92	00031
STRUCT STEEL	Structural Shop Dwgs	S SERIES; A SERIES	21OCT92	30OCT92	0		AAN	12NOV92	12NOV92	00032
STRUCT STEEL	Structural Shop Dwgs	S SERIES; A SERIES	21OCT92	30OCT92	0		AAN	12NOV92	12NOV92	00033
05000-400	Berlin Steel Misc. Metals	MANIS METAL WKS: 4254 M1;M2	06NOV92	16NOV92	0		AAN	12NOV92	12NOV92	00034
15800-003	AHU equip;Pumps; ARU equip	NA	10OCT92	20OCT92	0		APP	05NOV92	02NOV92	00021
15000-MSC	CRC Misc Items Submittals		07OCT92	20OCT92	0		APP	21OCT92	21OCT92	00011
PLUMBING FIXT'S	Kohler Package	NA	22OCT92	10NOV92	42	CRC	DIS	06NOV92	06NOV92	00029
SEISMIC/VIBRATE	Mason Industries Seismic	NA	28OCT92	07NOV92	0		AAN	10NOV92	10NOV92	00030
15000PLMB-RESBM	Plumbing Fixture Resubmitta	NA	24NOV92	30NOV92	0		AAN	08DEC92	08DEC92	00052
16160SWITCHGEAR	Switchgear advance copy		01DEC92		0		AAN	14DEC92	14DEC92	00057
08100	Hollow Metal	EASTERN METAL SHOP DWGS	10DEC92	20DEC92	0		AAN	14DEC92	14DEC92	00058
FRAZIER-003	Rack Layout Dwgs Final Subm	SPD-920940	17NOV92	25NOV92	0		AAN	25NOV92	25NOV92	00045
14302 JIB CRANE	Jib Crane		13NOV92	23NOV92	0		AAN	25NOV92	25NOV92	00044
14302 JIB CRANE	Jib Crane		13NOV92	23NOV92	0		AAN	25NOV92	25NOV92	00044
14630	Bridge Crane		01DEC92	10DEC92	0		APP	08DEC92	08DEC92	00053
07532; 07580	EPDM Roofing; Flashing	AS NOTED	13NOV92	24NOV92	0		APP	19NOV92	19NOV92	00040
07532; 07580	EPDM Roofing; Flashing	AS NOTED	13NOV92	24NOV92	0		APP	19NOV92	19NOV92	00040

07532; 07580	EPDM Roofing; Flashing	AS NOTED	13NOV92	24NOV92	0		APP 19NOV92	19NOV92	00040
07532; 07580	EPDM Roofing; Flashing	AS NOTED	13NOV92	24NOV92	0		APP 19NOV92	19NOV92	00040
07532; 07580	EPDM Roofing; Flashing	AS NOTED	13NOV92	24NOV92	0		APP 19NOV92	19NOV92	00040
07532; 07580	EPDM Roofing; Flashing	AS NOTED	13NOV92	24NOV92	0		APP 19NOV92	19NOV92	00040
07532; 07580	EPDM Roofing; Flashing	AS NOTED	13NOV92	24NOV92	0		APP 19NOV92	19NOV92	00040
07532; 07580	EPDM Roofing; Flashing	AS NOTED	13NOV92	24NOV92	0		APP 19NOV92	19NOV92	00040
07532; 07580	EPDM Roofing; Flashing	AS NOTED	13NOV92	24NOV92	0		APP 19NOV92	19NOV92	00040
07532; 07580	EPDM Roofing; Flashing	AS NOTED	13NOV92	24NOV92	0		APP 19NOV92	19NOV92	00040
08100	Hollow Metal	EASTERN METAL SHOP DWGS	10DEC92	20DEC92	0		AAN 10DEC92	09DEC92	00055
RACK WITH LOADS	Final Rack submittal with (	COMPLETE SET HD-921029	14DEC92	21DEC92	4 MAGUIR		NEW 14DEC92	14DEC92	00056
08332-001	Overhead Doors	NA	24NOV92	30NOV92	0		AAN 24NOV92	24NOV92	00041
08332-001	Overhead Doors	NA	24NOV92	30NOV92	0		AAN 24NOV92	24NOV92	00041
15000PLMB-RESBM	Plumbing Fixture Resubmitta	NA	24NOV92	30NOV92	0		AAN 24NOV92	24NOV92	00042
FINISH HARDWARE	HARCON Hardware submittal		14DEC92	21DEC92	3 MAGUIR		NEW 15DEC92	15DEC92	00059
FIRE ALARM/SOUN	Fire Alarm /Sound Equipment		14DEC92	21DEC92	3 MAGUIR		NEW 15DEC92	15DEC92	00060
FIRE ALARM/SOUN	Fire Alarm /Sound Equipment		14DEC92	21DEC92	3 MAGUIR		NEW 15DEC92	15DEC92	00060
							15DEC92	15DEC92	00060
							07OCT92	07OCT92	00006
							12OCT92	12OCT92	00007
							01DEC92	30NOV92	00047
							01DEC92	30NOV92	00047
							01DEC92	30NOV92	00047
03200	Matt Reinforcing	REVISED 450	06NOV92	16NOV92	0		AAN 06NOV92	06NOV92	00023
STRUCT STEEL	Structural Shop Dwgs	S SERIES; A SERIES	21OCT92	30OCT92	0		AAN 21OCT92	21OCT92	00009
11 161;164;165	Loading Dock Equipment		06NOV92	16NOV92	44 MAGUIR		NEW 06NOV92	06NOV92	00024

Figure 5.4 Shop drawing log created by transmittals.

equipment delivery dates fit into the overall time frame of the job. If they do, then these equipment delivery dates should be incorporated into the bar chart schedule and distributed to all subcontractors. The bar chart, often referred to as the *Gantt chart* (Fig. 5.5) after its originator Henry Gantt, is not a static endeavor. It will have to be updated from time to time as new information is obtained and as delays or schedule improvements occur. There are many types of projects that can be effectively administered by using a bar chart. For other projects, the critical path method (CPM) is recommended.

Critical path method (CPM)

The critical path method (CPM) of construction scheduling involves the preparation of a graphic display of all the operations required during the life of a project. A simplistic explanation of CPM can be described by the use of an arrow diagram. One end of the arrow indicates the start and the other end the completion of an activity. The length of the arrow indicates the length of the time apportioned to each activity. Some construction operations precede others on a straight-line basis and cannot start until a prior operation has been completed. Other operations can start prior to the completion of a preceding activity, and some operations are performed simultaneously or concurrently with others. Although this may sound rather elementary, it is the kind of thinking and evaluation necessary to construct a CPM network. In fact, one of the values achieved by the use of this schedule is the careful and analytical consideration of time and sequencing of each operation in the initial stages of the project as the CPM is being developed. Carrying the arrow concept further, each activity, or arrow, will have a start, stop, and hence duration time. When two or more arrows or activities meet, this meeting point is known as an *event*. Activity flows are terminated at events, and subsequent operations or phases move forward from one event to another. The events are assigned numbers which are used either manually or electronically to change event sequences or durations as the CPM program is monitored during the construction period. The various activities, arrows, and events used in the CPM schedule make up what is known as the *network*.

The CPM schedule shows the dependence of one operation on a preceding operation. For instance, if the excavation for the building's footings is scheduled to commence 3 days before forming and placing concrete begins, any delays due to weather or materials will be seen to cause subsequent operations to be delayed and extended in time. If there is to be a structural-steel framing system, the starting date for steel erection will be dependent on certain foundation work being completed. The CPM schedule will illustrate what effect weather delays will have on foundation work completion and structural-steel start and finish and the

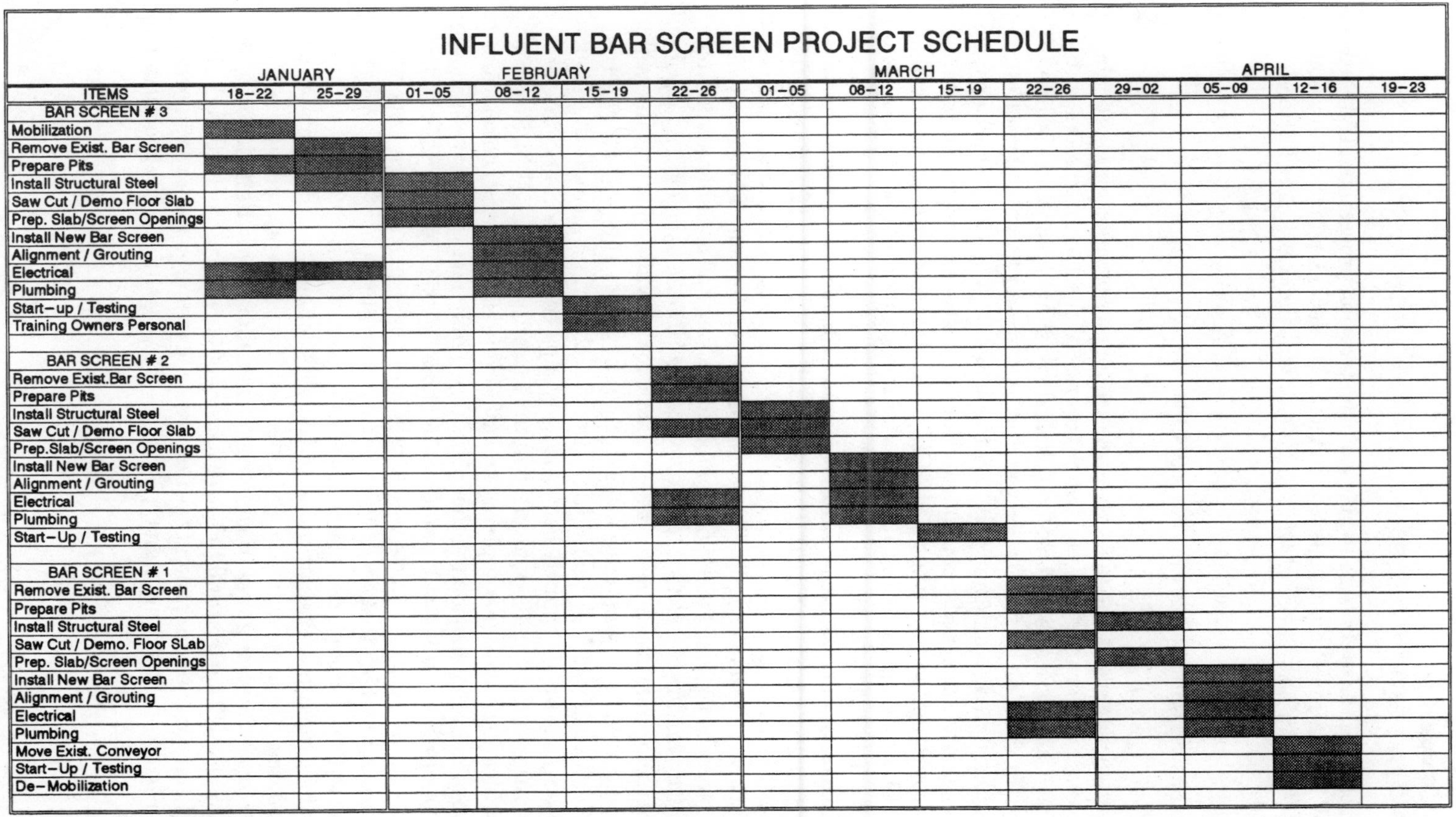

Figure 5.5 Gantt or bar chart.

relations of these changes to all other construction procedures. If there is no "float time," the project manager can decide whether the steel erection can be delayed or the concrete foundation work is to be accelerated.

The basic difference between bar and CPM charts

The dependence of one task, or work component, on another is probably the major difference between bar chart and CPM scheduling representation. Whereas the standard bar chart may show a continuous line of activity for a particular trade which starts at one point and continues uninterrupted to another point on the schedule, the CPM chart draws attention to the specific starting and ending dates for each major portion of a construction component. The CPM will also show, very dramatically, the effect of one starting date on the dates of prior and subsequent construction activities.

In bar chart presentations, it is common to display one continuous line for a trade such as electrical. The electrician will start work almost at the time the construction office trailer arrives on the site; the trailer will need temporary power for lights, heat, and office equipment. The electrician will then be required to supply temporary power and possibly temporary lighting for the concrete foundation crews. Although the electrical subcontractor may then leave the job site for a while, electricians will reappear with varying crew sizes during the life of the project. Accordingly, the bar chart will show the electrical schedule as a single line from trailer hookup to "punch list" with perhaps some landmark dates or activities highlighted along its length. In contrast, the CPM involves establishing dates for equipment and material deliveries and the relationship of their installation to other activities. This chart will also show how those other activities will commence or end in relation to prior tasks. This precedence of operations—which task will come first, which task will follow, and which tasks will be performed simultaneously—is really the heart of the CPM of job scheduling.

Along with the obvious value of the CPM chart for future planning purposes, the preparation of the chart will force the planners to isolate and focus on each phase of construction in such a way that the critical elements will surface and a clearer picture of how the project will be built will emerge. Building the project on paper may not be required in order to create a bar chart, but that type of analysis is essential to the production of a CPM chart.

Preparation of the CPM chart

Important elements of CPM planning are the dates when activities will occur, the length of time required to complete the activity, and the dates when the activities will require materials or equipment. Long-lead items will surface and have a definite impact on scheduling sequences. Subcontracted work involving materials and equipment that must be purchased must be reviewed and contracts awarded promptly so that shop drawing submission and equipment delivery dates can be more accurately defined. In fact, some CPM schedules include activities for shop drawing preparation, review, and anticipated delivery of related equipment. Until key subcontractors have been selected and contracts awarded, the CPM scheduling process will be in limbo.

With the cost of personal computers now in the $2000 range and with the proliferation of all kinds of software programs, small- and midsize contractors can now afford to prepare CPM charts in-house, and more and more clients are making the submission of a CPM chart a contract requirement. Although clients request CPM charts, they are quite seldom prepared to pick up the cost for this work, which can be substantial depending on the complexity of the project and the complexity of the schedule. Even though clients may not fully understand the presentation of a CPM chart, somehow they reason that by its preparation alone, the project will run smoothly. On very large projects, the cost of establishing and maintaining a CPM schedule could cost several hundred thousand dollars, and if the client is willing to pay for this service, it can become a valuable tool for all parties to the construction process. Problems occur when the contractor is expected to provide a complex CPM schedule but either did not include enough money in the general conditions to create and maintain the schedule, or when presented with the costs, the client demands the service but refuses to pay the full cost of the service.

Although some CPM schedules may be complex, by becoming familiar with basic schedule terminology some of the mystery will be lifted.

Activity flow—the sequence of work from one task to the other

Order of activity or order of precedence—an indication of which work event or task precedes or follows the other

Duration—the time it takes to complete a work task

Nodes—the graphic representation of specific tasks, displayed as either rectangles, hexagonals, or rounded boxes and usually containing a number identifying the task it represents; a node may also include start and finish dates

Early start—a date earlier than that initially anticipated for the start of an activity

Late start—a date indicating a start later than initially proposed but still allowing for on-time completion

Early completion—completion of a task prior to initially scheduled date

Late completion—completing later than originally scheduled

Float time—contingency time allotted to a specific work task or to a series of tasks to compensate for unforeseen circumstances

The importance of float time and who owns it

It will be a rare case indeed when every scheduled event on a construction project comes off as planned. Weather delays, labor disputes, problems with obtaining equipment and materials, and just plain mistakes all take their toll on job progress, and contingency time must be included in every schedule. In CPM terminology this contingency time is referred to as "float time," and who owns the float time can be very important. Does the contractor "own" the float time which can be used to make up for delays incurred during the life of the project, allowing the contractor to complete the project on schedule? Does the owner "own" the float time which is to be used to take the necessary time to respond to critical construction decisions as they arise during the project without affecting the completion date? This kind of question becomes very important when there are liquidated-damage clauses attached to the construction contract and the builder wishes to use the float time to offset delays and avoid penalties.

Consideration of who owns the float time is also important when bonus clauses are included in the construction contract. A builder who completes a project on time without ever having utilized any float time may have actually completed the project ahead of schedule and be eligible for the bonus if the float time belongs to the contractor rather than to the owner.

In Conclusion

A properly drafted CPM network has to include the following elements:

1. Dates when equipment, materials, and work force will be available.

2. The proper relation of one activity to another, in regard to sequence or precedence, and the time required to complete the activity.

3. Enough detail to create guidelines, but not so much as to create confusion. If more details are required for a specific phase, create a subnetwork.

4. Landmarks or important events critical to completion—the critical path.

5. Long-lead items that could become potential trouble spots.

A job schedule is produced and monitored to serve as a coordination tool, to create a roadmap of the way from job start to completion, to establish a method for monitoring job progress or lack thereof, and to have a means of recognizing, anticipating, and compensating for the many detours that will occur along the way. It is up to the project manager to determine which type of schedule will best suit the job.

Organizing in the Field

Part of the project manager's responsibility is to assist the job superintendent in organizing the field office at the beginning of the job. Along with making certain that there are ample pens, pencils, notepads, and payroll reporting and other field-related forms, the field office must be organized to receive and store all the paperwork and drawings that will be forthcoming from the office. There must be not only a place to store all these documents but also a storage method that will permit the quick retrieval of these documents when needed.

Shop drawings for a structural-steel, precast, or cast-in-place concrete structure will be voluminous. Drawings for ductwork and other aboveground and below-grade piping as well as equipment layout drawings must be filed for future use, along with all the equipment catalog booklets. Unless there is good organization in the field office, chances are that key drawings and documents will become lost—and always when they are needed the most.

A condensed version of the office job files should be prepared for the field office. Correspondence from the architect and engineer, memos from the office, job meeting minutes, and letters to the owner and architect should be filed in their respective folders. Equipment catalogs for the mechanical and electrical trades should be filed in their respective plumbing, HVAC, sprinkler, and electrical system folders. Often when the job superintendent has to answer a question from a subcontractor about a job-related issue, he will have to locate a drawing or other document. If everything has been filed at random in a cardboard box or in the bottom drawer of a file cabinet, it will be difficult or impossible for the superintendent to answer the question without contacting the project manager to obtain the information from office-filed documents. Plan racks are needed in the field office for current construction drawings and shop drawings. Shop drawings should be installed on the rack only when they have been approved by the architect or engineer. Any preliminary shop drawings that had been sent to the job for informational purpose should be discarded once the approved drawings have been received. If general revisions to the construction drawings have been made, it is critical that the drawings be sent to the field immediately and the outdated drawings rolled up and put away. These superseded drawings should not be discarded because they may be needed at some future date to ascertain the previous scope of work in case they are questioned by either subcontractor, architect, or client. The job superintendent must make certain that only current, approved drawings are on the plan rack. A subcontractor may come into the field office when the superintendent is not there and look for information in drawings that are considered or assumed to be current. If outdated drawings are in the plan rack and the subcontractor uses erroneous information, unnecessary problems can be created that could affect many trades.

Now that the office and field are properly organized, the project manager is ready to get to the business at hand: awarding subcontracts and issuing purchase orders for the materials needed to satisfy the project's immediate needs.

6

Buying Out
the Job

As a project moves through its various phases after a construction
contract has been executed, all the bids received from suppliers and
subcontractors will be reviewed so that contracts can be awarded and
other commitments firmed up to start the flow of labor and materials to
the job site.

Awarding Subcontracts

The process of awarding subcontracts is more complicated than merely
selecting the apparent low bidder and writing a contract. In order to
negotiate a contract for labor, equipment, and materials or just for
equipment or materials, the project manager must be thoroughly familiar
with all aspects of what must be purchased. Some construction companies
allow the project manager to "buy out the job"; other companies have
purchasing departments. In the latter case, the purchasing agent will be
wise to consult the project manager and review scope, terms, and
conditions before a contract is awarded.

The Subcontractor Interview Form

Construction projects are getting more and more complicated, and
specifications can be complex. All too often specification sections, after
outlining the scope of work contained therein, state "See other sections
for related work." To retain all the requirements of the plans and

specifications in one's head while reviewing the scope of work with a subcontractor is all but impossible for most of us. An easier way to retain and review scope issues is to prepare a subcontractor interview form (Fig. 6.1) well in advance of meeting with the subcontractor. A thorough review of the plans and specifications can be made and an individualized checklist prepared for each trade.

The form in Figure 6.1 pertains to structural and miscellaneous steel, and its purpose is to ensure that all items required of that particular subcontractor are covered during the interview, which will establish scope of work and corresponding cost in order to evaluate each bidder on an equal basis. In the case of the steel subcontractors, they will even be asked to stipulate how many tons of steel were included in their bid so that each subcontractor's tonnage figures can be compared. Once this interview has been completed, the subcontractors should be permitted to review the form and, if they agree to all the statements contained therein, should be requested to sign where indicated. This will preclude subcontractors from stating that they were misunderstood during the interview and did not state a certain fact or did not include or exclude specific items. Similar forms can be made for all other trades, but the basic intent of each form is to be able to compare similar scope and respective costs submitted by each subcontractor.

But before any contract negotiations can begin, all the bid information has to be organized and collated, and a simple way to do that is to prepare a bid summary sheet similar to the one shown in Fig. 6.2. The purpose of this sheet is to provide a means of comparing one quote with another to ensure sameness or highlight differences.

The Bid Summary Sheet

The bid summary sheet contains the project name, the work classification, and the budget estimate for the item to be purchased. In the first column, the names of all bidders submitting quotations will be listed and the various components to be included in their bids will be listed alongside. The last column will be used for the total, in dollars, of all listed components representing the scope of work included in that budget.

Figure 6.2 is an example of a bid summary sheet for drywall work and for batt insulation which is to be installed within these drywall partitions. At times, insulation may be listed in the drywall section as "related work in other sections," and if that is the case, from a practical standpoint it is wise to negotiate this work with the drywall subcontractor. We will assume that the architect issued Addendum 1, which includes some additional drywall work. Since the project is a private job, the state sales tax is to be included in the price and a column is added for that item.

Project		
Trade	Division and Section	Date
Subcontractor	Representative	(Area Code) Telephone
Base Bid Amount	Plans/Specs Dated	Addendum

Alternates	Unit Prices	
(1)	(1)	#1
(2)	(2)	#2
(3)	(3)	#3
(4)	(4)	#4

Sales Tax	Bond	
Yes No Amount $	Yes No Value $	Included Yes No

Scope of work — included but not limited to the following:
This form must be fully complete and initialed by Subcontractor & Contractor

Item	Yes	No	Exceptions as Noted
1. All structural steel shown on structural and architectural drawings.			
2. All steel required per mechanical / electrical drawings			
3. Included all rolled members, plates, bars, angles, channels, tees, pipes, tubular members, built up members, special shapes as required to conform to drawings and specifications.			
4. Loose lintels where called for on structural and architectural drawings.			
5. Quantity review — tonnage			
6. Additional steel allowed for ton.			
7. Erect structural steel			
8. a. Erector — self			
b. Erector — other			
9. Metal Deck a. Furnish			
b. Install			
c. Review metal deck scope sheet			
10. Furnish / install shear studs			
11. Review general notes on structural drawings.			

Final Agreed Amount

Contractor	Subcontractors Rep. Signature

Figure 6.1 Subcontractor interview form.

BID SUMMARY SHEET

JOB: GRISWOLD MANUFACTURING

TRADE: DRYWALL - BATT INSULATION

BUDGET: $140,000

BIDDER	DRYWALL	INSULATION	ADD #1	SALES TAX	TOTAL
BEST DRYWALL	$122,000	$11,000	$5,000	Incl.	$138,000
CGM ACOUSTICS	135,000	10,000	Incl.	Incl.	145,000
GYPSUM ASSOCIATE	133,000	No-($9700)*	Incl.	Incl.	142,700
L & M DRYWALL	141,000	9,800	Incl.	Incl.	150,800
R & S INSULATION	-	* $9,700	-	Incl.	
ACME INSULATORS	-	10,400	-	Incl.	

Figure 6.2 A bid summary sheet.

On the bid summary sheet, the columns to the right of the BIDDER column will be used to display the various items to be included in the quotation, such as drywall, insulation, Addendum 1, sales tax, and the total cost of all these items. If all subcontractors who submitted bids have included all the items requested, the bid tabulation will be simple; just compare the total at the far right. Many bids will not include all of the required parts, and some subcontractors will take exception to some items of work, which will be highlighted when the form is used.

By using the form and having to review "included" or "excluded" items, the project manager will have another check on the completeness of a subcontractor's quotation. When reviewing bids, for example, that do not specifically include or exclude Addendum 1 in this case, the subcontractor interview form can be referred to or the subcontractor can be contacted to verify whether Addendum 1 was included in their quotation.

The bid sheet also allows easy comparison of the methods of combining quotes to achieve the most cost-effective price. When variables do exist, without some form of spreadsheet tabulation, comparison analysis will be difficult. For example, a complicated roofing and moisture protection section of a specification may deal with a wide range of work items, and several different types of subcontractors may bid on portions of the work, not the complete scope. One subcontractor may include water-repellent coatings for the exterior brick walls as well as membrane or fluid-applied coatings on the precast concrete parking garage. The general contractor may be planning to apply the concrete foundation wall waterproofing but might also wish to see if a better price can be obtained from the roofing contractor. And although the water-repellent coating is included in Specification Section 7, a mason contractor quoting work under Specification Section 4, Masonry might also submit a price to apply that coating. Again, the bid tabulation sheet will make this kind of analysis much easier. Of course, price is not the only criterion. It might be better to apply foundation wall dampproofing with the company's own workers because there will be better control over the scheduling of backfilling operations on the exterior walls.

Some subcontractors, when submitting individual prices for a number of specified items, may indicate that if they are considered for all the items, they would be willing to offer a package price somewhat less than the sum of the separate quotes. Other subcontractors will state that although they are submitting separate prices for many items, they are doing so for clarification purposes only and will not contract for separate items at the same price. In other words, the project manager may have a limited ability to pick a low quote from one subcontractor and combine with a low quote on a separate item from another. This point needs to be clarified with each subcontractor when they submit quotes containing a list of included items with corresponding prices for each item.

Combining Work To Best Advantage

The example of the mason subcontractor submitting a price to apply water-repellent coatings raises another point of interest. There may be some merit other than monetary in combining items of work under one subcontractor, as in having the mason subcontractor apply any water-repellent coatings that may be required on the brick or blockwork which he has installed. That would place the responsibility for water-penetration problems squarely in the hands of one subcontractor—the mason.

Many different types of subcontractors can and do apply such coatings: painters, caulkers, restoration contractors, or specialized coating applicators. There have been times when one of these subcontractors has been hired to apply water-repellent coatings over another subcontractor's masonry work only to find that after application, the wall still allows water to penetrate. Some coating applicators have been known to disclaim any responsibility for these leaks, placing the blame squarely on the shoulders of the mason contractor and poorly laid-up masonry, bad mortar joints, improperly installed flashings, and so forth. In defense, the mason will claim that the applicator failed to apply the material in strict accordance with the manufacturer's recommendations and skimped on the proper quantity of material applied per square foot. This places the project manager in the position of judge and rarely is the argument settled without backcharges and the creation of ill feelings. But if the mason had been contracted to apply the sealing coating, responsibility for water leaks would lie solely with him.

A situation like this will generally occur when the building is nearing completion or has been completed and water leakage at that stage can seriously delay the start of the finishing trades, or if the building has been occupied, cause the owner's blood pressure to rise, so corrective action must be decisive and quick. Therefore, even if the bid submitted by the mason is the same as, or slightly higher than, the bid submitted by a painter or coatings applicator, think twice before making an award and consider the advantages of having the mason perform this work.

After a particular trade contract has been awarded, all the quotations pertaining to it should be attached to the back of the bid summary sheet and filed in the appropriate job file. Bid summary sheets can be referred to when a list of subcontractors for a particular phase of work must be selected on future projects and the project manager wants to see how competitive they were on the last several bid requests.

Subcontract It
or Do It Ourselves?

Depending on the capabilities and availability of the general contractor's work forces, the project manager can decide what work will be performed by those forces or should be subcontracted. Any number of factors can enter into this decision-making process.

1. Does the current work load presently under contract permit committing more work force to the new job, or will most of the work have to be subcontracted because of the company's heavy backlog?

2. Is the new job so far from the home base of operations that travel time, with all its additional costs, make local subcontractors more competitive as far as overall costs are concerned?

3. Is it possible to incorporate work normally performed with one's own forces into a subcontract so that the larger scope of work offered to subcontractors might result in bids which are lower than the estimate?

4. If the work is of such a nature that there is a potential for future problems, will it be less expensive in the long run to award the work to a more experienced company to which accountability can be transferred?

All these considerations have to be weighed before subcontractor negotiations can be started. Sometimes, a manager will say, "All the bids exceed our budget; let's do this job with our own forces." This can be a dangerous and ill-advised statement unless all the facts are reviewed and discussed. In normal market conditions subcontractors will generally add 10 percent overhead and 10 percent profit to their costs, and if this is the difference between the company's estimate and the low subcontractor quote, the decision to perform the work with the company's own forces is easier to make. But, after discounting the subcontractor's price by an amount assumed to represent overhead and profit, if their costs exceed the company's estimate by a substantial amount, and all other subcontractor quotes equal or exceed the one that was just dissected, could they be right and the company's estimate be wrong? The answer to this question should be considered carefully before embarking on the path to do the work with the company's own forces.

Combining Related Work Contained in Other Sections

In many cases, one section of the contract specifications will refer to related work in other sections. The related work may or may not fall within the scope of work quoted by a particular subcontractor or supplier, but the project manager may be well advised to consider the advantages of having it included as an alternate proposal. A drywall subcontract illustrates some of the elements to be considered in making a decision on what related work can be combined to advantage in one contract.

The standard Specification Section 09250 in Division 9—Finishes, usually contains work related to framing for gypsum drywall and the application of finishing or taping of the drywall. Insulation or soundattentuation blankets or batts within these walls will often be included in the drywall specification section or will be cross-referenced to an 07000 (Thermal and Moisture Protection) series specification section. The project manager should look beyond the obvious work to be included in a drywall subcontract and determine what other operations, at additional cost, might be included to the benefit of both parties. For instance, if the hollow metal door frames to be installed in the drywall partitions are of the setup and welded type, they are almost an integral part of the partition work. Because the installation of these frames and the installation of the drywall work are so interrelated, these frames must be on the job site prior to the start of the metal stud framing operations. The entire framing operation will proceed more smoothly if the drywall subcontractor installs the frames with his carpentry crews. The drywall subcontractor will find it advantageous because he can work at a steady pace and not have to be concerned with another crew, not under his control, that may or may not be there when he needs them. At the time of final negotiations, the cost to incorporate hollow metal frame installation into a drywall contract may not be significant on a unit frame basis. Once the decision to incorporate these frames into the subcontractor's scope of work has been made, the project manager must then ensure that the metal frames are on the job when needed to avoid delay claims being raised by the subcontractor. Late delivery may turn a small cost advantage into a substantial extra if the subcontractor has to double back and install the frames and complete the framing around the openings at a later date.

Another item that could be incorporated into a drywall contract, if it is required, is the wood or metal blocking installed in partitions prior to the drywall application. Blocking such as this is usually required for corridor handrails, toilet accessories, kitchen cabinet installations, and other heavy objects that need to be secured, attached, to finished walls. There again, if the drywall subcontractor has this work included in his contract, he can't claim delays if other crews, not under his control, have not installed the blocking far enough in advance, thereby slowing down his sheetrockers.

The general contractor's superintendent must assume responsibility for confirming the location of all concealed blocking, and the superintendent must also check on the quality and integrity of the installation to ensure that the items ultimately attached to the blocking will remain firm.

Key Questions to Ask Subcontractors While Negotiating

Besides the need for the project manager to ensure that subcontractors have incorporated the proper specifications sections in their bids, along with any scope increases or decreases, it is important that other criteria be acknowledged or clarified. If the subcontractor interview form has been prepared carefully and thoroughly, these questions will have been answered during the interview. If not, let's run through them again.

1. Have the latest contract drawings been reviewed, and do the subcontractors accept all the revision dates as being a part of their bid?

2. Have all addenda, if any were issued, been reviewed, acknowledged, and included in the bid?

3. If the project is exempt from state sales tax, does the bid reflect the exemption? If ti is not exempt, is sales tax included?

4. Are the subcontractors aware of the project construction schedule? It is important that they be apprised of the schedule so that they can anticipate when work will commence and when completion is scheduled, so they can include escalation for wages, materials, and equipment.

5. Are any exceptions being taken with respect to the work shown on the contract drawings or in the specifications? A subcontractor may have based their price on being able to substitute what they consider "or equal" products. Often these or-equal products will not be accepted by the architect or engineer. It must be established during the negotiation stage that if such a situation should arise, the subcontractor will be obliged to furnish the exact item specified at no additional cost. If that is agreeable to both parties, the contract price can be based on an or-equal product, subject to architect or engineer approval. If the product is rejected, the contract sum will either remain the same, or if so negotiated, increase by a mutually agreeable, and stipulated, sum.

Pitfalls to Avoid in Mechanical and Electrical Contract Negotiations

A project manager must be completely familiar with all aspects of the contract documents in order to make the most intelligent decisions on contract awards. In the case of mechanical and electrical trades, there are a number of items to be addressed beyond the basic work contained in their respective specification sections. Will the mechanical and electrical subcontractors be obliged, under the terms and conditions of their specification sections, to provide temporary utilities during construction? Is there a provision in the electrical specification section or the general conditions for electrical and mechanical trades section that requires the electrical subcontractor to provide temporary electrical facilities for power and lighting during construction? The project manager should read the fine print carefully because there will be times when the "temporary utilities" requirements may be designated in the contract specifications as the responsibility of the general contractor.

Even more confusing will be specifications that designate the "contractor" as having responsibility for installing temporary utilities, but there is no definition for the word *contractor*. Does the term mean *contractor* responsible for the electrical work, or does it mean *contractor* responsible for the entire project, i.e., the general contractor? Does the word *subcontractor* appear in other portions of the specifications which further confuses the issue?

These points must be clarified before final subcontractor negotiations begin. Each party, when negotiating, can assume that the definitions apply to the other, and the general contractor may end up issuing a change order to an electrical subcontractor to cover the costs of temporary utilities installation.

Although there may not be any question about the electrical subcontractor furnishing temporary lights during construction, if the specifications don't stipulate the foot-candle requirements or the specific number of 100-W bulbs to be installed per 100 ft^2 of floor space, that issue must also be addressed at negotiation time. Some electricians will state that, in the absence of any specifications on lighting levels, they will install a bare minimum which will usually be insufficient to provide safe working conditions. When the scope of the work is ill-defined, the project manager can write a subcontract clause to the effect that "temporary lighting is to be installed by the electrical subcontractor as required for proper working conditions and proper safety as defined by the general contractor."

When the project requires that all new utilities, such as electrical primary service, domestic and fire protection water mains, sanitary and storms sewers, and natural-gas mains are to be installed, determine whether all related costs such as trenching and backfilling, cutting and patching, tap-in or tie-in costs, and other utility company fees are included in the subcontractor's price. Even if the specifications are clear, it is wise to verify the inclusion of these items.

Another problem often occurs when an out-of-state architect or engineer has been engaged by the owner to prepare the mechanical and electrical specifications. These designers may not be familiar with all the utility company requirements in the state for which the design is being prepared, and these specifications may vary from the designer's home state.

This problem appears to be more prevalent in the mechanical and electrical specifications, but there can be other items of work that historically might be performed by a subcontractor in one state but not by a similar trade contractor in a neighboring state. For instance, in one state the plumbing subcontractor will trench and backfill in connection with his underground piping, but in an adjacent state this work is customarily performed by the general contractor.

When specifications prepared by out-of-state consultants are received, review them carefully with these points in mind. Also, when a project manager is working on a project away from his home state for the first time, information should be developed concerning historical practices of the various trades so that proper scope can be negotiated and included in the related subcontract agreements. The investigation of mechanical and electrical scope should extend to inquiring about the responsibility for paying fees in connection with new utilities such as tap-in, tie-in, connection, and hookup work.

Job Cleaning and the Contract

Keeping a job clean can be an expensive operation and, at certain times during construction, may have to be a continuous one. Job cleaning helps maintain good safety practices, and many of the job-related accidents that have occurred could have been prevented if better housekeeping measures had been in effect. Housekeeping has a direct effect on quality—a dirty site tends to create an atmosphere of lack of concern about the work under way, whereas a clean and tidy site creates an atmosphere of concern for neatness and quality.

Most specifications will contain provisions for cleaning and will assign to each trade the responsibility to clean the debris generated during the performance of their work. A central trash container may be supplied by the general contractor, and each subcontractor will use this container, or the various subcontractors may be required to furnish their own trash containers and pay for the removal of their debris. To avoid arguments at a later date, it is wise to insert a sentence or paragraph in the contract itself setting forth the procedures that are to be followed with respect to job cleanup.

Probably more backcharges to subcontractors are generated for job cleaning than for any other activity. The project manager would be wise to establish a time limit after which the general contractor, not being able to tolerate the subcontractor's lack of cleaning, will take over this operation and charge the subcontractor for all related costs. Such a clause might read as follows: "If after being given 24 hours' notice to thoroughly clean the premises of debris generated by your trade [insert the general contractor's name] will assume these obligations and backcharge your account for all costs associated with these cleaning operations."

Important Issues to Consider When
Preparing the Subcontractor's Contract

Whether required by contract with the owner or not, subcontractors should be requested to submit lien waivers with each request for payment, except the first request. Since lien waivers ostensibly state that monies previously received have been dispersed to pay for labor, materials, and equipment for the previous work period, it is understandable why this lien waiver cannot be submitted with the initial payment request. However, waivers for all subsequent payments must be presented. Even though a subcontractor group may have paid their subcontractor, say, in the case of an insulation company working for a mechanical subcontractor, there is no way of being assured that the insulation materials purchased by that second-tier subcontractor have been paid, unless lien waivers are requested from all second- and possibly third-tier subcontractors.

In times of economic stress, such as those being experienced by general contractors and subcontractors in the early 1990s, it is imperative that a general contractor have assurance that monies dispersed to subcontractors are dispersed down the entire construction "food chain." This can be accomplished by requesting a detailed schedule of values from each subcontractor performing significant portions of the work. This schedule of values should identify all specialty trade contractors working for the subcontractors and the amount of their contracts. The schedule of values should include the cost and name of the supplier of major pieces of equipment. If the subcontractor's financial status is unknown or weak, a suggestion can be made to pay for these major pieces of equipment by joint check. If the subcontractor does not agree to this suggestion, then ask for receipted bills indicating payment for the equipment, and these bills should be forthcoming prior to the payment following the one that was to cover such equipment payments. Also, request that a subcontractor cannot subcontract any work unless the general contractor is notified, in writing, beforehand, and approves, in writing.

Once all the questions have been asked and answered, subcontractor bids have been analyzed, and a contract award is to be made, the language and terms and conditions must be made clear to persons not present at the final negotiation meeting. Both the subcontractor foreman and the general contractor's superintendent will be the prime administrators of the subcontract agreement at the job site, and unless they are both familiar with its content, much confusion will be created.

The primary definition of contract scope and obligations will be reference to the plans and specifications. If the agreement that has been reached deviates from the plans and specifications, the deviations should be spelled out in the written agreement so that all parties who are to enforce the provisions at the job site are aware of the full extent of the scope of the work. All too often a subcontractor's foreman will state to the project superintendent, "Oh, I know that is included in the contract but your purchasing agent and my boss agreed that it was OK not to do it." If that's the case, include it in the contract. If all these clarifications of, additions to, or deletions from scope are written into the contract, there will be fewer discussions and disputes in the field about what was or was not included.

Purchase Orders

A purchase order is written when materials or equipment only is to be bought, as opposed to a contract in which both labor and materials-equipment are included in the purchase price. Purchase orders should contain certain basic information:

1. The vendor's name, address, telephone number, fax number, and the person to contact at the vendor's place of business if questions arise.

2. The project name and project job number (if there is one), purchase order number, and cost code for the product ordered (so that materials can be charged to a specific internal account for that job).

3. The project address, phone number, fax number, and superintendent's name.

4. The quantity of materials ordered, a brief description of the materials, a unit price, and the total price. Any trade or payment discounts should be included. Freight charges should be defined, either f.o.b. (free-on-board) job site or shipping point. Any taxes such as state sales tax should be included or indicated as not included. If the job is tax exempt, the exemption number ought to be included.

5. There should be a preprinted statement on the purchase order form that receipts for all deliveries must be obtained and mailed to the office with the invoice. (Verifying proof of delivery can sometimes be a problem, and duplicate signed receipts accompanying the invoice will be a big help if the vendor cooperates.)

6. There should be another preprinted statement on the purchase order form to the effect that prices stated on the purchase order are not

subject to change without prior notification, in writing, and presented prior to the delivery of the materials.

7. There should be a line for the signature of the person authorizing the purchase and some companies add another line so that the vendor can also sign as an acknowledgment.

The job superintendent should be consulted before a delivery date is placed on the purchase order, and if deliveries are to be made several weeks or months in the future, a statement can be added, such as "Do not ship until released by the job superintendent, Alex Donate (or whatever his name is)."

A copy of the purchase order will be distributed to the accounts payable department so that it can be compared with the invoice when received. Another copy can be filed in a purchase order file or in the file related to the materials purchase. A copy of each purchase order should be sent to the job site so that the superintendent is aware of what has been purchased and either anticipate its delivery or schedule future shipments when needed. Some materials such as extruded polystyrene board and batt insulation are so bulky that adequate storage areas may have to be created well in advance of receiving large quantities of these bulky materials.

Ordering when exact quantities are not known

When orders for some items such as framing lumber are placed, the actual quantities needed will most likely be different from the quantities estimated. Approximate quantities can be used to obtain pricing, but purchase orders, when issued, should not contain exact amounts of materials; the superintendent might find a significant overage or underage when the operation is nearing completion. Rather than specify an exact amount, indicate on the purchase order an amount that is stated to be approximate. Arrange the ordering so that releases can be made as required by the superintendent. The price will be subject to renegotiation only if the quantities shipped are, say, 25 percent less than indicated in the purchase order.

Partial releases may give the superintendent better control over waste. When smaller quantities of framing lumber, for instance, are on the job site, it is much easier to spot excessive waste because the stack of lumber will be depleted at a rate which will be disproportionate to the amount of work actually put into place. It may sometimes appear to be more costly to purchase large quantities of materials and have them delivered in a series of partial shipments, but that might be the most economical way to buy after a discussion with the project superintendent.

If there is any pilferage at the site, it will be easier to spot if smaller quantities are there. Of course, when storage space is at a premium on the job site, partial shipments will become a necessity.

Price protection and the purchase order

There are several ways in which purchase orders can be negotiated to obtain a full or partial measure of price protection. When purchasing transit or ready-mix concrete, it is not unusual to have the supplier guarantee the price for the duration of the project. Other factors, some of which might not be so apparent, should also be included when purchasing ready-mix concrete. When a project is being built in a section of the country where winter means cold weather, "winter concrete" will probably be used. The term *winter concrete* refers to concrete shipped from the plant during certain times of the year when temperatures are low and the ready-mix supplier heats the sand and aggregate before it goes into the mix and also adds hot water. Standard procedure calls for suppliers to charge an extra amount per cubic yard of concrete for this service.

Ready-mix plants also indicate to the customer that all concrete shipped between specified starting and ending dates will contain the heated materials at extra cost. Since not all ready-mix plants set the same start and end dates, and often have varying costs for this service, the total anticipated cost of winter concrete to the general contractor depends on which supplier is selected. By estimating how much concrete will be used during winter months, and reviewing each supplier's suggested price and winter concrete duration time, a proper pricing analysis can be made.

Special criteria involving kitchen appliance purchases

When kitchen and laundry appliances are being purchased in any substantial quantities, such as when a high-rise apartment project is under way, the manufacturer will quote prices which may escalate on a quarterly basis, every 3 months. Appliances must be ordered early to obtain roughing in information and price protection can be a very real problem since they are among the last items to be installed in the job. The project manager may be able to obtain price protection for one, two, three, or even four quarters. If the delivery of appliances will be further in the future, perhaps for a 2-year-duration housing project, the project manager will want to extend some type of price protection as far as possible. Appliance manufacturers will normally state that prices beyond a certain point in time are not expected to increase by more than a specific percent.

The purchase order can then be written with the current quoted price, the length of time for which that price is guaranteed, and a percent increase which will not exceed a certain figure for the period extending beyond the guarantee period. Another aspect of appliance purchasing that the project manager should be aware of is related to delivery and unloading procedures. The standard delivery practice is to include freight charges, for quantity purchases, in the cost of the appliances, i.e., f.o.b.-delivered. However, the unloading, uncrating, and disposal of crating materials and distribution of these appliances will fall to the general contractor, unless responsibility has been assigned elsewhere. In a large high-rise apartment project, these costs can be considerable and the costs do not end there.

If deliveries can be so arranged that the appliances can be distributed directly to each apartment on being unloaded from the truck instead of going into a holding area, some costs will be reduced. Some appliance suppliers offer unloading, uncrating, and debris removal service at a rather low additional cost per appliance. The project manager might consider this option if it is available and local trade restrictions don't apply.

Is price the only consideration?

The project manager's responsibility as it relates to purchasing materials must include not only competitive buying of comparable materials but also getting these materials on the site when needed. By reviewing the plans and specifications and discussing job progress with the field superintendent, a schedule of materials with corresponding delivery dates can be established. Enough time has to be allotted to obtain competitive pricing and allow for delivery time. Price may not be the overriding factor. In the case of framing lumber, a better grade might result in less waste and therefore actually cost less than a lower grade. Or there may be times when the less expensive material is not readily available and using a more expensive one will result in continued job progress. Although price is an important criterion in today's competitive market, consider these other factors as well.

The domino theory in purchasing

The purchase of one item may force the expeditious purchase of another item. If architectural or custom-grade veneer wood doors are to be purchased and the intention is to have them prefitted and premachined for the hardware, obviously other items will have to be purchased. Although it might not be necessary to purchase finished hardware now, a 14- to 16-week delivery date for certain types of architectural or custom-grade wood doors might make it necessary to accelerate certain other purchases such as door frames, if they are to be aluminum or hollow metal, as well as the finish hardware. Unless the wood door supplier has the appropriate information with which to prefit and premachine, they often will not even put the doors into a production schedule. The same thing is true of hollow metal doors.

Pitfalls to Avoid When Issuing Subcontracts and Purchase Orders

The negotiation and award of subcontracts and purchase orders is an important part of the construction process. When performed with knowledge and thoroughness, it can prevent future problems, both economic and schedule-wise. In this process there are certain pitfalls that the project manager should be aware of and avoid if at all possible:

1. Intelligent purchasing is based on knowing as much as possible about the item to be purchased. Rather than hurriedly attempt to purchase an item or subcontract, spend some time to research exactly what it is that must be bought. Look carefully at the drawings and specifications that pertain to the subject and related items. A little time spent investigating might save a great deal of time and money later on.

2. When a job is just getting started, there doesn't seem to be enough time to select subcontractors and to purchase materials. Set priorities and goals to establish what must be dealt with first. A priority list can be established on a daily basis. It can consist of several things that must be done that day, followed by other things of lower priority to be done if, when the priority items are dealt with, there is time to spare.

3. Immediately after a construction contract has been awarded, subcontractors will begin telephoning to discuss various phases of work. Invariably, landscaping or flooring contractors will be the first to call, and these two items are furthest from the project manager's thoughts at the time. In keeping with the concept of setting priorities, it is best to advise these callers to discuss their trade at a more opportune time and call back in a month or two. Don't be rude or too abrupt, but prioritizing time is essential, and lengthy discussions with subcontractors not needed immediately on the project is an unwise use of time.

4. Avoid "crisis management" whenever possible so that each contract or purchase order contains exactly what it was meant to contain. Again, this relates to proper planning and doing what is necessary to take care

of the immediate and near-term requirements first. By reviewing job sequences with the job superintendent, you can develop a list of items needed during the first several weeks.

5. Recognize the long-lead items and concentrate on them. Lumber prices can be obtained and analyzed, a purchase order can be written, and a delivery can be made sometimes within 24 hours, whereas other purchases require more time to assemble information and write an order. A late award of hollow metal door frames to be built into masonry partitions will certainly slow up the masonry operation or result in added costs, or both. Historically, long-delivery items such as an elevator must be given attention at the beginning of the job. With equipment deliveries of 5 months to 1 year after receipt of approved shop drawings, the ordering of elevators is important.

6. Don't delay the issuance of subcontracts. It is best to try to award as many contracts as possible, as soon as possible, starting with the most urgent ones and following with those less urgent. There is normally a lull period at the start of a job when either sitework or foundation work is in progress. This is the time to devote to subcontractor selections and material purchases. By devoting more time to make these awards, the project manager will be free to deal with the next demand on his time: job administration.

7. There are difficult decisions to make with respect to awards that exceed the budget estimates. It is easier to award contracts and purchase orders when they are in line with the budget estimate. Maybe some of the awards are below the estimate, and not too many exceed the estimate by a significant amount. The tough decisions come when certain subcontracted items or materials have been drastically under-estimated for whatever reason. There is a natural tendency to delay making these awards in the hope that some subcontractor will appear with a magical way to perform the work and submit a price to do so that fits into the budget. This seldom happens. When five or six qualified subcontractors have submitted prices that substantially exceed the budget, it must be assumed that the budget is suspect. If overbudget awards are not dealt with on a case-by-case basis but are delayed too long, additional costs may be incurred. This is a difficult problem to solve, and there are no easy answers or solutions to the problem, but positive steps must be taken to resolve the matter and resolve it in a timely fashion. Putting the problem at the bottom of the pile and leaving it there is not the way to handle it.

The entire purchasing activity is, needless to say, a very important part of the entire construction process. It should be attacked with the thoroughness and exactness appropriate to any phase of actual construction. It is an activity that can exercise the ingenuity and imagination of a project manager to the fullest extent.

7

Project Cost-Control Procedures

Once construction has started, subcontractor awards have been made, and many of the materials have been purchased, the project manager will want to develop a system to monitor all the job costs. The cost-monitoring process should be a continuous one so that, at various times during the job, the project manager can determine how well the projected profit is being effected. To look at the actual costs versus the estimated costs and projected profit, a cost-projection procedure can be established for each job currently under construction. The report can be set up by using data processing equipment, or, in the absence of computer operations for this purpose, a system of manual posting and tabulations can be established. The cost-projection report will have three basic components:

1. The field labor cost report containing costs for work performed by the company's own forces.

2. The materials report costs pertaining to material or equipment purchased such as ready-mix concrete, lumber, masonry materials, power tools, and hoisting equipment.

3. The subcontractor status report containing all existing and forthcoming subcontract awards.

The Field Labor Report

The field labor report, discussed in Chap. 4, is generated on a weekly basis since the information being reported is also used for weekly payroll preparation. When effectively and properly used, it shows how the weekly costs to perform certain activities or tasks compare with the estimated costs. The primary use of the field labor report is to generate unit-cost information for historical purposes. Since it records unit costs, it provides a comparison of actual costs with the unit costs contained in the estimate. Therefore, its other valuable function is to provide the project manager and project superintendent with a gauge of the weekly task costs as they are being accumulated and create a projected cost for each task. The field labor report allows the project manager and superintendent to monitor costs as they occur rather than wait until an operation has been completed to determine whether it has met the profit goals.

When the report is used as a component of a cost-projection system, its function is to allow the project manager to scrutinize each individual labor task, evaluate the cost to complete it, and hence project the total of all field labor. The following example illustrates the point:

> Labor to install roof blocking in the estimate has been determined to be $3.00/ft for an estimated 500 ft or 2 × 6-in fir lumber. The total cost of this operation is therefore $1500. If the blocking operation is 50 percent complete and the unit costs are averaging $3.50/ft, the costs will probably continue at that rate and the projected cost for the entire task can be assumed to be $1750, or $250 over budget.

When the costs are reviewed for projection purposes, the quantity of work in place and quantity of work remaining should be calculated. It might have been difficult for the estimating department to make an accurate takeoff for many of the rough carpentry items to determine the actual linear or square footage or board measure of lumber required. Since the total cost of the operation is based not only on estimated labor costs but also on total quantities, the total cost of work will vary if the quantities vary. In the case of roof blocking, field conditions or blocking requirements imposed by the roofing subcontractor may cause the quantities to increase or decrease.

Going back to the roof blocking example, if the project manager determined that 250 lineal ft of blocking has actually been put in place to date, but only 200 lineal ft remains to be installed, the total roof blocking cost, 450 ft × $3.50/ft projected cost, will equal $1575 versus an estimated $1500, producing only a $75 cost overrun. The magnitude of variations of blocking might not appear to be of major consequence in projecting costs, but it is the concept that should be learned. When this concept is applied to major cast-in-place concrete operations, wide variations in quantities used versus those estimated can have telling effects. A 5 percent variance when working with 10,000 yd^3 of concrete will result in a difference of 500 yd^3, and if concrete costs $75.00/yd^3, that 5 percent equates to $37,500, a not so insignificant number.

If there appears to be considerable variation between estimated and actual quantities, the project manager should pursue the matter further to determine whether the estimating department is calculating quantities properly or the field is incurring too much waste.

The Field Materials Report

A field materials report is needed in conjunction with the labor report. It will contain material purchases and costs to date, plus additional costs to purchase the balance of a particular item for the completion of the task or operation. The field materials report will also contain the actual price paid for the item as compared to the estimated unit cost. The estimated unit cost for ready-mix concrete might have been figured at $75.00/yd^3 and based on an estimated requirement of 5000 yd^3, the total cost of concrete materials will be $375,000. If market conditions change and the price of concrete becomes more competitive, resulting in an actual cost of $71.00, a $20,000 savings can be projected if the quantity used versus the estimated quantity remains the same. Conversely, if the price increases, losses will be incurred, quantities remaining equal.

The tabulation of materials purchased to date, consumed to date, and required to complete an operation can get a little involved. The first problem has to do with coding the material delivery receipts.

Field coding of materials received

When materials are delivered to the job site, the delivery receipts should be coded by the job superintendent or his designated assistant. The quantity received should, if at all possible, be checked against the quantity on the ticket. The cost code should be written on the ticket if it is known. If the code has not been given to the field, the exact operation or task for which the materials will be used should be plainly written on the ticket. Then, when the ticket is received in the office and attached to the invoice for approval and payment, the project manager can assign the correct code number.

There will be times when proper segregation and coding will be either difficult or impractical to record accurately. During a concrete foundation operation, when continuous footings, column footings, pilasters, and piers are being poured in quantity throughout the day, accurate apportioning of what concrete went where will be difficult except where a field engineer or clerk has been assigned the task. That is doubly true when lumber is received and is to be used for various rough carpentry and blocking operations.

The best way to analyze materials that may become commingled is to treat the material category in its entirety, that is, compare total foundation concrete material estimates with total foundation concrete used to date and project the amount required to complete the foundations on that basis. These kinds of quantity calculations can be done with the job superintendent over the telephone or during a job visit.

The supplier's billing cycle

The second problem in calculating materials used to date has to do with the supplier's billing cycle. If material suppliers do not invoice promptly, the delivery receipts are the only source of information on how much material was delivered to the job during a certain period of time. If any delivery tickets were lost, misplaced, or not sent to the office (a not too uncommon occurrence), the quantity of materials delivered may not be accurate. A supplier might have a billing cycle that does not relate to a calendar month, as when deliveries made after the 25th of the month will not be billed in that month but will be sent out the following month. If the project manager is trying to establish material costs to date and reviews the supplier's invoice only in-house, some of the invoices may not have been submitted, and therefore all costs will not have been accounted for. If, for instance, large concrete pours are occurring daily, significant costs may be excluded from the cost projection if the project manager relies only on in-house invoices. Suppliers can be contacted and asked to review their accounts receivable to determine what new charges may have been entered that have not yet been billed.

The Subcontractor Status Report

The third report needed to complete the cost-projection procedure is the subcontractor status report. It will contain a list of all subcontracted work by trade designation and the budget estimates corresponding to the items. As subcontracts are awarded, the amount of the contract will be placed alongside the budgeted figure and the difference between the two expressed as a gain or loss. At the end of the report there will be a place to indicate the total amount of all subcontracted items and a total of all contracts awarded to date. A third column can be used to indicate the total effect of all contracts let to date, the net gain or net loss, and the dollar impact of these deviations. This report is usually compiled on a monthly basis as opposed to the field labor report, which is basically a weekly status report. When the report is reviewed, it can also act as a tickler file to alert the project manager to contracts that remain to be awarded.

The subcontractor status report can provide another bit of useful information once all the contracts have been awarded. The difference between the actual and the estimated costs of a subcontract can be expressed as a percentage. The percent for each contract and for the totals of estimated versus actual costs will represent the percentage of subcontractor buyouts. As more and more projects are completed and these buyout percentages are calculated, a pattern will evolve. And this pattern could be a revealing report on the general contractor's reputation in the subcontractor marketplace.

If the percentage of buyouts exceeds 10 percent, then a closer look at subcontractor relationships is warranted. Some general contractors have a reputation for pressuring subcontractors into drastically reducing their prices once they have been awarded a construction contract. When a general contractor (GC) gets this reputation, many subcontractors will inflate their bids so that, if and when the GC is awarded a contract, they will have bargaining room to, in effect, lower their prices to where they should have been in the first place. The "bargaining" GC then feels that he has achieved his goal. If buyout percentages are too high, on a consistent basis, is your company gaining a reputation that might need improvement?

In a competitive bidding market, a GC relies on competitive subcontractor bids. The bargaining GC will assemble subcontractor bids prior to the final estimate review, and as part of the company's bidding strategy, total the amount of subcontracted work and arbitrarily deduct a specific amount from the total estimated costs. The general contractor will, in effect, have "bought" out the job at bid time in the hope of becoming a low bidder. But if the subcontractor quotes received were inflated in anticipation of a bargaining session later on but the GC has already discounted their bids, then this is something like a dog chasing its tail—getting nowhere and accomplishing nothing.

When buyout percentages have been, historically, in the 5 to 7 percent range and a $5 million job is being bid, of which $3.5 million is subcontracted work, it is possible to be noncompetitive by as much as $175,000 because of this one factor, inflated bids from subcontractors.

The Management
Recapitulation Report

A meaningful synopsis of a cost projection can be assembled in a very concise way. A management report indicating the anticipated profitability of a project versus the estimated profit can really contain only one line:

ABC Manufacturing Company—
Cost Projection Report 5

Estimated profit $250,000
Projected profit $245,000

Although the purpose of management reports is to get to the heart of the matter, this is probably too concise a report. If further information is requested, the worksheets showing how the profit projection was determined can be reviewed. Following utilization of the field labor, field material, and subcontractor status reports, a cover sheet on which total labor, material, and subcontractor estimated amounts are listed and the projected cost of each category is placed alongside the corresponding item, a concise report can be produced.

A simple recapitulation sheet containing each project's name, the contract or adjusted contract sum, the cost, and hence the difference between the two—the profit—can be prepared for multiple projects. A simple job status form can be similar to the one shown in Fig. 7.1—a hypothetical job status report for the month of January 1994. A quick look at the report will provide management with a clear picture of all current projects and their projected profits. When change orders have been issued and approved, the contract price will increase, or possibly decrease. This can be recapitulated by merely indicating the actual contract amount as being higher, or possibly lower, than the estimated contract amount as in the case of both the Simplex Company and Delta Corporation shown in Fig. 7.1. The fact that the actual contract price increased from the estimated price can also be footnoted on this form with a notation that certain change orders have been included in the actual contract amount for a particular project.

Preparing Cost-Projection Forms

The wide diversity of computer software these days can create the format required to set up cost-projection forms, but no matter which form the cost projection takes, it needs to include certain basic bits of information. This format can best be illustrated by the manually prepared sheets used as examples and displayed in Figs. 7.2 to 7.5. These sheets have been prepared for a hypothetical project called "Acme Manufacturing" and consist of cost projection reports for general conditions, materials, and subcontracted items and a management recapitulation sheet. The only other report required, is the field labor report. The field labor report shown in Fig. 7.6 could serve as the cost-projection worksheet. On a weekly basis all labor costs for a specific work task have been posted to the

	JOB STATUS REPORT FOR THE PERIOD — January 1-31,1994						
PROJECT	ESTIMATED			ACTUAL			
	CONTRACT	COST	PROFIT	CONTRACT	COST	PROFIT	
ACME ELECTRONIC	$2,875,000	$2,728,000	$147,000	$2,875,000	$2,710,000	$165,000	
H & R MFG.	475,000	435,000	40,000	475,000	450,000	25,000	
SIMPLEX CO.	4,870,000	4,619,000	231,000	4,995,000	4,750,000	245,000	
UNITED TIE	120,000	100,000	20,000	120,000	105,000	15,000	
DELTA CORP.	3,555,000	3,276,500	278,000	3,695,000	3,405,000	290,000	

Figure 7.1 Job status report.

GENERAL CONDITIONS

PROJECT: __ACME MANUFACTURING__

COST PROJECTION NO. __1__

DATE: __Nov. 15, 1993__

GENERAL CONDITIONS	ESTIMATED		TO DATE		TO COMPLETE		TOTAL		GAIN \<LOSS\>
	UNIT	COST	UNIT	COST	UNIT	COST	QUANTITY	COST	
LABOR									
Supt.	600/wk	41,600	15 wks	12,000	37 wks	29,600	52 wk	41,600	—
Engineering	LS	1,500	—	780	1	420	LS	1,200	+300
Project Sign	LS	500	—	450	1	-0-	LS	450	+50
Temp. Protect	LS	8,000	—	4,000	1	4,000	LS	8,000	—
Temp. Heat	750/Mon	3,000	3 Mos	3,000	1 Mos	1,000	4 Mos	4,000	\<1,000\>
Cleaning	520 Mhrs	10,400	100 Mhrs	2,000	88	10,000	600 Mhrs	12,000	\<1,600\>
MATERIALS									
Engineering	LS	500	—	500	-	0	LS	500	—
Temp. Protect	LS	3500	—	2500	-	1500	LS	4,000	\<500\>
Temp. Heat	2000/Mo	8,000	3 Mos.	6,000	1 Mos.	2,000	4 Mos.	8,000	—
Cleaning	LS	1,500	—	800	1	700	LS	1,500	—
Total		78,500		32,030		49,220		81,250	\<2750\>

Figure 7.2 Manually prepared cost projection for general conditions.

MATERIALS REPORT

PROJECT: __Acme Manufacturing__

COST PROJECTION NO. __1__

DATE: __Nov. 15, 1993__

MATERIALS	ESTIMATED		TO DATE		TO COMPLETE		TOTAL		GAIN <LOSS>
	QUANTITY	COST	QUANTITY	COST	QUANTITY	COST	QUANTITY	COST	
CONCRETE									
3,000 psi	105 CY @ $67.50	$7087.50	25 CY @ 65.00	$1625.-	80 CY	5200.-	105 CY	6825.-	$262.50
4,000 psi	50 CY @ $71.25	3562.50	15 CY @ 70.00	1050.-	35 CY	$2450.-	50 CY	$3500.-	$62.50
REBARS	10 Tons @ $450.-	4500.-	10 T @ 450.-	$4500.-	-	-	10 T	4500	-
PLYWOOD 5/8" CDX	1600 SF @ $.80	1280.-	1000 SF @ .75	$750.-	600 SF	$450.-	1600 SF	$1200	$80.-
TOTAL		16,430						16,025	+$405.-

Figure 7.3   Cost projection for materials.

SUBCONTRACTORS STATUS REPORT

PROJECT: **AcME MANUFACTURING**

COST PROJECTION NO. **1**

DATE: **Nov. 15, 1993**

SUBCONTRACTOR	CONTRACT AMOUNT	COST TO COMPLETE	TOTAL COST	ESTIMATE	GAIN <LOSS>
EXCAVATION BRIGGS BROS.	65,000	2,000	67,000	65,000	(2000)
PAVING ELM CITY	18,000	—	18,000	18,000	—
STRUCTURAL STEEL FEROX STEEL	105,000	—	105,000	105,000	—
MASONRY D & R MASONS	85,000	2500	87,500	75,000	(12,500)
GLASS/GLAZING	20,000	—	20,000	21,500	1,500
DRYWALL	47,000 ?	Not Yet Awarded	47,000	—
PAINTING	15,000 ?	Not Yet Awarded	15,000	—
FLOORING	12,000 ?	Not Yet Awarded	12,000	—
PLUMBING ARCO PLUMBING	58,000	—	58,000	55,000	(3000)
HVAC HAVCO.	75,000	5,000	80,000	75,000	(5000)
ELECTRICAL	71,000	—	71,000	72,000	1000
TOTAL	571,000	9500	580,500	560,500	(20,000)

Figure 7.4 Subcontract cost-projection analysis.

field labor report, and the latest such report will be used when the monthly cost-projection report is being prepared. Actual costs to date and corresponding unit costs culled from this report will be extended and multiplied by the actual quantities of each task to be completed. When a work task has not yet started, the estimated unit costs and quantities should be used to arrive at the completed cost.

Of the sheets illustrated, it is to be noted that a separate report has been prepared for the general conditions segment of the estimate. General conditions are affected by time, and therefore a realistic project completion schedule has to be updated before this report can be completed. Certain time-related items such as superintendent's salary, telephone expenses, and other field office expenses, along with progress cleaning, must be properly projected.

Among the major cost items in the general conditions category are temporary heating and cooling of the structure under construction and the cost to furnish electrical power for the various trades working on the project. Temporary light and power costs commence when the job trailer is first placed on the site, and these costs continue and accelerate as various trade contractors increase their electrical power demands. Temporary heating costs begin to increase dramatically as cold weather approaches and large portions of the building have to be heated to allow drywall taping operations to continue and other finishing operations to progress. These costs in buildings of substantial size can run into tens of thousands of dollars each month and must therefore be calculated and projected accurately.

When hot and humid weather begins and finishing trades are working in the building, ventilating and air-conditioning equipment will have to

SUMMARY SHEET

PROJECT: **ACME MANUFACTURING**

COST PROJECTION NO. **I**

DATE: **Nov. 15, 1993**

ITEM	PROJECTED COST	ESTIMATED COST	GAIN	LOSS
GEN'L CONDITIONS				
LABOR	67,250	65,000		⟨2250⟩
MATERIALS	14,000	13,500		⟨500⟩
FIELD LABOR	24,000	22,000		⟨2000⟩
MATERIALS	16,025	16,430	405	
SUBCONTRACTS	580,500	560,500		⟨20,000⟩
TOTAL COST	701,775	677,430		⟨24,345⟩
O H & P	43,398	67,743		⟨24,345⟩
CONTRACT AMT.	$745,173	$745,173		

Figure 7.5 Cost-projection summary sheet containing general conditions, materials, and subcontracts.

COST CODE/TYP	DESCRIPTION	U/M	QTY	ESTIMATED UCOST	COST	ACTUAL TO DATE QTY	UCOST	COST	PROJECTED COST -- TO COMP	GAIN/LOSS	LST 100 C/O PCT
03256 L	F/S STEP FTGS.	U	7	12.14	85	92	2.96	272	0	187-	
03258 L	FORM PIERS		0	.00	0	396	.16	62	0	62-	
03262 L	F/S FOUNDATION WALLS	SF	28,097	1.93	54,327	35,865	.96	34,357	0	19,970	
03264 L	FORM KEYWAYS	LF	580	1.41	815	234	.12	28	42	745	
03274 L	STRIP FOOTINGS		0	.00	0	757	1.52	1,154	0	1,154-	
03298 L	REPAIR/REWORK FORMS		0	.00	0	0	.00	39	0	39-	
03299 L	SHORING		0	.00	0	0	.00	34	0	34-	
03302 L	PL&FIN COL. FTGS.	CY	1,114	5.50	6,128	631	1.70	1,071	821	4,236	
03304 L	PL&FIN CONT. FTGS.	CY	43	6.05	260	244	2.82	687	0	427-	
03312 L	PL&FIN FOUND. WALLS	CY	572	7.69	4,400	712	5.02	3,571	0	829	
03352 L	SET ANCHOR BOLTS	LS	0	.00	1,600	133	20.91	2,781	0	1,181-	
03354 L	SET/GROUT BASE PLATE		0	.00	0	0	.00	169	0	169-	
03356 L	RUB WALLS	SF	14,000	.46	6,420	0	.00	51	6,369	0	
03362 L	FORM FND. HAUNCH	LF	492	2.00	985	1,032	2.16	2,226	0	1,241-	
03430 L	BONDBREAKER/EXP JNT	LF	1,400	.00	0	0	.00	0	0	0	ADJ.
03440 L	MESH FOR S.O.G	SF	39,750	.00	0	0	.00	0	0	0	ADJ.
03535 L	MESH FOR SUPP. SLAB	SF	135,000	.00	0	0	.00	0	0	0	ADJ.
06012 L	BLOCKING-ROOF&CORNIC	LF	0	.00	916	0	.00	0	916	0	
06031 L	TAPE&SPACKEL SHT. RK	SF	0	.00	0	0	.00	46	0	46-	
06055 L	OAK BUMPERS	LF	0	.00	3,511	0	.00	0	3,511	0	

Figure 7.6 Field labor report.

be made operative to rid the building of excess moisture. If acoustical ceiling pads are installed in a moisture-laden building, they will quickly cup so badly that replacement will be necessary. Cooling costs can be substantial and also must be calculated and projected accurately. Looking at the material report for the Acme Manufacturing job, there are entries for only concrete, reinforcing steel, and plywood to illustrate how three different units of material measurement are reported: cubic yards, tonnage, and square footage. Since the ⅝-in CDX plywood has been ordered but not yet used on the site, it is assumed that the estimated quantity will be the actual quantity. Since the material was estimated at $0.80/ft^2 and was purchased for $0.75/ft^2, a slight gain has been registered.

The subcontractor status report will list all the subcontracted items for the job, not just the eight shown in Fig. 7.4. The project manager should be realistic in projecting the costs to complete any of these items. If it appears that, on the basis of bids received to date, it will not be possible to award a contract for an amount equal to the estimate, and therefore a loss will occur, indicate the anticipated loss. The management report (Fig. 7.5) will recapitulate projected costs for the entire project and will indicate the projected total cost versus the estimated cost for general conditions, labor and materials, field labor and materials, and each subcontracted item. Only when the total or projected costs are added can it be determined whether they are less or greater than the estimated costs and will therefore result in a profit adjustment, greater or smaller than anticipated.

Figures 7.6, 7.7, and 7.8 display various electronic-data-processed (EDP) cost reports that are used to complete the field labor portions of the monthly cost projections. A typical field material report is shown in Fig. 7.9, and Fig. 7.10 is a cost report where labor, materials, and subcontracted work is contained in one report. In this report, the letter designations in the "Apl" (application) column define C—contract or subcontracted work, E—equipment costs, L—labor, T—sales tax, B—labor burden, M—materials, and O—other. Figures 7.11 to 7.13 show EDP-prepared subcontractor status, management recapitulation, and overall (general) recapitulation reports, respectively.

Assigning Cost-Code Numbers for Unassigned Tasks

There will be times when certain work tasks are required in the field but the work has not been assigned a cost-code number. Either the particular task was missed during the process of estimating the job, or field conditions are such that this additional task is now required. When the job superintendent uncovers a situation like this, the project manager

L A B O R   T O T A L   R E P O R T

PERIOD ENDING:

JOB #	ESTIMATED --HOURS	--TOTAL	ACTUAL TO DATE --HOURS	--TOTAL	THIS WEEK --HOURS	TOTAL	% CMP	EST COST TO COMP	EST FIN PROJ	GAIN /LOSS
00000 GENERAL CONDITIONS	0	8,182	127	1,811	47	426		7,075	8,885	-703
01000 SUPERVISION	0	33,500	402	9,360	73	1,023		24,140	33,500	0
02000 UNLOADING	0	2,170	0	0	0	0		2,170	2,170	0
04000 EARTHWORK	0	5,110	193	1,791	0	0		10,380	12,170	-7,060
05000 FORMWORK	0	47,384	1,591	27,247	54	546		49,173	76,420	-29,036
06000 CONCRETE WORK	0	20,478	90	1,657	0	0		19,752	21,407	-929
08000 REINFORCING	0	1,831	8	85	2	17		1,746	1,831	0
12000 ROUGH CARPENTRY	0	10,269	0	0	0	0		10,269	10,269	0
13000 MILLWORK-WOOD DOORS	0	51,555	0	0	0	0		51,555	51,555	0
14000 THERMAL & MOISTURE BARR	0	997	24	304	2	25		2,182	2,486	-1,489
15000 HOLLOW METAL	0	7,524	0	0	0	0		7,524	7,524	0
16000 WINDOWS & MIRRORS	0	5,400	0	0	0	0		5,400	5,400	0
17000 SPECIALTIES	0	2,600	0	0	0	0		2,600	2,600	0
18000 BUILDING EQUIPMENT	0	720	0	0	0	0		720	720	0
19000 FURNISHINGS	0	2,520	0	0	0	0		2,520	2,520	0
20000 BACKCHARGES	0	0	13	157	0	0		0	157	-157
22000 EXTRAS	0	259	2	276	0	0		0	276	-17
JOB TOTALS	0	200,499	2,450	42,688	178	2,037		197,206	239,890	-39,391

Figure 7.7   EDP-prepared labor cost report with totals by category.

ITEM	EST QTY	EST UCOST	EST TOTAL	ACT QTY	ACT UCOST	ACT TOTAL	WK QTY	WK UCOST	WK TOTAL CMP	% CMP	EST COST TO COMP	EST COST FIN PROJ	GAIN/LOSS
02180 UNLOAD HOLLOW METAL - EA	285	0.75	214	0	0.00	0	0	0.00	0	0	214	214	0
		0.00	0		0.00	0		0.00	0				
02190 UNLOAD WINDOWS - EA	216	1.00	216	0	0.00	0	0	0.00	0	0	216	216	0
		0.00	0		0.00	0		0.00	0				
02220 UNLOAD MISC. - LS	0	0.00	469	0	0.00	0	0	0.00	0	0	469	469	0
		0.00	0		0.00	0		0.00	0				
02230 UNLOAD FINISH HARDWARE - LS	0	0.00	208	0	0.00	0	0	0.00	0	0	208	208	0
		0.00	0		0.00	0		0.00	0				
04100 HAND EXCAVATION - CY	300	9.00	2,700	0	0.00	303	0	0.00	0	11	2,397	2,700	0
		0.00	0		0.00	34		0.00	0				
04101 HAND BACKFILL - CY	276	5.00	1,381	52	9.90	515	0	0.00	0	19	2,218	2,732	-1,351
		0.00	0		1.00	52		0.00	0				
04102 HAND COMPACTION - SF	25,726	0.04	1,029	660	0.23	155	0	0.00	0	3	5,765	5,920	-4,891
		0.00	0		38.82	17		0.00	0				
04156 PLACE STONE UNDER SLAB	0	0.00	0	0	0.00	558	0	0.00	0		0	558	-558
		0.00	0		0.00	64		0.00	0				
04200 WATER PUMPING - LS	0	0.00	0	0	0.00	260	0	0.00	0		0	260	-260
		0.00	0		0.00	26		0.00	0				
05100 FORM WALL FOOTINGS - SF	5,418	1.22	6,599	2,684	1.85	4,970	0	0.00	0	50	5,058	10,028	-3,429
		0.00	0		15.88	169		0.00	0				
05204 FORM WALLS 8'-12' - SF	27,207	1.19	32,270	10,414	2.11	21,943	240	2.20	529	38	35,433	57,376	-25,106
		0.00	0		7.45	1,398		4.62	52				
05222 FORM CURVED WALLS 4'-8' - SF	610	2.00	1,220	0	0.00	0	0	0.00	0	0	1,220	1,220	0
		0.00	0		0.00	0		0.00	0				
05300 FORM PIERS 0-4' - SF	371	1.22	452	111	1.37	152	0	0.00	0	30	356	508	-56
		0.00	0		13.88	8		0.00	0				
05324 FORM ROUND COLUMNS 8'-12' - LF	11	4.00	44	0	0.00	0	0	0.00	0		44	44	0
		0.00	0		0.00	0		0.00	0				
05504 FORM SUPPORTED SLAB 8'-12' - SF	976	1.25	1,220	0	0.00	0	0	0.00	0	0	1,220	1,220	0
		0.00	0		0.00	0		0.00	0				

Figure 7.8 EDP-prepared labor report with different format.

COST CODE/TYP	DESCRIPTION	U/M	ESTIMATED QTY	ESTIMATED UCOST	ESTIMATED COST	ACTUAL TO DATE QTY	ACTUAL TO DATE UCOST	ACTUAL TO DATE COST	PROJECTED COST TO COMP	PROJECTED COST GAIN/LOSS	LST 100 PCT C/O
03252 M	FORM/STRIP COL. FTGS	SF	8,300	.50	4,150	4,712	.38	1,796	1,363	991	
03254 M	F/S CONT. FTGS.	SF	1,160	.80	930	2,037	.43	877	0	53	
03256 M	F/S STEP FTGS.	U	T	10.00	70	92	.00	0	70	0	
03262 M	F/S FOUNDATION WALLS	SF	28,097	.90	25,285	36,525	1.22	44,632	0	19,347-	
03264 M	F/S KEYWAYS	LF	580	.41	235	235	.00	0	235	0	
03274 M	STRIP FTGS.	SF	0	.00	0	377	.27	102	0	102-	
03275 M	PUMP FND'S	DAY	6	900.00	5,400	0	.00	2,160	3,240	0	
03302 M	PL&FIN COL. FTGS.	CY	1,114	45.00	50,130	631	41.49	26,183	20,040	3,907	
03304 M	PL&FIN CONT. FTGS.	CY	43	45.00	1,935	244	50.39	12,296	0	10,361-	
03308 M	PL & FIN PIERS	CY	0	.00	0	0	.00	0	0	0	
03312 M	PL/FIN FOUND. WALLS	CY	572	45.00	25,740	661	43.02	28,434	0	2,694-	
03352 M	SET ANCHOR BOLTS	LS	0	.00	155	133	.76	101	0	54	
03356 M	RUB WALLS	SF	14,000	.01	140	0	.00	0	140	0	
03362 M	FORN FND. HAUNCH	LF	492	1.02	500	372	6.56	2,439	787	2,726-	
03430 M	BONDBREAKER/EXP. JNT	LF	1,400	.35	490	0	.00	0	490	0	
03440 M	MESH FOR S.O.G.	SF	39,750	.00	0	0	.00	0	0	0	ADJ.
03455 M	CONC.FOR SL/3000 PSI	CY	580	45.00	26,100	.	.00	0	26,100	0	
03458 M	PUMP	DAY	3	900.00	2,700	0	.00	4,275	0	1,575-	
03470 M	APPLY CURING COMPOUN	SF	35,844	.03	1,075	0	.00	0	1,075	0	
03505 M	PUMP SUPPORTED SLAB	DAY	11	.00	0	0	.00	0	0	0	ADJ.
03535 M	MESH FOR SUPP. SLAB	SF	135,000	.08	10,485	0	.00	0	10,485	0	ADJ.

Figure 7.9 EDP-prepared field materials report.

JOBS IN PROGRESS/BUDGET REPORT

JOB #:

CODE	DESCRIPTION	APL	ORIG EST	C/O EST	TOTAL EST	NON-CONT COSTS	ORIGINAL CONTRACTS	CONTRACT CHANGES	TOTAL COMMITMENT	DIFFERENCE
02220	STRUCTURE EXC. + BACKFILL	C	1,250		1,250	0	0	0	0	
02220	STRUCTURE EXC. + BACKFILL	E	82,873		82,873	2,419	0	0	2,419	80,455
02220	STRUCTURE EXC. + BACKFILL	L	28,128		28,128	2,136	0	0	2,136	25,992
02220	STRUCTURE EXC. + BACKFILL	T	13,486		13,486	0	0	0	0	
	TASK TOTAL:		135,582	0	135,582	5,375	0	0	5,375	130,207
02271	RIP RAP	B	2,000		2,000	0	0	0	0	
02271	RIP RAP	E	3,900		3,900	0	0	0	0	
02271	RIP RAP	L	5,800		5,800	0	0	0	0	
	TASK TOTAL:		11,700	0	11,700	0	0	0	0	11,700
02400	DRAINAGE	B	1,101		1,101	274	0	0	274	827
02400	DRAINAGE	C	2,899		2,899	0	320	0	320	2,579
02400	DRAINAGE	L	4,345		4,345	614	0	0	614	3,731
	TASK TOTAL:		8,345	0	8,345	888	320	0	1,207	7,138
02401	DEWATERING	B	5,400		5,400	624	0	0	624	4,776
02401	DEWATERING	L	15,400		15,400	1,367	0	0	1,367	14,034
02401	DEWATERING	M	0			849	0	0	849	849-
02401	DEWATERING	O	0			0	0	0	0	
	TASK TOTAL:		20,800	0	20,800	2,839	0	0	2,839	17,961
02441	LAWN IRRIGATION	S	17,800		17,800	0	17,000	0	17,000	800
02445	FENCES AND GATES	B	10,500		10,500	0	0	0	0	
02452	SIGNAGE (PERMANENT)	C	10,000		10,000	0	0	0	0	
02456	PARKING BUMPERS	B	259		259	0	0	0	0	
02456	PARKING BUMPERS	C	4,000		4,000	0	0	0	0	
02456	PARKING BUMPERS	L	741		741	0	0	0	0	
	TASK TOTAL:		5,000	0	5,000	0	0	0	0	5,000
02476	SITE CONCRETE	B	13,516		13,516	160	0	0	160	13,356
02476	SITE CONCRETE	C	6,400		6,400	0	618	0	618	5,782
02476	SITE CONCRETE	L	45,148		45,148	369	0	0	369	44,779
02476	SITE CONCRETE	M	0			451	0	0	451	451-
	TASK TOTAL:		65,064	0	65,064	980	618	0	1,598	63,466
02480	LANDSCAPING	S	85,300		85,300	0	0	0	0	
02480	LANDSCAPING	T	8,000		8,000	0	0	0	0	
	TASK TOTAL:		93,300	0	93,300	0	0	0	0	93,300
02500	PAVING	B	2,100		2,100	0	0	0	0	

Figure 7.10 EDP-prepared job cost report with labor, materials, and subcontractors on same report.

COST CODE	DESCRIPTION	ESTIMATED	---AWARD---	---VARIANCE----	COMMENT	LOC PCT
01013	FINAL CLEANING	1,500	.00	.00	NO AWARD	
	TOTAL GENERAL CONDITIONS	1,500	.00	.00		
02002	CLEARING	5,000	1,854.00	3,146.00		
02004	PLANTING	30,000	39,607.00	9,607.00-		
02006	SEEDING	10,000	9,718.00	282.00		
02010	BITUMINOUS PAVING	98,960	85,900.00	13,060.00		
02012	LINE PAINT-PAVING	1,005	.00	.00	NO AWARD	
	TOTAL SITE WORK	144,965	137,079.00	6,881.00		
02066	SITE SUBCONTRACTOR	174,900	170,439.50	4,460.50		
	TOTAL EXCAVATE / BACKFILL / GRADE	174,900	170,439.50	4,460.50		
02132	UNDERGROUND SPRINKLE	0	10,850.00	10,850.00-		Y
02135	WALKS & CURBS	16,410	13,692.00	2,718.00		
	TOTAL SITE IMPROVEMENTS	16,410	24,542.00	8,132.00-		
03102	MESH	3,990	3,696.00	294.00		Y
03104	REBAR	5,000	5,000.00	.00		Y
	TOTAL REBAR PLACEMENT	8,990	8,696.00	294.00		
03499	SLAB ON GRADE-SUB.	4,900	4,200.00	700.00		Y
	TOTAL SLAB ON GRADE	4,900	4,200.00	700.00		
03560	MTL.PAN STAIRS&LAND.	400	.00	.00	NO AWARD	Y
03570	SUPPORTED SLAB	12,830	16,278.32	3,448.32-		Y
	TOTAL SUPPORTED SLAB	13,230	16,278.32	3,448.32-		
04010	BUILDING MASONRY	108,500	109,180.00	680.00-		
	TOTAL MASONRY	108,500	109,180.00	680.00-		
05010	STRUCTURAL STEEL	361,500	317,371.68	44,128.32		Y
	TOTAL STRUCTURAL STEEL	361,500	317,371.68	44,128.32		
06026	SPRAY FIREPROOF-SYST	0	2,500.00	2,500.00-		
	TOTAL ROUGH CARPENTRY	0	2,500.00	2,500.00-		
06116	P.O. #08361	6,150	5,450.00	700.00		
06122	COUNTER TOPS, STOOLS	24,040	23,005.00	1,035.00		
	TOTAL MILLWORK INSTALLATION	30,190	28,455.00	1,735.00		
07050	ROOFING	42,000	40,500.00	1,500.00		
	TOTAL MOISTURE PROTECTION	42,000	40,500.00	1,500.00		

COST GROUP/TYPE	ESTIMATED COST	ACTUAL TO DATE OR AWARDED	PROJECTED COST TO COMP	GAIN/LOSS	SUB CONTRACT VARIANCE
GENERAL CONDITIONS					
LABOR	30,350	19,747	14,036	3,433-	
MATERIAL	10,386	15,547	8,094	13,255-	
EQUIPMENT	0	5,400	0	5,400-	
SUB CONTRACT	6,500	.00			.00
SITE WORK					
LABOR	0	179	0	179-	
MATERIAL	0	0	0	0	
EQUIPMENT	0	0	0	0	
SUB CONTRACT	49,906	38,284.00			11,622.00
EXCAVATE / BACKFILL / GRADE					
LABOR	0	41	0	41-	
MATERIAL	0	0	0	0	
EQUIPMENT	0	0	0	0	
SUB CONTRACT	107,094	122,796.00			15,702.00-
SITE IMPROVEMENTS					
LABOR	0	0	0	0	
MATERIAL	0	132	0	132-	
EQUIPMENT	0	0	0	0	
SUB CONTRACT	7,815	3,300.00			4,515.00-
CONCRETE FOUNDATIONS					
LABOR	0	17,467	0	17,467-	
MATERIAL	0	0	0	0	
EQUIPMENT	0	0	0	0	
SUB CONTRACT	0	.00			.00
REBAR PLACEMENT					
LABOR	0	291	0	291-	
MATERIAL	0	65	0	65-	
EQUIPMENT	0	0	0	0	
SUB CONTRACT	70,000	70,000.00			.00
FORMWORK					
LABOR	70,132	41,822	3,343	24,967	
MATERIAL	36,070	49,567	4,908	18,405-	
EQUIPMENT	0	0	0	0	
SUB CONTRACT	0	.00			.00
CONCRETE PLACEMENT					
LABOR	10,788	5,329	821	4,638	
MATERIAL	77,805	66,913	20,040	9,148-	
EQUIPMENT	0	0	0	0	
SUB CONTRACT	0	.00			.00
MISCELLANEOUS ITEMS					
LABOR	9,005	5,227	6,369	2,591-	
MATERIAL	795	2,540	927	2,672-	
EQUIPMENT	0	0	0	0	
SUB CONTRACT	0	.00			.00

Figure 7.12 EDP-prepared management recapitulation report.

		------ESTIMATED------ TOTAL	------ACTUAL TO DATE------ TOTAL	------THIS WEEK------ TOTAL	% CMP	EST COST TD COMP	EST COST FIN PROJ	GAIN /LOSS
00000	GENERAL CONDITIONS	8,182	2,336	149	28	6,970	9,306	-1,124
01000	SUPERVISION	33,500	10,832	531	32	22,668	33,900	0
02000	UNLOADING	2,170	0	0	0	2,170	2,170	0
01000	EARTHWORK	5,110	1,826	26	15	10,344	12,169	-7,059
05000	FORMWORK	47,384	31,450	1,513	66	36,273	67,723	-20,339
06000	CONCRETE WORK	20,478	1,911	74	9	19,209	21,119	-641
08000	REINFORCING	1,831	85	0	5	1,746	1,831	0
12000	ROUGH CARPENTRY	10,269	0	0	0	10,269	10,269	0
13000	MILLWORK-WOOD DOORS	51,955	0	0	0	51,955	51,955	0
14000	THERMAL & MOISTURE BARRIERS	997	304	0	31	675	979	18
15000	HOLLOW METAL	7,934	0	0	0	7,934	7,934	0
16000	WINDOWS & MIRRORS	5,400	0	0	0	5,400	5,400	0
17000	SPECIALTIES	2,600	0	0	0	2,600	2,600	0
18000	BUILDING EQUIPMENT	720	0	0	0	720	720	0
19000	FURNISHINGS	2,520	0	0	0	2,520	2,520	0
20000	BACKCHARGES	0	157	0	100	0	157	-157
22000	EXTRAS	259	276	0	100	0	276	-17
	JOB TOTALS	200,499	49,177	2,293	21	180,643	229,818	-29,319

Figure 7.13 EDP-prepared recapitulation sheet.

should be contacted for instructions. The project manager may decide to incorporate this new task into one to which a cost-code number has already been established, or a new cost-code number may be assigned to this task.

As all work units are reported, they will begin to show items of work being reported which were not included in the estimate. If and when other missing items surface during the course of construction, the superintendent should be encouraged to call the office for direction in assigning cost codes. The superintendent should be given the authority to arbitrarily assign cost-code numbers if the project manager is not available and the information is required for payroll processing. When a project has been completed, the final report should be handed to the estimating department for their review.

Incorporating Change Orders into the Cost Projections

Depending on which form of cost-reporting system is being used, the method by which change order work is incorporated will vary. The project manager or the company's management team might not care to keep change-order work separate, whereas other managers like to see how change-order estimates compare to change-order actual costs.

Two types of change orders will be involved in cost projection work. One is the type issued to subcontractors or suppliers for which no corresponding change order will be forthcoming from the owner to increase the contract sum. The other is the type issued to subcontractors and suppliers to cover additional work which will be paid for by the owner, therefore increasing the contract amount. In the first instance, the project manager could have overlooked an item that should have been included in the subcontractor's scope of work, but was inadvertently omitted. As an example, the provision for the installation of temporary power might not have been included in the electrical specification section but was indicated in another section of the specifications as being the responsibility of the general contractor. If this item was not discussed with and incorporated into the electrical subcontractor's contract initially, a change order must be written to increase the scope of work and add the amount of the temporary power installation to the electrician's contract. This adjustment will show up on the subcontractor status report as an increase in cost but without an increase in estimated costs. As for change orders that will increase costs and contract sums, does the project manager wish to keep these costs segregated or incorporate them into the general category to which they belong? A complicated change order might include four or five subcontracted items plus work that requires more or different materials, portions of which are to be installed by the general contractor's own forces. A typical change order used to illustrate this point is as follows:

Electrical work		$3,500
Plumbing		4,500
HVAC		1,500
Flooring		1,000
General construction		
Labor	$1,500	
Burden (40%)	600	
Materials	$1,000	
Tax	60	$ 3,160
		$13,660
Overhead and profit, 15%		2,049
Total		$15,709

If cost projections are being prepared by manual means, one way to keep track of the change-order costs is to assign a separate code to each change order. Then all costs associated with the change order will receive the same cost-code number. For example, 09900 series cost code can be set aside for change orders. The first change order for a particular project can be assigned cost code 09901, and change order 2 will be assigned cost code 09902. All costs incurred to complete the work outlined in change order 1 will therefore be coded 09901 and will be posted against the estimated cost of the work.

This system may not work when electronic data processing is being used. Problems may arise when a change order to an owner contains work that will be subcontracted to several different trades. A change order involving work by multiple trades must be cost-coded so that each trade's contract is updated. Let's say that a change order requested by an owner amounts to $10,000 without the contractor's overhead and profit, and involves HVAC work worth $6500, plumbing work for $1000, and electrical work amounting to $2500. When a change order to the owner is issued for $10,000 plus overhead and profit, the cost of this work must be distributed where it belongs, and all trades receiving a change order for this work will have that portion of the change relating to their work cost-coded to their original contract. If the HVAC subcontractor's contract has been coded 15500, it is possible to use the last two digits to highlight changes to that contract; therefore, change order 1 to his account would be coded 15501.

The method by which cost-control and cost-projection procedures are put into place will vary with the individual company needs, staffing availability, and accounting techniques, but every construction company should implement some form of cost and job profit forecasting.

8

Change-Order and Liquidated-Damage Clauses

This chapter concerns the change-order and liquidated-damage clauses that are contained in some contracts. On the surface it might appear that the two subjects are unrelated, because one has to do with changes in the contract obligations, and the other, with penalties levied for late delivery of a construction project. The American Institute of Architects (AIA) General Conditions contract (Document A201), revised in 1987, contains Article 7—Changes in the Work, which deals with the process in depth.

A *change order* is defined as a written order to the contractor, which has been signed by the owner and architect, issued after the contract has been signed and authorizing a change in the scope of the work or an adjustment in the contract sum or contract time, or both. Because the general contractor's goal will be to complete a project on time, or submit a change order to request an extension in contract time, if the contract contains a liquidated-damages clause, these two seemingly unconnected aspects of the construction process do possess a common thread.

Change Orders—the Textbook Approach

One major problem in change-order work concerns the disparity between the theoretical way change orders should be processed and the practical manner in which they are usually handled. Article 7 of the AIA General Conditions document states that a change order is a "written instrument prepared by the architect and signed by the Owner, Contractor, and Architect stating their agreement" to a change in the work, the cost of this work, and the extension of time, if any, required to put this work in place.

If one follows the rules, a change order's life starts when the architect submits a proposal request in which it is requested that the contractor submit a proposal for all costs to perform the work outlined in the request. Each such proposal is numbered sequentially by the architect, and this number is referred to in the contractor's cost proposal or estimate. After this cost estimate is reviewed and approved by the architect, a formal change order, usually AIA Document G701, is prepared and sent to the contractor for signing. It is then returned to the architect, who signs it and sends it on to the owner for signature. When this fully executed document is returned to the contractor, then—and only then—the contractor is authorized to proceed with the work. This is a rather lengthy and time-consuming process by which to get the work done, and change-order work normally has an urgency about it.

Speeding Up the Process

The procedure described above is cumbersome and impractical from a time standpoint, and the architect can speed things up by issuing a construction change directive, AIA Form G7143, which authorizes the contractor to proceed with the work promptly with costs to be determined by one of several means so that a formal change order can be written at a later date. This form, however, still has to be signed by the architect and the owner before the work is officially authorized, so that even the architect's attempt to speed up the process will take some time.

The Verbal Authorization

The most common approach to authorizing change-order work is the verbal commitment or directive. The architect sends a sketch to the contract or discusses a possible change in the work with the project manager, who in turn prepares a cost estimate for the work. This may involve the contractor's own cost estimates, including subcontractors' prices, or a combination of both. The contractor's allowable markup for overhead and profit will be added to the net cost, and the total price will be telephoned to the architect or passed on verbally at a job meeting. The architect will consult with the owner and advise the project manager whether the price is acceptable and the work should proceed or whether the price is not acceptable and arrive at a compromise scope and price so that the work can get started.

At this point, the project manager should confirm the instructions he received, including the price, by sending a letter to the architect, unless the architect has already initiated a confirming letter. The project manager's confirming letter can be short and simple and might include the following:

> Pursuant to the issuance of a formal change order, as of this date, (name of contractor) is to proceed to (describe the nature of the extra work) based on your verbal authorization to do so. The cost of this work, as mutually agreed on, is $_____ and includes the general contractor's overhead and profit. It does not appear that this work will have any impact on the construction schedule (or if it will have an impact, state so here). It will be appreciated if a formal change order can be issued at your earliest convenience.

The project manager should remember that although there has now been a verbal authorization to proceed followed by a written confirmation, it is still important to obtain a formal change order as rapidly as possible. The extra work may be completed promptly, but it cannot be included on the monthly requisition for payment until the formal change order has been duly executed by all parties. For that reason alone, it is wise to press for prompt processing of the formal change order.

There are certain facets of change-order preparation that should be given more than just casual thought. The question of what constitutes allowable costs and overhead and profit percentages is not always clearly answered. Some contracts do not include specific lists of items constituting acceptable contractor "costs," and what may be applied against these costs for markup, and overhead and profit. Specific instructions and directions for change-order procedures, if there are any, will usually be contained in the bid documents or the supplementary general conditions within the bid documents. By looking through Article 7 the project manager can see if there are any provisions for change-order preparation that might have been overlooked.

When preparing a cost estimate for change-order work the project manager should consider the following:

1. Will the work contained in this change order affect the completion time of the project?

2. What is the net cost of the work? (The term *net cost* is explained more fully below.)

3. What other costs besides "bricks and mortar" should be included in the estimate?

4. Does the cost of this work have any effect on the payment and performance bond or on insurance requirements?

5. What fees can be included in this change order work?

Completion Time and the Change Order

Are the nature and timing of the change order work apt to affect the completion date for this project? Will they extend the completion date, or will they actually decrease construction time? These questions should be asked even if a liquidated-damages clause is not part of the contract. There is a line item near the bottom of the change-order form that pertains to contract time; the project manager is to indicate whether the contract time will be increased, be decreased, or remain unchanged by the issuance of the change order. A space is included to insert the number of days for the anticipated decrease or increase. Another line item directly below that one on the AIA change-order form has a space in which to insert a revised date of substantial completion, if that will change.

Theoretically, an increase in contract completion time would mean that a request could be made for reimbursement of the portion of the general contractor's general requirements that is related to time. The project manager, if the changes are going to extend the length of the job, could include the following as cost of the work: additional supervision, additional field office expenses (including office trailer rental), added temporary utility costs, added sanitary control costs, cleaning costs, and in some cases additional project management costs.

If the nature of the change orders is such that it might be debatable whether the completion time will be extended, another approach might be tried. Get the architect to agree to the job completion extension time with the proviso that, if the project is complete within the original contract time frame, no claim will be made for additional general requirement cost reimbursement. If the completion extends beyond the date established in the contract or in the initial job progress schedule, there will be reimbursement of general requirements for the time extension agreed on.

One word of caution about requesting time extensions. Members of the project team can change during the life of a construction job, and although the project manager may have developed a fine working relationship with the original team, new faces can appear, and either the previously friendly relationships turn cool or go all the way to cold. If the architect or owner's representative had previously stated that formal time extensions were not necessary, because if the time came that they were needed, they would agree to them, the new team may completely disavow these verbal commitments. To avoid any such situation it is wise to prepare for the worst and request time extensions if they are justified. A project manager can always use the "hit by a car" excuse so as not to imply that the owner-architect representative can't be trusted. Simply stated, if there is mutual agreement that a job extension is warranted, it should be so indicated in

the change order; suppose one of the team members is "hit
tomorrow and there is no documentation of the verbal commi

What Is Net Cost?

Net cost is usually interpreted as the cost of materials; including sales tax
and delivery charges; the cost of labor, including Social Security benefits,
unemployment insurance taxes, fringe benefits established by collective
bargaining agreements or company policies, Workmen's Compensation
insurance, bond premiums, and rental of tools and equipment; and fees
levied by local, state, and federal agencies. Overhead costs are sometimes
viewed differently by each company. Project management may be included in the estimate as a general condition expense, while other
companies figure it as a corporate expense. The project superintendent's
salary plus any other field-stationed time clerks are usually considered a
general requirement cost; however, the cost of a secretary stationed in a
field office may not be so easy to define. All expenses connected to the
operation of the general contractors main or branch office are historically
defined as overhead costs, which also includes the top executives whose
responsibility is overall management of the company. Although some cost
and overhead items are fairly clearcut, the job superintendent's salary
and related expenses might very well be a gray area. Depending on the
nature of the anticipated change, the job superintendent may be required
to spend more time supervising the change and may need an additional
carpenter or labor supervisor to take over some other supervisory function temporarily. Obviously, a change order involving the installation of
four more 120-V electrical outlets will not place an added burden on the
superintendent. But what about the change in design of continuous
footings and foundation walls to a system of spread footings, pilasters, and
grade beams because of unsuitable subsurface soil conditions which have
just been uncovered? And what about large quantities of interior partitions which are to be changed and will in turn require the relocating of a
great deal of mechanical and electrical work already in place? Depending
on the magnitude of the changes and the added demand placed on
supervision, a strong case can be made for including additional supervisory costs in the cost of the work.

Don't overlook a cost sometimes referred to as "small tools." Will some
hand tools need to be purchased to complete this change-order work?
Generally hand tools are viewed as expendable; once used on the job, they
have no further value. Will additional or different kinds of power tools be
required to perform this work? Power tools are not considered expendable
but are considered as having residual value after the job is complete, but
a charge representing true depreciation of the tool or tools can be included

in the cost of work. Often a general contractor, rather than listing specific tools and related costs, will add a small percentage to each change-order estimate to include the cost of "small tools."

What Costs Other Than Bricks and Mortar Should Be Considered?

Will an additional fee have to be paid to increase the cost of the building permit? If a building permit has been issued for the core and shell of an office building with tenant improvements to be installed at a later date, the local building department will assuredly require an additional sum for the revised building permit. Some building departments request a copy of the building's completed costs so that an adjustment can be made in the cost of the permit.

When substantial completion status is reached and the architect stipulates that date in writing, the building's temporary utilities—gas, water, electricity, and telephone systems—are usually transferred to the building owner's account. If change-order work takes place after this transfer of utilities, the project manager need not be concerned with these utility costs as a part of the change-order work. If substantial completion has not been reached and certified, it is essential that additional heating or cooling costs resulting from the proposed change-order work be included. If electric welders are required to complete the change-order work, or any other equipment will be used that may require considerable power consumption, these costs should be factored into the cost of the work.

And don't forget the cost of fasteners, nails, screws, and bolts! More than one project manager has been shocked to find a $2000 invoice for stainless-steel expansion bolts that were used in change-order work, but were not included in the estimate sent to the architect.

Does the Cost of Work Affect the Payment and Performance Bond Premiums?

If the project in question required a payment and performance bond at the outset, the premium for the bond was based on the original contract amount. Many insurance companies will monitor the project costs to determine whether the contract amount has been increased by the addition of approved change orders. The cost of the bond premium may be increased if there have been enough change orders of sufficient magnitude to warrant an increase. The project manager should check with the company's insurance agent to determine what impact a large-dollar change order will have on the premium so that it can be included as a cost in the change-order preparation.

What Fees Can Be Included in Change-Order Work?

The procedure and method of costing and the allowable overhead and profit percentage are normally established in the bid documents. Typical restrictions in these bid documents or supplementary general conditions may be as follows:

> The undersigned (general contractor) agrees that the total percentage for overhead and profit which can be added to the net cost of the work shall be
>
> For work performed by his own forces   ___%
> For subcontracted work   ___%
>
> The undersigned (GC) also agrees that, for subcontracted work, the total overhead and profit percentages added by the subcontractor will not exceed the percentages indicated above.

In some cases, specific allowable overhead and profit percentages are stipulated for subcontracted work with these percentages decreasing as the cost of the work increases.

When completing the bid document information, the general contractor is, in effect, establishing the overhead and profit percentages that a subcontractor will be allowed to charge for change-order work. When subcontract agreements are being negotiated, after the construction contract has been signed, the subcontractor must be made aware of the restrictions that will be placed on the overhead and profit structure.

Along with the requirement for specific percentages to be applied for overhead and profit, the architect may also insert a clause that will affect the way overhead and profit are computed. A statement may be added that when changes in the work result in some cost increases and some cost decreases, the overhead and profit calculations will not be applied until the net change is established. Let's look at a hypothetical case involving three cost increases of $500, $2800, and $450 and two credits or cost decreases of $1100 and $384. Assume a fee of 10 percent for overhead and 5 percent for profit. By adding overhead and profit into each individual cost increase and then deducting credits, we can compute as follows:

Cost	$500.00	$2800.00	$450.00
10% overhead	50.00	280.00	45.00
	$550.00	$3080.00	$495.00
5% profit	27.50	154.00	24.75
	$577.50	$3234.00	$519.75

Adding these three items together will total	$4331.25
Deducting the two credit items	1484.00
Net add for these changes	$2847.25

The architect, by inserting the statement about overhead and profit being applied to the net change, would alter the request for $2847.25 as indicated above, and would dictate that the cost be tabulated differently:

Cost of all add items, $500, $2800, $450	$3,750.00
Cost of deduct or credit items	1,484.00
Net change	$2,266.00
10% overhead	226.60
	$2,492.60
5% profit	124.63
Net add for these changes	$2,617.23

By calculating the latter way, the cost of the total change is $230 less than by the first method.

The Construction Change Directive

Article 7 of the 1987 edition of the AIA General Conditions document contains a new term for change-order work: the construction change directive. This directive is an order signed by the architect and the owner directing the contractor to effect a change in the scope of work when there is an absence of agreement among all parties as to the terms of a change order, which usually means disagreement over the cost of the work.

The cost of the work contained in the construction change directive is to be determined by a mutually accepted lump sum, by unit prices if contained in the contract, by "costs to be determined in a manner agreed upon by the parties" (whatever that means!), or by a method prescribed in a subsequent paragraph.

When contractor and architect-owner cannot agree on an acceptable cost for the work, the architect may request an itemized accounting of costs, which shall include the following:

1. Cost of labor and related fringe benefits

2. Cost of materials, supplies, and equipment, including cost to transport to the job site

3. Rental costs of machinery and equipment, exclusive of hand tools whether these tools are rented from the contractor or other sources

4. Costs of bond and insurance premiums, permits and fees, and taxes

5. Additional costs of supervision and field office personnel directly attributable to the change-order work

A reasonable allowance for the contractor's overhead and profit is to be added to these costs. The construction change directive appears to be a fair way to treat change-order work when the cost is being questioned.

State and Federal Agency Change Orders

When work is performed for municipal, state, or federal agencies, additional restrictions, qualifications, and procedures can be expected. The Connecticut Department of Housing, in the author's home state, for example, states that a change order involving the rehabilitation of a building for middle-income housing can be instituted when one of the following conditions occurs:

1. The time required to complete the project must be increased because of conditions beyond the control of the contracting parties.

2. Revisions in the plans and specifications, ordered by the local housing authority with the approval of Department of Housing (DOH), result in an increase or decrease in the cost of construction.

3. Unpredictable underground or superstructure conditions which will increase or decrease the cost of construction are encountered.

Some state housing agencies require that change orders be signed and dated by all interested parties in the order of their interest. This could set up a situation whereby the following signatures are needed in the order of their listing:

1. The chairperson of the local housing authority

2. The general contractor

3. The architect

4. The chief of construction of the state

5. The manager of development

6. The director of housing

As can be imagined, this could be a time-consuming exercise. A change order issued by the U.S. Department of Housing and Urban Development (HUD) contains a statement whereby the mortgagee (owner) certifies that a sum of money necessary to cover the cost of the change order is on deposit. This restriction is very helpful when a not-for-profit sponsor is involved in the project in that it assures the general contractor that monies will be available to pay for work over and above the initial contract sum. But this provision can be a two-edged sword. If the mortgagee (owner) does not have sufficient funds to cover the cost of a change involving unforeseen conditions that are required to keep the job going, the general contractor may have only two choices: proceed with the necessary work in the hope that funds will come available, or stop the job and commence legal action.

Roadblocks to Change-Order Approval

Why is the change-order process so fraught with problems and frustrations? After all, what could be simpler? The owner or architect would like to make a change in the work under contract, the nature of the work is discussed, a price is submitted and agreed on, and the work is completed and is paid for on the next requisition.

Another change-order scenario has the general contractor uncovering a discrepancy, omission, or conflict in the contract documents and requesting that the architect review the problem and discuss the additional costs to correct the situation so that a change order can be issued.

The greater portion of change-order work is usually generated by the owner or architect, when a complete, well-coordinated set of plans and specifications has been the basis on which a construction contract was prepared. Most general contractors would prefer to go through a project without the disruptions and delays that can be caused by change-order work. The exception to this rule is when a general contractor finds that the construction plans and specifications are deficient in that they do not fully cover the scope of the actual job requirements and such significant additional work is required that additional compensation is justified. This situation probably sets up the first roadblock in the relationship between contractor, architect, and owner.

The ability to view problems from the other person's perspective can be particularly important when it comes to change-order requests. Let's look at it from the general contractor's viewpoint first. A small or midsize general contractor may be estimating many jobs at the same time and only a certain amount of time is allotted to each estimating effort. The estimating department will be estimating exactly what is shown on the drawings, and there may not be time to analyze whether a certain detail will work. It is the general contractor's responsibility to price out what is on the drawings, and the responsibility for proper functioning is left up to the design professionals.

If the general contractor is awarded the job and, on commencing construction, finds that the design documents are incomplete, why shouldn't the contractor be allowed to request the additional funds necessary to complete that portion of the work? He must assume that the plans and specifications which were to be estimated represented a complete project that had been assembled and checked by design professionals for accuracy, completeness, and compliance with all applicable codes and regulations.

The architect-engineer viewpoint

In the preparation of drawings and specifications for the construction of a sophisticated project, by constraints of time and money, it is almost impossible for the architect to include all the construction details. If the drawings are too exact, they might not give the contractor any latitude to adapt to field conditions. The architect recognizes these facts and establishes certain ground rules to cover some of the contingencies, but by their very nature they may also create some of the problems associated with change-order work.

The first potential area of conflict between contractor and architect is addressed in the bidding documents. There are usually statements intended to discourage change orders. Instructions to bidder statements generally include a phrase that directs the contractor to notify the architect, in writing, of any ambiguities, inconsistencies, or errors in the bid documents, prior to submission of the bid.

The next warning is usually contained in the bid proposal, which states that the undersigned general contractor is to affirm by signature that all the contract documents have been examined, and all rights to plead any misunderstandings of these documents are hereby waived. From there we go to the "supplementary general conditions of the contract for construction," which will, in most cases, contain phrases to the effect that should the general contractor discover any contradictions, ambiguities, errors, or inconsistencies in or between any of the contract drawings, before proceeding with the work, the architect will be notified and requested to render an interpretation of these matters. Failing to do so, the contractor will have no excuse for not carrying out the work in a satisfactory manner as interpreted by the architect.

Still other supplementary conditions state that all drawings are a working part of the specifications and any questions or disagreements as to the true intent of the specifications or drawings, or the kind or quality of work required, shall be decided by the architect and/or local authority, whose interpretation shall be *final, conclusive, and binding on all parties.*

That is very unilateral and nonnegotiable language! The architect, knowing that the drawings might lack some specific details, would like to be protected from that unscrupulous contractor who might be looking to take any and every opportunity to generate change orders. Possibly that honest, hard-working contractor needs protection from that less-than-perfect design consultant.

What is the solution?

If it is impossible for the architect and engineer to issue a perfect set of plans and specifications, complete in every single aspect, it is also impossible for the general contractor, during the bidding process, to comply with all the investigations for completeness of design as required by the architect in the bid documents. It would appear that the best solution to the controversies that arise over change-order work would be to require both contractor and architect to be *reasonable* in their approaches to these problems of extra cost items.

Is it reasonable to assume that it is the contractor's responsibility to ensure that the mechanical and electrical drawings have been properly coordinated with each other and with the architectural drawings? If during construction it is determined that the ductwork, sprinklers, and light fixtures can't fit in the space above the proposed ceiling and additional costs are involved in rerouting some ductwork or piping, is this not the basis for an unarguable change-order request? On the other hand, if additional window blocking is required for proper and secure window installation, and this blocking detail is not specifically shown on the drawings, is this a legitimate claim for an extra cost request?

The answer to the first question is "yes." The contractor cannot and should not be held responsible for the coordination of multidisciplinary drawings that is necessary to make certain that everything will fit in an allotted space. This does not seem a *reasonable* responsibility to be assumed by the general contractor. The answer to the second question is "no." It does not seem *reasonable* for an architect to assume responsibility for the complete detailing of window blocking, since an experienced and competent general contractor ought to be able to develop the proper wood blocking details as field conditions dictate. Both questions should be viewed with an eye to what is reasonable; and if that kind of approach can be developed, some of the difficulties in implementing and approving change-order work may be eliminated.

The project manager should also bear in mind that the architect does not relish having to go back to the client, the owner, and reveal that extra costs might be involved because of omissions on the drawings or details that lack clarity. There are usually compromise positions that all parties can take to resolve these problems. One approach that the project manager can take is that, if a detail or missing items had in fact been shown on the drawings at bid time, all the bids would probably have included additional costs for the items. Therefore, the initial project cost would have been higher. Since that was not the case, it is merely a question of including the costs now instead of having them in the initial bid.

There are a few terms connected with change-order work that may surface, particularly when there are problems getting change-order work approved. One such term is *quantum meruit,* and another is *unjust enrichment,* and they present the project manager with another approach to obtaining change-order approval.

Quantum Meruit

The Latin term *quantum meruit,* pronounced "quantum mare-o-it," is also referred to as "quasicontract." Both terms refer to recovering costs for benefits received rather than from the contract between two parties. The theory of quantum meruit, in the legal community, is that damages or claims for money by a contractor in connection with such things as change-order work will be based on the value of the work performed. If there is a dispute between owner and contractor over change-order work and whether it was authorized, the contractor can base a request for payment on the quantity and quality of work performed or in question.

Unjust Enrichment

This theory differs somewhat from the theory of quantum meruit in that unjust enrichment will be used to measure damages or contractors' claims by the amount by which the owner has been enriched. There may come a time when the project manager will proceed with change-order work based on a good-faith commitment from either the architect or the owner. Let us assume that this oral agreement to do the extra work was never confirmed in a letter or memorandum. Now that the work is complete, the project manager is requesting that a change order be issued so that payment for the work can be requisitioned. Repeated requests go unanswered for some reason; and since there was no written authorization to do the work, the project manager is now concerned about being reimbursed for the cost of the work and the associated contractor's fees.

Let us assume that the change involved upgrading the birch hollow core doors, as specified by the contract documents, to oak veneer, solid core doors. There were 10 doors involved, and the additional cost per door amounted to $150; therefore, the total cost of this extra work was $1500 plus the contractor's fee. The owner, very clearly, has had the project's value enriched by this substitution, and if it looks as though the owner will not issue a change order for this work, the project manager should familiarize the owner owner and architect with the legal concept of unjust enrichment. The owner may argue about the costs associated with this change and request documentation to substantiate every aspect of the $1500 cost, but the argument that value has not been added to the job by virtue of this change cannot be denied or dismissed. This is one approach to be pursued in order to get that written change order issued and approved.

Betterments and Enrichments

Another pair of terms related to change-order work are *betterments* and *enrichments*. The two terms are occasionally used in connection with change orders; and if they are not questioned thoroughly, they could have a substantial effect on a change-order request. HUD has a specific form for change orders known as FHA Form 243, Request for Construction Changes, Project Mortgage. On the reverse side of this form there are instructions and conditions for acceptance by HUD. The form states that, to be acceptable by HUD, the proposed change order must actually be due to necessity, be an appropriate betterment, or qualify as an equivalent.

There have also been private construction contracts with language that limits the acceptance of change orders to items constituting betterments and enrichments. This type of restrictive clause may also state that the contract sum cannot be increased for any change in the work in order to comply with building, fire, safety, or similar laws and ordinances. In other words, if the owner wanted to substitute oak doors for birch doors, that would be considered a betterment and the change order would be processed. If the fire marshal or building inspector conducted an inspection prior to the issuance of a certificate of occupancy and requested that additional exit or emergency lights be installed, along with more fire alarm pull stations or fire or smoke detectors, the general contractor might not be able to submit a claim for the additional costs involved in complying with these requests. The owner may take the position that this change did not make the project any "better" and was needed to comply with the local ordinances as interpreted by the local officials. The contractor, on the other hand, will certainly argue that these extra cost items were indeed betterments. Without them, a certificate of occupancy would not have been issued, and therefore the building would have had no value at all. The project was enriched when the certificate of occupancy was issued after the work was done.

It would appear that these types of code compliance items must be the responsibility of the owner's consultants. Article 3 of the 1987 edition of the AIA General Conditions seems to back this up. Paragraph 3.7.3 clearly states that it is not the contractor's responsibility to ascertain that the plans and specifications comply with applicable statutes, codes, and ordinances. But time and time again, local building officials and fire marshals review and approve drawings prior to the issuance of building permits. After they conduct a walk-through in the closing days of construction, however, they often require that various life-safety items be added or modified. If those items result in added costs, the owner must recognize that the costs are reimbursable to the contractor. The time to uncover and discuss the restrictive contract language referred to above is when the contract is being reviewed at the beginning of the job, not at the end, but contractors, not willing to risk being argumentative at the beginning of a project, often find themselves immersed in problems at job's end.

Liquidated-Damages Clause

The liquidated-damages clause is a provision inserted into the construction contract stipulating that a certain monetary penalty will be leveled against the contractor for each day that the project completion is extended beyond the agreed date, taking into account mutually agreed-on time extensions.

A typical liquidated-damages clause

A liquidated-damages clause will usually be inserted into the paragraph referring to contract time in either government or private construction contracts. It will probably be similar to the following:

> If the work is not substantially completed in accordance with the drawings and specifications, including any authorized changes, by the date specified above, or by such date to which the contract time may be extended, the contract sum stated in Article (whichever article contains the contract sum) shall be reduced by $__ (the daily amount of damages) as liquidated damages for each day of delay until the date of substantial completion.

Although the intent is to have the contractor pay the owner for damages incurred due to late delivery of the building, the liquidated-damages clause states that the total amount of damages will, in actuality, be deducted from the final payment, since it has the effect of decreasing the contract sum.

Purpose of liquidated-damages clause

It was first thought that by having a liquidated-damages clause in a contract, the contractor would have more reason to complete a project on time. If he didn't, the owner's damages represented by the daily dollar amount of liquidated damages would be compensation for late delivery without recourse to legal action. That has not always been the case, inasmuch as the courts have been used to interpret and determine what constitutes the proper application of the liquidated-damages clause. One of the key elements of the liquidated-damages claim is "complete, including any authorized changes." The question of contract time that can and should be extended by change orders has already been discussed, but what about the other justifiable reasons for extending contract completion time?

Job Delays

There are three basic categories of construction project delays in the eyes of the law:

1. *Excusable.*   The contractor is granted a time extension, but no monetary compensation.

2. *Concurrent.*   Delays occur, but neither contractor nor owner can collect monies for damages.

3. *Compensable.*   Delays for which either owner or contractor is entitled to additional monies.

Excusable delays

Excusable delays will allow the contractor to extend the completion date of the contract but may not allow him to recover costs associated with the delays. The following constitute excusable delays:

1. Acts of God

2. Fires and other accidents

3. Illness or death of one or more of the contractors

4. Transportation delays over which the contractor has no control

5. Labor strikes or disputes

6. Unusually severe weather

Concurrent delays

The contractor generally assumes some delays for weather conditions and for periods of labor non-availability. When delays are concurrently caused by the failure of the owner to honor his contractual obligations and the contractor's lack of performance, the courts have been prone to rule that each party must bear its own losses because of the delays incurred. In other words, if the owner is remiss in meeting the requisition payment schedule contained in the contract and the contractor arbitrarily, without any written notice, slows the job down because of the late payments, neither party will be able to collect on the damages attributable to their delays.

Compensable delays

Compensable delays, according to the courts, are those delays for which damages can be claimed. Compensable delays include delays caused by elements beyond the control of the contractor, but within the control of the owner; changes in the work, access to the site, and site conditions differing materially from those specified in the contract. Specific court cases established some delays as "compensable"; these are cited below.

- Delays in the approval of shop drawings submitted by the contractor. [*Specialty Assembling and Packing Co. v. United States,*274,Ct.Cl. 153 (166).]

- Delays caused by owner's improper inspection procedures. [*Gannon Co. v. United States,* 189 Ct.Cl. 328 (1969).]

- Inadequate or defective drawings or specifications. [*United States v. Spearin,* 248 U.S. 132 (1918) and *J. D. Hedin Construction Co. v. United States,* 171 Ct.Cl.70 (1965).]

- Contract changes when the nature of the work changed affects the original or unchanged work and causes an extension of time. [*Conduit and Foundation Corp. v. State of New York,* 425 N.Y.S. 2d 874 (App. Div. 1980).]

- Owner work-force interference. The owner, in accordance with the provisions of the contract, is allowed to award separate contracts for work on the project, and this work interferes with the general contractor's work. Such a situation could arise on a union construction job when an owner engages nonunion subcontractors and jurisdictional disputes lead to work stoppage. [*Bateson Construction Co. v. United States,* 319 F.2d 135 (Ct.Cl.1963).]

Establishing the Time Frame for Liquidated Damages

When do liquidated damages commence, and when do they cease? The date for commencement is stated in the contract, and this date can be extended only by agreed-on extensions of time and excusable delays. When do liquidated damages stop? They stop when the project reaches the stage of substantial completion as determined by the architect in accordance with the provisions of Article 9.8 of the AIA General Conditions document. If there is a disagreement between the contractor and the architect as to what constitutes substantial completion, the responsibility falls to the general contractor to establish that the project in contention was completed to the point at which it could be used for the purposes for which it was intended.

Some contracts may state that liquidated damages will remain in effect until the project is 100 percent complete and all current punch-list items are also complete. This provision may not be enforceable since the courts have generally gone along with the substantial completion concept.

Enforcement of the Clause

Liquidated-damages clauses will not be enforced by the courts if they are construed to be used as a penalty. Even though the language states that the liquidated-damages clause is not a penalty clause, that's immaterial. Certain criteria must be present for the clause to be acceptable:

1. The amount fixed as the daily dollar amount of damages must be a reasonable assessment of the costs the owner will incur if the project is not completed on time.

2. The effects of the breach of contract (inability to finish on time) must be very difficult to establish at the time of contract preparation.

The amount of the liquidated damages must bear a relation to the real, and not imagined, harm that may be caused to the owner if completion is not adhered to. In a case known as *Harty v. Bye*, 483 P.2d 458 (1971), the Supreme Court of Oregon ruled that, although a contract contained liquidated damages and the contractor did not complete the project on time, the owner was unable to substantiate any proof of actual losses due to the late completion. In another court case known as *Nomellini Construction Company v. Department of Water Resources*, 96 Cal. 682 (1971), neither party could establish the amount of damages which were incurred as a result of the other party's delays. The court said that if it is not able to discern a clearcut distinction between the damages caused by the parties, then liquidated damages cannot be assessed.

A further illustration of unenforceability is the case of *Mosler Safe Company v. Maiden Lane Safe Deposit Co.*, 199 N.Y. 479 (1910). There was a liquidated-damages clause in the construction contract, and when the contractor completed the work later than the date specified in the contract, payment was requested in full per the contract amount. The owner wanted to invoke liquidated damages. During the court action, the contractors stated that they had been delayed because the architect required the work to be installed in a manner different from that in the contract drawings. The contractors also claimed that the architect delayed the job by not acting promptly on shop drawings submitted for review. The court ruled that, when delays are caused by both parties, it will attempt to apportion the damages and will refuse to enforce the liquidated-damages provision of the contract.

Documentation Required for Liquidated Damages

With respect to excusable delays, delays which will extend the contract time but will not support a claim for additional monies, the project manager should submit a written request for job extensions whenever they occur, even though it appears at the time that the job is well ahead of schedule.

When a request for job time extension is made, there may be no immediate response from the architect. If no response has been received after a week or so, it is a good idea to write another letter referring to the first request and stating that if there is no response to this second request within 5 working days after receipt of the request, it is assumed that the delays have been accepted and therefore the contract completion time will be extended by the requested number of days. This will trigger a fast response!

When weather is the basis for requesting job delays, it is important that the job superintendent document the daily time sheet or daily diary properly. The report or diary should have an entry such as "No work day due to extremely heavy rains from 6:30 A.M. to 10:30 A.M." If any workers have reported for duty awaiting a decision on whether the day will be considered a no-work day, that also should be noted in the report. When a claim for weather delays is made, copies of the primary documents should be attached to the request.

9

Project Documentation

The proper documentation of a construction project entails maintaining sufficient records to effect a history of the construction process. "Proper documentation" does not mean creating endless reams of paper to fill endless filing cabinets. It does mean making certain that when important events are about to happen, are happening, or have happened, they are correctly and promptly recorded. The key words are "important" as to events, and "correctly" as to recorded. Unfortunately, there are no hard-and-fast rules governing what to document and what not to document, but, hopefully, this chapter will assist the project manager in making those decisions.

Proper or adequate documentation of a construction project involves maintaining sufficient records to account for the actions and inactions of all participants to the process. This documentation will provide the following benefits:

1. Create a history of the project which can be referred to when similar jobs with similar problems are encountered.

2. Provide enough information so that, if project reassignments are made within the organization, a new project manager can trace the job history to date and continue the administration of the project easily.

3. Provide more than merely the reliance on one's memory to reconstruct various segments of a project's activity long after it has been completed.

4. Reduce the possibility of future misunderstandings, disagreements, or disputes by committing important events or verbal communications to written ones.

5. Be available in the event of litigation. The United States is known as a litigious nation; one prone to engage in lawsuits. The construction industry is such that exposure to that risk is very high; and if litigation is being considered, proper documentation will be invaluable.

Proper record keeping is important with respect to the project manager's relations with

The owner

The architect and engineer

Government authorities

Subcontractors and suppliers

Field operations

Office personnel

Documentation to the Owner

The form and content of any documentation will vary with the general contractor's relationship with the owner. When the architect is the owner's agent or representative, most owner-related communications will pass through the architect. Some owners, even though they have contracted for the full services of an architect during construction, may request copies of all documents which the general contractor sends to the architect. There may even be an owner who will bypass the architect and give instructions directly to the contractor. If that does happen, the project manager must advise the architect of the situation; and when a response is made to the owner's request or instructions, a copy should be sent to the architect.

In the case of a cost-plus or guaranteed-maximum-price (GMP) contract, both the owner and the architect will want to be kept aware of any significant cost increases or decreases. Under a lump-sum contract, the owner will have no interest in how actual costs are related to estimated costs, except when change orders are involved.

When a cost-plus or GMP contract is in effect, the final selection of subcontractors may be subject to approval by the owner; if so, copies of the quotes along with the project manager's recommendation will have to be forwarded to the owner. The letter accompanying the quotes should contain a tabulation of the scope and prices so that each quoted price represents equal scope. Included in the letter should be a time frame required for a response—within 5 working days, 72 hours, or whatever time is necessary so that a subcontractor award can be made in order to maintain job progress.

There may be a time when a project manager will not recommend the low bidder. The low bidder might not be too much lower than a second bidder who has a record of much better performance and is less prone to request "extras" for questionable times. If that is the case, the reasons for selecting someone other than the low bidder should be stated in the recommendation forwarded to the owner.

The owner's responsibility to the contractor

The owner has more than a responsibility to pay the monthly requisitions; there is an obligation to pay the contractor on time, and there is the responsibility to have made arrangements for financing prior to the start of construction. By and large, the owner's obligations to a general contractor begin after a construction contract has been signed. If formal bidding instructions were issued when general contractors were requested to submit bids, there may have been a statement in those instructions that any bids submitted are to remain valid for 30, 45, or 60 days. Depending on the time frame indicated in the bid documents, the general contractor will be notified, in writing, that they are the apparent low bidder and have been selected to do the work, or the contractor may be advised that their bid is not acceptable to the owner and the reasons for nonacceptability clearly stated. If the owner does not make either statement within the prescribed period of time, the contractor will be under no obligation to accept an award if it is offered. Who would wish to do that? Well, just suppose that, on review of their bid, the general contractor discovers that a major item of work has been inadvertently omitted from the estimate. The contractors may very well wish to withdraw their bid but not forfeit their bid bond, if one was required. If the owner fails to abide by the bid notification procedure, this would be the time to examine one's bid to determine whether a contract would be accepted if offered. If it would not be accepted, the first and last bit of owner correspondence will be generated: a letter from the contractor to the owner indicating a desire to withdraw the bid.

The owner also has an obligation, in most cases, to provide certain surveys and easement information to the contractor. Since these documents will be needed shortly after contract signing, the contractor should request them and, if they are not forthcoming, follow up with a letter indicating the urgency of the request. Once a construction contract is signed, the conventional team of design and supervising consultants will enter the picture. Most future documentation will take place with these owner representatives.

Documentation to the owner from a construction manager

When a construction manager contract has been awarded to a general contractor, relations with the owner and related documentation will take on a new dimension. The construction manager's contractor will now become the owner's agent and consultant in matters related to construction. Because of that relationship the documentation takes on a different perspective. The construction manager's daily activities as the owner's agent will require the CM to prepare reports, schedules, and various analyses, along with recommendations pertaining to contract awards, subcontractor requests for extras, and decisions related to the project. The construction manager will monitor costs during construction, review and comment on job progress, and advise the owner with respect to the acceptability of monthly billings submitted by suppliers and subcontractors.

Documentation to the Architect and Engineer

Correspondence with the architect and his consultants, a principal cog in the construction machinery, will constitute one of the most voluminous parts of the entire record-keeping process. The following list contains most of the categories of items that will require the project manager's attention. When "architect" is mentioned, "engineer" may also apply.

1. *Shop drawing flows.*   A proper shop drawing log must be maintained by the project manager to monitor the flow of shop drawings: when they are received, how many copies and what type of drawing, the date when they were forwarded to the architect, the date when they are received after being reviewed, and the disposition of the reviewed drawings. The log must be reviewed periodically; and when the shop drawings have lingered too long at the architect's office, the project manager must request more rapid handling. There are many types and forms of shop drawing logs, and Figs. 9.1 and 9.2 represent two of them. Computer software packages often contain shop drawing log configurations, or a form can be quite easily prepared by someone in the office.

2. *Requests for clarifications of plans and specifications.*   Known as *requests for information* or requests for clarification (RFIs or RFCs), these forms are often used to obtain interpretation of those portions of the plans and specifications that are unclear, vague, or in conflict with

SHOP DRAWING RECORD

	SUBMISSION DATE	GENERAL CONSTRUCTION	JOB NUMBERS:
1		PLUMBING	CON'TR._____
2		HEATING & VENTILATING	
3		ELECTRICAL	
4		STRUCTURAL STEEL	

PROJECT:

CONTRACTOR:

SPACE TO BE COMPLETED BY CONTRACTOR

SPACE TO BE COMPLETED :

SPECIFI-CATION REFER-ENCE	NO. COPIES	SHOP DRAWING DESCRIPTION	DRAWING NUMBER	DATE RECEIVED DWG'S. FROM CON-TRACTOR	NO. COPIES	DATE SENT DWG'S. TO ENGINEER	NO. COPIES	DATE RECEIVED DWG'S. BACK FROM ENGR.	NO. COPIES	APPROVED	APPROVED AS NOTED	RESUBMIT FOR FINAL APPROVAL	Disapproved RESUBMIT	DATE RETURNED TO CON-TRACTOR	NO. COPIES	1 COPY TO CLERK OF WORKS

REMARKS:

Figure 9.1 Shop drawing log.

PROJECT NO:1978 NAME: Apex Manufacturing Co. P.M. John Farnham

SHOP DRAWING REPORT SYSTEM
GENERAL LISTING (REPORT # 1)

CSI NO.	VENDOR NAME	DRAWING DESCRIPTION	SUBMIS NO	DRAWING NO.	QTY	TYPE	DATE RECEIVED	DATE DUE	CPM DATE	DATE RETURNED	ACTION	REMARKS	REC NO
5100	BERLIN	STEEL	2	1127	1	PRINT	03/25/92	04/07/92	/	03/26/92		AA	2397
5100	BERLIN	STEEL	1	1128	1	PRINT	12/26/91	01/09/92	/	12/26/91		AC	1508
5100	BERLIN	STEEL	2	1128	1	PRINT	03/25/92	04/07/92	/	03/26/92		AA	2398
5100	BERLIN	STEEL	1	1129	1	PRINT	12/26/91	01/09/92	/	12/31/91		AC	1509
5100	BERLIN	STEEL	2	1129	1	PRINT	03/25/92	04/07/92	/	03/26/92		AA	2399
5100	BERLIN	STEEL	1	113	1	CATALOGE	10/17/91	10/30/91	/	10/23/91		AB	165
5100	BERLIN	STEEL	2	1130	1	PRINT	12/26/91	01/09/92	/	12/31/91		AC	1510
5100	BERLIN	STEEL	1	1130	1	PRINT	03/25/92	04/07/92	/	03/26/92		AA	2400
5100	BERLIN	STEEL	1	1131	1	PRINT	12/26/91	01/09/92	/	12/31/91		AB	1511
5100	BERLIN	STEEL	1	1132	1	PRINT	12/26/91	01/09/92	/	12/31/91		AA	1512
5100	BERLIN	STEEL	1	1133	1	PRINT	12/26/91	01/09/92	/	12/31/91		AA	1513
5100	BERLIN	STEEL	1	1134	1	PRINT	12/26/91	01/09/92	/	12/31/91		AB	1514
5100	BERLIN	STEEL	1	1135	1	PRINT	12/26/91	01/09/92	/	12/31/91		AA	1515
5100	BERLIN	STEEL	1	1136	1	PRINT	12/26/91	01/09/92	/	12/31/91		AA	1516
5100	BERLIN	STEEL	1	1137	1	PRINT	12/26/91	01/09/92	/	12/31/91		AB	1517
5100	BERLIN	STEEL	1	1138	1	PRINT	12/26/91	01/09/92	/	12/31/91		AA	1518
5100	BERLIN	STEEL	1	1139	1	PRINT	12/26/91	01/09/92	/	12/31/91		AB	1519
5100	BERLIN	STEEL	1	114	1	CATALOGE	10/17/91	10/30/91	/	10/23/91		AB	166
5100	BERLIN	STEEL	1	1140	1	PRINT	12/26/91	01/09/92	/	12/31/91		AA	1520
5100	BERLIN	STEEL	1	1141	1	PRINT	12/26/91	01/09/92	/	12/31/91		AA	1521
5100	BERLIN	STEEL	1	1142	1	PRINT	12/26/91	01/09/92	/	12/31/91		AA	1522
5100	BERLIN	STEEL	1	1143	1	PRINT	12/26/91	01/09/92	/	12/31/91		AA	1523
5100	BERLIN	STEEL	1	1144	1	CATALOGE	11/25/91	12/09/91	/	11/27/91		AA	1027
5100	BERLIN	STEEL	1	1145	1	PRINT	12/26/91	01/09/92	/	12/31/91		AA	1524
5100	BERLIN	STEEL	1	1146	1	PRINT	12/26/91	01/09/92	/	12/31/91		AA	1525
5100	BERLIN	STEEL	1	1147	1	PRINT	12/26/91	01/09/92	/	12/31/91		AA	1526
5100	BERLIN	STEEL	1	1148	1	PRINT	12/26/91	01/09/92	/	12/31/91		AA	1527
5100	BERLIN	STEEL	1	1149	1	PRINT	12/26/91	01/09/92	/	12/31/91		AB	1528
5100	BERLIN	STEEL	1	115	1	CATALOGE	10/17/91	10/30/91	/	10/23/91		AA	167
5100	BERLIN	STEEL	1	1150	1	PRINT	12/26/91	01/09/92	/	12/31/91		AA	1529
5100	BERLIN	STEEL	1	1151	1	PRINT	12/26/91	01/09/92	/	12/31/91		AA	1530
5100	BERLIN	STEEL	1	1152	1	PRINT	12/26/91	01/09/92	/	12/31/91		AA	1531
5100	BERLIN	STEEL	1	1153	1	PRINT	12/26/91	01/09/92	/	12/31/91		AA	1532
5100	BERLIN	STEEL	1	1154	1	PRINT	12/26/91	01/09/92	/	12/31/91		AA	1533
5100	BERLIN	STEEL	1	1155	1	PRINT	12/26/91	01/09/92	/	12/31/91		AA	1534
5100	BERLIN	STEEL	1	1156	1	PRINT	12/26/91	01/09/92	/	12/31/91		AA	1535
5100	BERLIN	STEEL	1	1157	1	PRINT	12/26/91	01/09/92	/	12/31/91		AA	1536
5100	BERLIN	STEEL	1	1158	1	PRINT	12/26/91	01/09/92	/	12/31/91		AA	1537
5100	BERLIN	STEEL	1	1159	1	PRINT	12/26/91	01/09/92	/	12/31/91		AB	1538
5100	BERLIN	STEEL	1	116	1	CATALOGE	10/17/91	10/30/91	/	10/23/91		AA	168
5100	BERLIN	STEEL	1	1160	1	PRINT	12/26/91	01/09/92	/	12/31/91		AA	1539
5100	BERLIN	STEEL	1	1161	1	PRINT	12/26/91	01/09/92	/	12/31/91		AA	1540
5100	BERLIN	STEEL	1	1162	1	PRINT	12/26/91	01/09/92	/	12/31/91		AA	1541
5100	BERLIN	STEEL	1	1163	1	PRINT	12/26/91	01/09/92	/	12/31/91		AA	1542
5100	BERLIN	STEEL	1	1164	1	PRINT	12/26/91	01/09/92	/	12/31/91		AA	1543
5100	BERLIN	STEEL	1	1165	1	CATALOGE	12/12/91	12/26/91	/	12/23/91		AA	1318

Figure 9.2 Computer-generated shop drawing log (for structural steel).

one another. In such a case, an RFC or RFI should be directed to the architect who, contractually, is the interpreter of the contract documents. A log of all outgoing RFCs and RFIs should be maintained so that they can be tracked to determine whether they are being promptly responded to by the architect. Project managers can expect RFCs and RFIs to be generated by various subcontractors on the job, and these should be passed on to the architect and logged in as well. A periodic review of all outstanding RFCs and RFIs is essential, and the weekly job meeting is the proper forum to review request for information or clarification status. Figures 9.3 and 9.4 are representative samples of RFIs and RFCs.

3. *Requests for decision involving field conditions.* When a field condition that may require a change in a construction detail or procedure or a dimensional change arises, a request for clarification often takes the form of a field information memo (FIM). FIMs are often used when a contractor wishes to change a construction detail and must create a sketch in order to convey this information to the architect and, conversely, when an architect considers making a minor change, or addition to the plans, this data can be transmitted to the contractor's field office via a FIM. When dimensional changes are involved or construction details are to be changed, all such requests to the architect, and a copy of the response to the request, should be filed in an "as-built data" file so that this information can be retrieved and used in the preparation of the as built drawings required at the end of a project. When a FIM file is first started, all FIMs should be numbered and filed sequentially.

4. *Field inspections requested by contractor or architect.* There will be a time when one or the other party will want to have an item of work inspected before being covered or enclosed. This is in addition to the inspections required by local building officials during the course of construction. There may be a specific structural detail or mechanical piping installation that the project manager would like to have inspected before it is enclosed so that the architect or engineer can approve the installation. If that is the case, put the request in writing and ask for written approval. The general conditions of a contract generally state that if a portion of the work has been covered without being inspected as the architect had requested, the contractor might have to uncover the area in question so that it can be inspected. The cost to uncover and recover may have to be borne by the general contractor.

5. *Distribution of instructions issued by the architect.* During the job visits, the architect may issue verbal or written instructions or may prepare freehand sketches to clarify or change certain details. If those instructions, sketches, and the like are not confirmed in writing by the architect, they should be confirmed by the project manager. Other parties might need to know about them, and they should be sent copies of any

REQUEST FOR INFORMATION

RFI No._____

DATE:_____

PROJECT NAME: _____

LOCATION: _____

TO:

****

TRANSMITTED BY:

RESPONSE REQUIRED BY:

****

REQUEST FOR INFORMATION AS FOLLOWS:

****

_____
SENDERS SIGNATURE

Figure 9.3 A request for information (RFI) form.

REQUEST FOR CLARIFICATION

FRANK MERCEDE & SONS, INC.   RCI NO._____
860 CANAL STREET
STAMFORD, CT 06902
TELEPHONE: 203/967-2000   DATE:_____
FAX: 203/353-8737

Project name: _____

Location: _____

_____

RFC Directed To:_____

_____

Respond To:_____

REQUEST FOR CLARIFICATION AS FOLLOWS:
****

                                              _____
                                              Senders Signature

Figure 9.4 A request for clarification (RFC) form.

pertinent information. When it appears that any of these field-originated changes may have a cost or schedule impact, the need for documentation becomes more evident.

6. *Resolution of problems created by insufficient drawing coordination.*   Coordination problems happen frequently, and they reflect the complexity of today's construction. Making things fit in confined areas requires a great deal of time and effort. When it is apparent that not all the mechanical and electrical components will fit above a suspended ceiling, for example, the project manager should present the facts, as they are known, to the architect so that a resolution can be obtained. If the project manager can suggest a solution, and additional costs are involved, those recommendations and related costs should be included in the letter. When an immediate response is required, a telephone call is warranted, but the discussion should always be backed up by fax or mailed letter. Some contracts require the general contractor to coordinate all shop drawings, which may include structural steel, ductwork, piping, electrical conduits, lighting, and fire protection systems. If that is the case, each trade could be assigned a certain space or elevation under the steel beams so that they can commence shop drawing preparation. Periodic coordination meetings should be held with all subcontractors involved and progress shop drawing prints circulated for everyone's review and comment. Once a coordinated set is prepared, each subcontractor should sign the drawings indicating acceptance of each other's space requirements. But even then conflicts may occur and must be resolved quickly.

7. *Cost proposal or cost estimate requests.*   All cost proposals or estimates, if presented verbally, should be confirmed in writing so that there is no misunderstanding of the amount of the quote or the scope of the work contained in the quote. All such cost proposals should be numbered sequentially for ease of identification, review, and future reference. Once a formal quotation is submitted, the project manager must monitor the response time to ensure that the proposal is either accepted or rejected promptly. There may be a time when either an architect or the owner will take an exceptionally long time to review cost proposals, and job progress may be affected if work is being delayed in the area where change is being considered. Or if work in the area continues to progress, and a late acceptance for change-order work is received, retrofitting may be required at an additional expense to the general contractor, who probably will not be able to collect these added costs from the owner. "Why didn't you tell me you needed approval in a hurry; if you had told me, I would have responded promptly." That will be the answer from the owner to the request for additional costs. When cost proposal reviews are frequently delayed, the project manager should put some kind of time restraint on acceptance by the owner, possibly adding a statement such as "If this proposal is not acted on within 10

days after receipt, at the option of the general contractor, it may be modified or withdrawn."

8. *Conditions which occur and impact on completion time.* When a contract contains liquidated-damages clauses, all justifiable delays must be documented as they occur. Even when the contracts do not contain the clause, delays due to conditions beyond the contractor's control should be documented in some fashion, possibly in the superintendent's log book. When there are work stoppages due to strikes or other types of labor disputes, the architect should be notified in writing on the day the strike or dispute occurs. This notification can state that when the length and effect of the strike or dispute is established, another notification will be sent reflecting the effect, if any, on the construction schedule. Prolonged labor disputes can have serious financial consequences; and since the length of these disputes cannot be known in advance, any such job action must be documented when it occurs with updates as it progresses.

9. *Contracts containing allowance items and "alternates."* Many contracts will contain "alternates" that the owner can elect to accept or reject. When it appears that a decision is required, the project manager should notify the architect, in writing, that a decision regarding the acceptance of a specific alternate is required and must be made within a certain period of time or else job progress may be impeded and extra costs may be incurred by the general contractor, who may require reimbursement for these extra costs. With regard to allowance items, the project manager has to review the contract to determine how they are to be handled. Will the architect be soliciting bids and selecting a supplier so that the general contractor can issue a contract or purchase order, or is the project manager supposed to obtain bids and present them to the architect for review and approval? Depending on their nature, some of the allowance items might be more critical than others. Finish hardware is a common allowance item; and since an approved hardware schedule is required before hollow metal doors and frames are fabricated, it becomes a critical allowance item. Often, an architect, rather than hire a hardware consultant, will prefer to work with a hardware supplier suggested by the general contractor and develop a schedule that fits within the hardware allowance. Carpet selections might be another important item. Since architects like to select colors by coordinating all interior schemes, delivery times required for certain types of carpeting must be taken into consideration. Again, if a contract contains liquidated-damages clauses, delays in job progress may occur when allowance items are not handled properly. It is, therefore, important that attention be given to allowances and alternates and any delays be documented.

10. *Unforeseen subsurface or unusual conditions.* Whenever conditions encountered below the surface or above ground are, in the opinion of the project manager, unusual, or at variance with the norm, or of a

peculiar nature that may have a cost impact on the work to be performed, a letter should be sent to the architect. If groundwater is observed during excavation and it does not appear to be significant at the time, it is best to document its existence. During a dry spell there may be only a trickle, but after a significant rainfall there could be a river. Document!

11. *Disputes, claims, or requests for arbitration.* Although covered more fully in Chap. 10, suffice it to say that today's congenial relationship with an architect, owner, or subcontractor can deteriorate rapidly for any number of reasons—usually triggered by money problems. If conditions that have a potential for dispute in the future arise, document them even though the relationships among all parties to the contract are perfect. Conditions which may be disputable should not have any effect on the good relationship that currently exists, but documentation may be extremely important in the future if that congenial atmosphere disappears. And when that happens, everyone's memory seems to be selective, recalling only those facts that support their position, but forgetting other factors that were not in their favor.

12. *Monthly requisitions.* The project manager must obtain agreement on the requisition format at the inception of the project and then assemble and submit requisitions promptly. Some architects prefer to review a preliminary "pencil" copy of a requisition with the project manager a few days in advance of the formal submission. Either through prior discussions or pencil copies, the project manager should promptly submit the monthly requisition with a letter or transmittal so that there is a record of the date when the requestion was sent. Then late payments cannot be attributable to the "late" submission of the requisition by the general contractor.

13. *Documentation of job closeout requirements.* Proper compliance with the contract closeout procedures and proper documentation of those procedures are necessary to trigger the contractor's final payment and start the clock ticking on any retainage requirements. There will be requirements for as-built drawings, owner's operating manuals for equipment, equipment maintenance manuals, and warranties and guarantees, most of which must be supplied by subcontractors. Requests for these materials should be made by letter or transmittal well in advance of the completion of the project. When subcontractors don't respond to repeated requests for this information, remind them that final payment from the owner will not be forthcoming until all this documentation is forwarded to the architect, and when the general contractor's final payment is delayed, so will the subcontractor's be delayed. When submitting all the lien waivers and other certificates to the architect as part of the closing document package, always retain a copy and transmit the documents via letter or transmittal. If the contract stipulates that extra materials for maintenance or replacement purposes are required, such as floor tile,

carpet scraps over a certain size, ceiling tiles, and paint stock, whenever possible, obtain a signed receipt from the owner's representative that the "attic stock" has been delivered.

Documentation to Subcontractors

Most general contractors will subcontract the greater portion of work to qualified subcontractors, and therefore the project manager will assume the responsibility for the administration of all these contracts. Indeed, monitoring subcontractor performance will occupy the major portion of the project manager's time as construction demands and schedules accelerate. Since all subcontractors are independent businesspeople, they have their own problems and concerns related not only to one job but also to the ones they are working on with other general contractors.

A binding relationship with a subcontractor begins when contract negotiations lead to an award of a subcontract agreement. The formal, written contract will contain the terms and conditions expected from both parties to the contract. It is important that the general contractor, through the project manager, be aware of the provisions contained in the contract that is being prepared for the subcontractor's signature. Conversely, the subcontractor should be aware of the provisions of the contract being presented for acceptance. Most subcontract agreements in use by general contractors today are either prepared by or reviewed by legal consultants. Although these lengthy legal forms can vary from contractor to contractor, they all seem to contain more or less the same type of language to protect the contractor from poor subcontractor performance. Of course, when a subcontract agreement is being entered into, it is not with the thought that serious problems will occur. There will always be a few minor problems or possibly a major problem during the administration of a subcontract agreement, but during the normal give-and-take during construction, the contract and the work contained therein is usually completed satisfactorily.

Someone once said that contracts with restrictive and protective clauses are not needed for the "good guys" but only for the "bad guys." The only problem is that sometimes it is very difficult to determine beforehand who will fit into which category. Proper documentation of subcontractor relations and performance, as it relates to contract language, is an important element of the project manager's administrative responsibilities.

The normal subcontractor agreement contains provisions for progress payment schedules, scope of work included and the cost of the work, insurance requirements, and compliance with local and federal laws and labor practices, along with a long list of standard work practices. The standard boilerplate language will be supplemented by specific job requirements such as

1. The precise scope of work to be included in the contract

2. The time frame in which the work is to take place

3. The name of the owner of the project, the date of the contract between the owner and general contractor, the name of the architect, and the name and address of the project

4. The contract sum, requisition period, and possibly percent retainage to be applied to the monthly payment requests

5. Any addenda that might apply

6. A tax-exempt status, if applicable

The first significant conflict can occur over the contract documents referred to in the subcontract agreement. Has the subcontractor acknowledged that his price does reflect the scope of work in the latest drawings which have been referred to in the subcontract agreement? Frequently a subcontractor will sign a subcontract agreement, start to perform work, and somewhere in the early stages of construction indicate that he had not really reviewed and accepted the contract set of drawings, but had in fact been working from earlier drawings. Now that he has seen the latest drawings, specifications, or addenda, there will have to be an increase in the price. Situations like this, which arise all too often, can be eliminated if the subcontractor interview form described in Chap. 6 is put into use.

The first question always asked by the project manager in such an instance when a subcontractor takes issue to the scope of the work is, "But why did you sign our subcontract agreement containing the proper contract drawings for the sum of money mutually agreed on?" The answers will range from, "I guess I didn't notice the difference in drawing dates" to "I never received a set of the latest drawings; I based my price on the set given to me at bid time" or to "I just don't know." No matter what the answer is, the project manager will usually try to resolve the problem amicably and possibly allow an adjustment to be made in the contract sum, if the second bidder would have still been too high, taking into account this price adjustment. The situation should also alert the project manager to the fact that the subcontractor should be monitored very closely and all future relations with him should be carefully documented.

Avoiding problems related to subcontractor misunderstandings

One way to avoid misunderstandings is to make certain that whenever plans and specifications are sent to a subcontractor for review or pricing, the transmittal includes not only the specific documents being sent but also the date of each document. If and when it comes to contract signing, there will be a record to confirm or deny the allegation that the most recent drawings were never received and therefore the quoted price did not include the work on these drawings. The use of transmittals during the bidding process will also allow the project manager to keep track of where all the drawings are so that they can be collected after the bidding process is over.

If there could be any misinterpretation of what is expected of the subcontractor, write it out plainly in the subcontract agreement. For instance, if the specifications require an electrician to be available during working hours to turn the temporary electric power on or off, this might require more specific information in the contract. What is the normal workday? If the electrician's workday ends at 3:30 P.M. but other trades normally work until 4:00 P.M., agree on whose "normal workday" will be used. If it is the intention to have the electrician stand by until 4:00 P.M. every day to turn off the temporary power supply, state this clearly in the contract so that all parties completely understand their obligations.

The time frame for subcontractor work—anticipated start and completion—is an important part of the contract. Inserting the dates avoids any misunderstanding that the price quoted anticipates a specific starting date and that any increased labor rates for work performed during the period have been taken into account. The cost of materials required for the work also will take into account the time frame required for the construction period.

Linking the subcontractor agreement with the owner's contract

Most subcontract agreements include a provision that links the agreement with the terms and conditions of the general contractor's contractual agreement with the owner. In fact, Article 5 of the 1987 edition of AIA Document A201, the General Conditions, goes a step further and directs the general contractor to "make available to each proposed Subcontractor, prior to the execution of the subcontract agreement, copies of the Contract Documents to which the Subcontractor will be bound and, upon written request of the Subcontractor, identify to the Subcontractor terms and conditions of the proposed subcontract agreement which may be at variance with the Contract Documents."

The subcontractor's payment schedule should be tied to the payment schedule from the owner to the general contractor. The general contractor's philosophy is "We can't pay you on the date agreed on in the contract if we have not yet received payment from the owner." The subcontractor's answer may well be that they have a contract with the general contractor and not the owner, and unless they are made aware of the fact that their payment schedule is tied directly to the owner's, future disagreements will certainly occur.

There are movements in several state legislatures to enact laws that do away with the "pay when paid" custom, and it would be wise to check with the company attorney to determine whether such a law has been enacted in the state in which your company resides.

Subcontractor performance—the major concern

One of the more restrictive clauses inserted into most subcontract agreements has to do with the remedies to correct a subcontractor's poor or otherwise unacceptable performance. The general contractor must be able to control the performance of a lagging subcontractor so that the entire project's progress is not severely affected. The following three common clauses concern nonperformance, and the context of one of them, more or less, should be in every subcontractor agreement:

Contract 1.   Should the subcontractor be adjudged bankrupt or insolvent or repeatedly fail to prosecute the work hereunder with promptness and diligence in keeping with the then-existing work schedule, contractor may take possession of all materials, equipment, tools, construction equipment, and machinery of the subcontractor after serving three (3) days written notice to that effect and may through itself or others provide labor, equipment, and materials to prosecute and finish the work hereunder.

Contract 2.   Should the subcontractor fail to prosecute the work or any part thereof with promptness and diligence, or fail to supply a sufficiency of properly skilled workers or materials of proper quality or fail in any other respect to comply with the contract documents, the contractor shall be at liberty, after seventy-two (72) hours written notice to the subcontractor to provide such labor and materials as may be necessary to complete the work and to deduct the cost and expense thereof from any money then due or thereafter to become due to the subcontractor.

Contract 3.   Should the subcontractor be adjudged bankrupt or should the subcontractor at any time refuse or neglect to supply a sufficient number of properly skilled workmen or sufficient materials of the proper quality, or fail in any respect to prosecute the work with promptness and diligence in keeping with the job progress schedule, or allow a lien to be filed against the building or cause by any action the stoppage of or interference with the work of other trades, or fail in the opinion of the contractor in the performance of any of the agreements contained herein, or fail to comply with any order given to him by the contractor or architect in accordance with the provisions of this subcontract, the contractor shall be entitled to provide for the account of the subcontractor and without terminating this subcontract, any such labor and materials, after 24 hours notice to that effect, and to deduct the cost thereof from any money then due or thereafter to become due, or the contractor at his option at any time may terminate this subcontract after 24 hours notice to that effect.

The Associated General Contractors of America (AGC) publishes several subcontractor contract agreement forms which are available from any local AGC chapter at nominal cost:

AGC Document 600	Subcontract for Building Construction
AGC Document 601	Subcontract for Use on Federal Construction
AGC Document 603	Subcontract (Short Form)
AGC Document 606	Subcontract Performance Bond
AGC Document 607	Subcontract Payment B

The three forms of subcontractor performance clauses set forth above contain the same basic conditions needed to trigger the contractor's intervention. One contract states 3 days' notice is needed to do so, another specifies 72 hours, and another specifies 24 hours, and the AGC contracts require 3 days. Any contract containing a period required for written notice should indicate whether calendar days or working days are to be used to determine the waiting period. AGC Document 600 clearly states that three (3) working days' notice is required before the contractor is free to take action. The project manager must clearly understand the nature of any such clauses and be able to ensure that corrective action is not preemptive.

Danger Signs and How to Interpret Them

What are the danger signs that in most cases portend trouble with subcontractor's? In order to prepare for the worst, if need be, watch for the following danger signs and be prepared to document any problems if further action is needed:

1. *Lack of adequate work force.*   There may always be disagreements between the general contractor and the subcontractor about what constitutes adequate work force. We are not talking about having 12 workers on the job instead of 10. We are talking about there being two workers on the job for the last week, when there clearly was a need for five times that number. Because of insufficient manpower in this particular trade, other trades have been affected. If a subcontractor is experiencing financial difficulties, it will be most noticeable in the size of the work crews. Workers have to be paid weekly; no pay, no work. Whereas material or equipment suppliers may be requested to extend their credit terms from 30 days to 45, 60, or even 90 days, this latitude does not apply to weekly payrolls. When the subcontractor work crews are not large enough to maintain job progress, notify the subcontractor in writing; if the situation persists, invoke the provisions of the contract regarding performance. The contractor then starts the clock as far as his ability to take control of the work is concerned. At this point, it is probably wise to have a heart-to-heart talk with the subcontractor. If the problem is a temporary shortage of funds, it may be possible to advance monies for weekly payroll until the problem is resolved. Perhaps some other equitable solution can be worked out.

2. *Delays in submitting shop drawings.*   A subcontractor, after being awarded a contract, will start purchasing of materials and equipment and will try to "package" various materials and equipment with one or two vendors to obtain the best possible price for the larger dollar value of the package. Under normal conditions this could take time for the subcontractor to obtain the most advantageous price, and usually shop drawings for a major piece of equipment are obtained from the vendor once an order has been placed. Prolonged negotiations with a vendor, and therefore prolonged delays in the submission of a shop drawing, could mean that the subcontractor either does not have a very efficient purchasing technique or is desperately trying to get lower price quotations because the added profit is needed to compensate for the low profit margin included in the initial estimate. Or, worse yet, the subcontractor is searching for a supply house or manufacturer's representative to accept his order because of a poor credit rating. If shop drawings are not being submitted in a reasonable, timely manner, a letter should be sent to the subcontractor advising him that any further delays in the submission of a particular shop drawing or group of drawings will seriously affect the progress of the job and that submission is expected on or about a certain date. If the drawings are not received within that time period, write another letter

invoking the proper paragraph of the contract pertaining to nonperformance and delay of the job.

3. *Inability to provide day-to-day working materials.* If, along with reduced manpower, adequate working materials are not provided from day to day, or if this happens consistently with adequate work force, there could be big problems. We are talking, for example, about a plumbing contractor having trouble keeping the job supplied with small quantities of small-diameter pipe and fittings, even though the foreman calls the office daily requesting these supplies. After sending the subcontractor written notice of this poor performance, a telephone call to the subcontractor's supplier might be helpful in determining or confirming the problem connected with the shortage of supplies.

4. *Requests for joint checks.* Requests from subcontractors to have joint checks issued are not necessarily danger signs. A valued subcontractor might be dealing with a new supplier who would feel more comfortable with joint checks in payment for supplies in his first transactions with the subcontractor. A subcontractor might be involved in that first big job and may need the added assurance of a joint check to obtain materials which normally would be beyond the company's present credit limit. Joint checks are not objectionable from the general contractor's viewpoint, in that there is added assurance that payment issued to pay for specific materials will be used for that purpose. The danger sign will come when a subcontractor with whom you have long been doing business suddenly asks that joint check agreements be signed for most of the materials and equipment on the new job. Another danger sign, with respect to joint checks, is when a subcontractor, halfway through a job, asks to have joint checks made out in favor of a supplier who has been supplying materials to the job without that requirement. But whenever joint checks are to be issued, the subcontractor should be requested to sign a statement agreeing to this procedure and that letter should be kept in their contract file.

5. *Delinquent payroll deduction notices.* If the subcontractor in question is party to a collective bargaining agreement and it is demonstrated that legitimate payroll contributions are not being made in compliance with the agreement, the project manager had better find out why they are not being made. Of course, this would also be true of monies owed to local, state, or federal agencies who have informed the general contractor that the contributions are in arrears. The subcontractor should be asked to explain the circumstances surrounding the allegations and submit plans for making the required contributions. Since the general contractor may be liable for these monies if the subcontractor defaults, a properly written letter outlining the problems should be sent to the subcontractor. The letter should state that the general contractor may withhold funds sufficient to satisfy the payroll contributions should the need arise.

6. *Requests from the subcontractor or supplier for immediate payment.*   If the subcontractor has been routinely submitting monthly requisition requests and receiving payment within the normal pay period time but suddenly asks for accelerated payment schedules, find out why. It could be a temporary problem caused by late payments from other general contractors or the beginning of a larger problem.

With reference to paragraph 6 (above), was the subcontractor's bid substantially less than competitor's bids? Here we are not talking about the subcontractor who submitted a bid for $95,000 when the other four subcontractor quotes ranged from $105,000 to $120,000. Discounting the highest bid of $120,000, there is a variation of close to 14 percent between low and high bidders, not an inordinate amount. What would concerned us would be someone submitting a bid of $75,000 in the same scenario and being 21 percent lower than the second bid and possibly 31 percent lower than the third lowest bidder. If that $75,000 bid were accepted, the project manager's danger antenna should be raised all the way.

Some general contractors, when faced with a decision whether to accept a substantially lower bid or discard it, will look at the situation differently. One general contractor will reason that if this very-low-price subcontractor is selected and the potential savings look tempting, the subcontractor probably omitted some item of work and will not be able to complete the job. Any additional costs to complete the work after the subcontractor defaults will, more than likely, total more than the second bidder's price; therefore this "low" bidder should be disqualified.

Another general contractor will reason that maybe this very-low-priced subcontractor does know what he is doing and could possibly complete the work resulting in a large savings accruing to the general contractor. However, if the subcontractor does not know what he is doing and defaults at or near the end of the contract obligations and another subcontractor can be engaged to complete the work, the total cost might still be less than the second bidder's price. If that is the case, the project manager should thoroughly investigate whether the defaulted subcontractor has actually dispersed all the money received from the general contractor, to date, to any subcontractors he may have hired for the project as well as to materials and equipment vendors up to the point of default. The project manager may find that the perceived costs to complete will be considerably higher than originally anticipated

This is a Las Vegas decision that one makes and then has to live with. The odds can be reduced substantially, if the extremely low bidder is called into the office before an award is actually made so that his bid can be carefully scrutinized to determine why it was significantly lower than that of his competitors. If a major portion of the work had been inadvertently omitted from the subcontractor's estimate, then the general contractor's decision may be somewhat easier to make.

But when things begin to go wrong, document everything, every day, including typewritten memorandums of telephone conversations, because everything will be needed.

Documentation When Major Drawing Revisions Are Made

There may be a time when a series of revisions will be made to a few or all of the architectural, mechanical, and electrical drawings when interior work at the site is progressing rapidly. This can happen if an interior designer is engaged by the owner to provide furniture layouts and additional design assistance primarily in the office environment. The furniture drawings will show desk and workstation locations and possibly task lighting, MIS cabling and terminal locations, and telephone and other business equipment placements. Any demountable partitions, of partial or full height, may require the relocation of HVAC ceiling diffusers, both supply and exhaust, and sprinkler head and recessed lighting relocations. Electrical switch and receptacle locations may need rearranging along with wall-mounted temperature-sensing devices, and that, of course, would have an impact on the installation of drywall and related wall finishes.

When such a situation arises, the project manager is faced with a number of immediate problems. They revolve around keeping the job progress momentum going while pricing out the changes and obtaining approval to proceed with the approved changes. The first priority is to distribute the drawings to the job superintendent and all subcontractors who might be affected by the changes. A note should be entered on the transmittal to each subcontractor that the reviewing and pricing of any changes must be done with a specific time frame and on an expedited basis. Changes that either add or delete scope must be identified clearly, and precise labor and material cost breakdowns will be required. The more explicit and definitive these estimates are, the faster the review process by the architect and owner will be once the cost proposal is submitted by the general contractor. Also, the subcontractors should be requested to refrain from installing any work in the areas under consideration if work crews can be conveniently shifted to other parts of the building. Assuming there is ongoing work in the areas considered for change, the architect and owner should be made aware of the need for a prompt review and response when the cost proposal is issued, and a statement to that effect should be included in the cost proposal. It is best to schedule a meeting with the architect and/or owner when the cost proposal is submitted so that any issues raised can be dealt with rapidly. If prompt decisions are not made, there could be an impact on job progress or additional costs incurred to make the changes and these issues should be addressed at that meeting.

Another general revision often takes place when an open-office-type contract is being administered for a speculative office building and the owner finds a tenant or two who require sophisticated improvements to the open space. Floor plans will have to be submitted by the tenant for owner approval and conformance with existing work letters, and further tenant negotiations with the owner might have to take place.

The project manager may have to advise all subcontractors to refrain from working in the affected areas while these tenant-owner negotiations are in progress. The project manager and the job superintendent must be able to plan the work schedule in such a way that subcontractor crews will not be reduced in size, while the owner-tenant negotiations are taking place. Any estimates for tenant work must have complete cost breakdowns to make for easier scrutiny and evaluation by the owner. The project manager, when submitting cost proposals, should include a response time to ensure compliance with the contract job progress schedule.

Documentation Required By Local, State, or Federal Agencies

Documentation involving local agencies will be concerned primarily with obtaining a building permit at the beginning of a project, recording of the various inspections to be made during construction, and at the completion of the project, when a certificate of occupancy is to be issued.

State and federal agencies will have their own requirements for the submission of forms, schedules, releases, affidavits, ordinances, and equal-opportunity and small-business set-aside compliance records. At the beginning of a project, there may be a long list of documents that must be filed within a certain time frame. If these sometimes tedious and lengthy procedures are not fully complied with, either requisitions for the first requisition for payment will be withheld or seriously delayed. At the completion of these projects numerous forms and certifications are required prior to release of the contractor's final payment. Certified payroll is a requisite to ensure that the various government-required pay scales are being enforced.

The project manager should carefully read the general and supplementary conditions contained in the specification books for these kinds of projects. Highlighting the forms' submissions requirements and other documents required before, during, and after completion of the project should be noted at that time.

Davis-Bacon Act

The certified payroll requirement contained in government projects stems from the existence of the Davis-Bacon Act, which applies to construction contracts being financed with federal funds in whole or in part. The Davis-Bacon Act became law during President Herbert Hoover's administration in 1931, when economic conditions were not very good. The Act required that all laborers and mechanics employed on the site of federally funded construction projects in excess of $5000, later amended to $2000, must be paid rates determined to be prevailing in that area. The U.S. Department of Labor determined what the prevailing rates were, and those wage scales were inserted into the bidding documents so that contractors bidding on the project were aware of them. The Act stipulated that the secretary of labor should determine the rates prevailing in the immediate neighborhood of the construction site. Today, the prevailing wage scale is not only regional but also contains differing wage scales for similar tradesmen working in various parts of a state, a confirmation of the original intent of the law to correlate wages to neighborhoods. The prevailing wage scales have more or less paralleled union wage scales, so that contractors who plan to use union labor on federally funded projects have little concern with compliance with the Davis-Bacon Act. Nonunion or open-shop contractors must not only be concerned with meeting the wage provisions of the Act but must also consider the fringe benefits that are to be either provided or paid for in kind. There have been repeated cries for repeal of the Davis-Bacon Act. Critics cite the fact that by its insistence on mandating prevailing wages on all federally funded projects, the Act inflates the total cost of government funded projects by billions of dollars each year.

Complying with Government Requirements

In order to ensure compliance with all the documents required when a government project is started and when it is closing, it is wise to review the job specifications thoroughly before construction commences. Close attention should be paid to all provisions in the general conditions, supplementary conditions, special conditions, and general standards. Make a typewritten checklist of all the required documents and when they will be needed. It could follow this format:

1. Contract signing
   a. Within 10 days submit schedule of values for requisition approval.
   b. Project sign must be installed before first requisition is submitted.

 c. Field office must contain separated space for office, and telephone for inspectors, or inspectors may require their own trailers.

 d. Prevailing wages scales are to be posted prominently, with Executive Orders 3,17 (and others), Public Act 79-606—Notice of Nonsegregated Facilities placed outside the office trailer.

 e. To be submitted before construction starts:

  (1) Estimated progress schedule (sometimes "S" curve is required, or statement of proposed monthly draws)

  (2) List of subcontractors to date (update as required)

  (3) Surety bonds

  (4) Schedule of values

  (5) Insurance certificates

  (6) Site logistics plan

2. During construction

 a. Weekly certified payroll

 b. Monthly manpower utilization reports

 c. Requisitions to be submitted by 20th of month projecting costs for work in place to the end of the month; seven copies (or more) to be submitted.

 d. List of any other forms that are to be maintained during construction

3. Due before substantial completion

 a. Certificate of compliance

 b. Architect certificate of substantial completion along with list of escrow items and punch list

 c. Product warranties and guarantees

 d. Any other closing document requirements that must be met

This list should be posted prominently in the project managers work area so that it is a constant reminder of the data required at certain landmarks.

Field Documentation

As far as the office and field operations are concerned, the job superintendent must be kept apprised of what the project manager is doing as it relates to his areas of responsibility. A good rule of thumb is for the project manager to ask himself, "If I were the job super on the site, is this something I would need to know in order to run the job effectively?" If the answer is "yes," send the information to the field. Any sketches or revised drawings issued by the architect and engineer should be sent to the job site promptly, and the transmittal should indicate what action is required. All approved shop drawings and equipment catalog specification sheets will be sent to the job with accompanying transmittals. If any verbal commitment is made between the project manager and a consultant or subcontractor, the job superintendent must know about it in order to manage the work effectively.

The Superintendent's Daily Record

Every superintendent must keep a daily record of job activity if for no other reason than to keep track of workers on the job and the hours they have worked so that weekly payrolls can be prepared. Most job superintendents keep more elaborate records in the form of either a daily diary or a daily report. The diary or report, if maintained consistently every day, will fulfill the definition of a business record and may be introduced into a legal proceeding as evidence if necessary. Some contractors prefer to use a bound daily diary to keep a narrative record of the day's job activities. A page is allotted for every day and the volume covers a calendar year. If a project starts in November of one year and is completed 6 months later, two bound volumes will constitute a complete diary.

The company's time sheet can be so arranged that payroll information can be printed on one side and the other side can be devoted to the daily report. One copy is sent to the office for payroll preparation and a duplicate filed in the job file. A third copy is retained in the field. No matter what form the daily log or diary takes, the following information must be reported on it:

1. Weather conditions

2. Any visitors to the job, identified by name, affiliation, and purpose of the visit (even company personnel)

3. Subcontractors on the job that day, number of workers in their crews, activities performed, and areas in which they are working

4. Deliveries received at the site, materials, equipment, and supplies

5. Any unusual or noteworthy event which took place

6. Any accidents incurred, even though separate accident reports will have been filed

7. Inspections, by whom, for what reasons, and results, if known

Bound daily diary books made specifically for use on construction projects can be purchased and used by the job superintendent in the field. The project manager can also use this diary book in the office to record telephone conversations with the superintendent and for discussions with the various project consultants and subcontractors.

Photographs: Important Documentary Components

Photographs of job progress or construction details can be a valuable adjunct to the documentation of a project. Some specifications require a general contractor to take progress photographs on a regular basis, and generally these pictures are black-and-white and sized 8 × 11 in. Even if it is not a project requirement, many contractors regularly take job photographs for a variety of reasons:

1. To further document job progress or lack of it

2. To record the uncovering of unusual conditions

3. To act as further substantiation of a change-order request

4. To record a complex construction process to show compliance with the contract documents and "best practices of the trade"

Many general contractors will use various photographs for in-house training sessions or in future sales and marketing brochures as well as lobby wall decorations. Although by no means the primary job document, progress photographs can be an invaluable addition to the overall project documentation file.

Documenting lack of progress

In the administration of contracts with liquidated-damages clauses, it may very well be important to document lack of progress for reasons that are beyond the contractor's control, such as weather or labor disputes. If a job is in the excavation, sitework, or foundation stage, a torrential rainfall can cause more damage than the loss of one workday.

Photographs will vividly depict the aftermath. During work stoppages due to labor disputes or strikes, photographs can serve several purposes:

1. Document the effect of the strike, not only on the disputed trade but on trades that may have joined the dispute in sympathy, which may

constitute an illegal secondary boycott. The photographs can show how progress of seemingly unrelated work is affected.

2. Sometimes during labor disputes, tempers flare, fights break out, or equipment and supplies are vandalized. Photographs of such occurrences may be helpful in respect to insurance claims.

Photographs during rehabilitation work

Photographs can be especially helpful in documenting conditions uncovered during the demolition stage of a rehabilitation project. When contract drawings show a nonbearing wall and the wall is discovered to be bearing, a photograph will display the problems that may exist. Photographs are also useful to document structural cracks which exist prior to the start of demolition and to show cracks uncovered by removal of wall finishes. The cost of 2, 12, or 20 photographs can be a relatively low-cost insurance policy. When taking closeup detailed photographs it is sometimes difficult to establish scale of the detail being photographed and its relation to the surrounding area. It will help to insert a carpenter's scale or engineer's rule or metal tape into the photographed area so that scale is established. For example, if a description of the crack is "about 14 in long and varies from $1/8$ to $1/2$ in along its length," a closeup photograph of the crack with a scale alongside will be more illustrative.

A log of the exact location of the detailed photographs should be kept. When the project manager receives the prints, he should diagrammatically indicate on the reverse side of the print, exactly where the detail is located in relation to column lines, room location, and other details. If that is not done as soon as possible, it will be surprising to find how difficult it is to reconstruct the location of a detail a month or two later.

Unsuitable subsurface conditions are other areas that can be effectively portrayed with photographs. Photographic documentation of underground water conditions and buried debris or other underground obstructions can be a strong backup for change-order requests.

All photographs taken as job progress documents or to show details or defects should follow these guidelines:

1. Size to be 8 × 11 in

2. Unless there is a specific need or reason for color, black-and-white photography should be used, as it is higher-resolution and results in more clarity.

3. Each photograph should have a title block containing the date it was taken, project name and location, general contractor's name, and an orientation of the photograph.

When overall or exterior views are being taken, a photographer can superimpose a scaled-down outline of the building or footprint in the corner of the negative and place an arrow in this outline indicating the location and orientation of the view.

Videotape photography

The rapid advances made in the development of videocameras, camcorders, and the rather inexpensive cost of these cameras has made them a popular item for general contractors. Videotaping can also create, simultaneously, a sound track which can be used to describe in detail what is being filmed. Visual presentation of unusual weather conditions as they are occurring can be dramatic, indeed.

Unusual conditions being encountered during the sitework or excavation phase of a project can also be graphically presented by videotape photography. Visual presentation of actual work in progress, dwelling on a particular area or operation and supplemented by a descriptive narrative, is probably the best form of on-site progress documentation.

10

Claims, Disputes, Arbitration, and Mediation

At some time or another, every project manager will be exposed to a legal problem. The problem might arise at any point during the construction process: before the process starts, while it is in progress, or after it has been completed. Although it might be the general contractors' intent to avoid it at all costs, litigation may be forced on them. A project manager who has been doing a proper job of documentation and is somewhat familiar with legal terminology, court rulings, and past practices will be better prepared to deal with the inevitable dispute.

The purpose of this chapter is not to create lawyers out of project managers; the practice of law is best left to the legal profession. The project manager, in the day-to-day administration of construction activities, matter-of-factly issues and receives a great number of legal documents. This chapter will make the project manager more aware of the responsibility that goes with the administration of contracts, purchase orders, and directives.

What Triggers Claims and Disputes?

The main reasons for the misunderstandings leading to claims and disputes are as follows:

1. Plans and specifications that contain errors, omissions, ambiguities, or requirements that don't or won't fit the actual conditions

2. Incomplete or inaccurate responses or nonresponses to questions or resolutions of problems presented by one party to the contract to another party to the contract

3. Inadequate administration of responsibilities by the owner, architect, engineer, contractor, subcontractors, or vendors

4. Unwillingness or inability to comply with the intent of the contract or to adhere to industry standards in performance of the work

5. Site conditions which differ materially from those described in the contract documents

6. Existing building conditions which differ materially from those shown in the contract documents

7. Extra work or change-order work

8. Breaches of contract by any party to the contract

9. Disruptions, delays, or acceleration to the work which causes the work to deviate from the normal prescheduled sequence

10. Inadequate financial strength of any of the parties to the contract

If and when any of these misunderstandings occur, every reasonable effort should be made to resolve them with the normal give and take that ought be expected from all parties to the contract. Only when all efforts at resolution have failed is there a need to consult the company attorney. Consultation at this early stage could save a great deal of time and money. If there will be a need for legal consultation or legal action, the project manager should make certain that the following documents have been either prepared and are assembled or can be speedily brought up to date:

1. Any and all requests for payments, from all parties

2. Daily reports, daily logs, daily diaries

3. Inspections and test reports

4. Time sheets for labor and equipment expended on the job site

5. Job progress schedules—preliminary, updated, and current

6. Transmittals and correspondence to owner, architect, engineer, and subcontractors

7. Shop drawings and shop drawing logs with transmittals pertaining to the drawings

8. Job meeting minutes

9. Interoffice memos, field memos, and telephone conversation memos

10. Estimates, bids, quotations, and either written or telephoned bids

11. Change-order requests, change-order proposals, change-order estimates, and all backup data for the estimates

12. Job progress photographs

13. Copies of all contracts issued or in progress, and all purchase orders issued or in progress

14. Any as-built drawings, either complete or with the as-built conditions recorded to date

These are the documents that will be needed if legal action is to be taken. If they have been prepared properly as the job progressed, the lawyer's job will be much easier and he or she will be able to render a decision with regard to the validity of the claim or counterclaim more rapidly.

Oral Contracts

Although we have been talking primarily about contracts and the misunderstandings caused by misinterpretations, there does not have to be a written contract to create a problem. Oral contracts also are recognized as creating obligations between two parties. A case tried in North Carolina was based on an architect performing work for an owner without benefit of a written contract. The owner, a developer, had requested that the architect do some preliminary work on a condominium project. The architect, according to the owner, had prepared such an involved contract for the design work that it was rejected by the owner as being too complex, but the owner did agree to sign a more simple contract if presented to him. The architect's fees, at this time, were not a subject of disagreement, and the owner directed the architect to proceed with the design work. Months later the owner advised the architect that another architect had been engaged to work on the project. By that time, the initial architect had completed a major portion of the design work and had submitted an invoice for the work to date to the owner. When the owner refused to pay the amount of the invoice, the architect filed suit, claiming breach of contract.

The North Carolina trial court dismissed the case for reason of the absence of a contract between owner and architect, but the North Carolina Court of Appeals did not agree. The appeals court said that even though a written contract does not exist, the architect can have an enforceable oral agreement. Therefore, the court ruled that a jury trial was in order. The appeals court went even further in stating that if the jury were to agree that an oral contract did not exist, the architect could still pursue the recovery of the actual value of the services which were performed in connection with the project design [*Willis v. Russell,* 315 S.S. 2nd 91 (North Carolina Appellate Court, 1984)].

The Bid Proposal Process

Disputes can and will arise even before a contract is awarded. In fact, a dispute can occur at the time a bid proposal is submitted prior to or at the time of formal bid openings. In private and public construction work, a formal bid procedure is often established: bids are to be submitted on a preissued bid proposal form; the form is to be completed and signed by an officer of the company, sealed in an envelope, and presented to the official to receive the bid by a designated time on a designated day. Sometimes a bid bond is required, or in the absence thereof, a certified check. The purpose of the bid bond is to ensure the owner that, if the contractor's bid is accepted, the owner will be protected against damages due to the inability of the apparent low bidder to go forward with construction after a contract is awarded. Other documents may also be required, and if they have not been submitted on the proper form, completed in accordance with the bidding instructions, any deviations from the designated format may be a cause for bid disqualification.

Do late bids count?

How many times has the project manager dashed from the office to the place where the bids are to be submitted. Instructions from the office are to get to a phone near the office where the bids will be opened and call the home office for final instructions and late-breaking price adjustments to the bid. Sometimes the project manager will leave the office with nothing but a blank bid form and will have to fill in not only the total project price but 10 or 15 alternates, two pages of units prices, and a page or two of allowances and acknowledgment of receipt of various addenda. When the project manager arrives at the bid-opening office and finds that all available phones are occupied, a cold sweat begins to form. "What will happen if I can't get to a phone in time and I can't get the prices tabulated on the form and into the clerk within the 5 minutes I have remaining?" The availability of a cellular phone or mobile telephone has not made the task any easier in all cases. How many times has a project manager relied on these kinds of phones only to have their transmission or reception go haywire at the most crucial time, and when reception does improve, the bid submission time has passed. Don't despair! Complete the form as quickly as possible, and run, don't walk, to the clerk receiving the bids, turn it in, and have the bid time-stamped. Just because a bid is received after the exact specified times does not mean that it will be disqualified.

In private bid situations, the owner is free to waive many prebid qualifications. In public bid situations, the courts have ruled that the public bidding regulations are there for the public's benefit. If a bid is received a few minutes late and there is no evidence of fraud, collusion, or intent to deceive, all is not lost. If the local authority refuses to accept the late bid, an immediate protest must be filed. It can be voiced in the presence of the official refusing to accept the bid, and as quickly as possible followed up with a written protest setting forth the exact circumstances involved in the late submission. The project manager should attend the bid opening, taking careful notes of all competitive pricing read off by the public official in charge. If this late bid happens to be the low bid but it appears that it may be rejected because it was submitted late, and if the job is important to the contractor, it may very well pay to investigate a formal, legal protest and challenge. It is possible that the courts might rule that it is in the public's best interest to accept the low bid even though the late factor could be considered a violation of the bidding procedure. In fact, if other "minor" deviations are noted during the bid opening process and either another contractor requests that the bid be disqualified, or the public official opening the bids indicates the bid may be disqualified, continue to take notes relating to the other bids as they are read off, return to the office, and discuss lodging a protest. If the "nonconforming" bid is significantly lower than the second bid, the public agency may decide to interview the contractor to ascertain that all other aspects of the project have been met; the contractor understood the scope of work to be bid, has included costs for all this work, and is reputable builder. The agency may rule that it is in the best interest of the community to accept this bid even though "minor" discrepancy in the bidding documents did exist. Emphasis must be placed on the word "minor."

Who is the low bidder?

Unless the bid documents state otherwise, the low bidder on a lump-sum bid is the low bidder. When the bid proposal contains not only a lump-sum price but also prices for alternates, as both additions and deductions, the determination as to who is low bidder becomes less than clear. In the absence of any language to the contrary, usually the owner can pick and choose the alternates that will be accepted. Therefore, the low bidder may not be apparent until all the accepted alternates are totaled with the base bid. There may be a time when the "apparent low bidder" wishes they were not, and that brings up another point.

Withdrawing a bid

In the rush of putting a bid together, it is not uncommon to leave out a few items. If these items are minor, and if the general contractor is a low bidder, they will usually accept the contract and chalk up the omissions to experience. However, the situation might take on a different twist if a bid bond or deposit check was required, and, on opening the sealed bids, the contractor finds that they were low bidder by such a substantial amount that something must have been radically wrong with the way in which their estimate was assembled. If a reputable contractor finds that their price is, say, $250,000 lower than the next bidder's price of $1,000,000 and the third and fourth bidder's quotes are similar to those of the second bidder, there is reason for alarm. The contractor will immediately take into consideration the bid bond or deposit check and consider the possibility of forfeiture of the bond or check rather than agree to accept a contract that has a serious flaw in it. Neither choice is very palatable, but does the contractor have any other?

In the case of *M. F. Kemper Construction Co. v. City of Los Angeles,* 376 Cal.2d 696, 235 P.2d 7 (1951), the contractor erroneously omitted a $330,000 item from their estimate, causing them to be $250,000 lower than the second bidder. The contractor contacted the Public Works Department a few hours after discovering their estimating mistake and requested that their bid be withdrawn and their bid bond returned. The City of Los Angeles decided to award the contract to the second bidder and directed the erroneous bidder to forfeit their bid bond. Needless to say, a lawsuit followed. The court made a distinction between errors in judgment and mathematical or clerical errors. On the basis of the evidence submitted, the court judged the $330,000 error to be a justifiable one and allowed the contractor to withdraw the bid and not forfeit their bond. It was the contractor's responsibility, however, to prove that a clerical error had, in fact, been made and that accounted for the erroneously low bid.

It would appear to be critically important that adding machine tapes, scrap paper with calculations on it, bid tabulation sheets, and other related matters be kept until well after a contract award has been made and accepted by the contractor.

Verbal Subcontractor Quotations

During the preparation of a bid, a sizable number of subcontractor proposals will be received over the telephone and recorded on the general contractor's telephone bid form. This form should contain the subcontractor's name, address, phone and fax numbers, and the name of the person relaying the subcontractor's bid. When the bids are being received, sometimes the corresponding scope is not recorded on the form, but when the bid has been assembled and submitted and the hectic activity is over, all these telephone bids should be reviewed for completeness and any missing information obtained from the subcontractors that day and inserted on their respective bid forms. There may come a time when a general contractor will receive a low bid from a subcontractor and incorporate that quote in a "winning" bid. Now assume that, because of that low subcontractor bid, or other bids, the contractor is designated as apparent low bidder. If a contract is subsequently awarded to the general contractor, the competitive subcontractors will be requested to submit formal written quotations if they have not already done so. This normal procedure can create an unpleasant surprise if one of the low-bidding subcontractors responds that because of an error in their bid or because some other work was just received, he wishes to withdraw his previous quotation and will not entertain entering into a contract with the general contractor. Without a written proposal for that subcontractor, can anything be done? You bet it can!

The principle of promissory estoppel may apply and render the oral contract enforceable. The word *estoppel* is defined in the dictionary as "an impediment that prevents a person from doing something contrary to his own previous assertion to do so." Under this doctrine, the offerer (subcontractor) can be held liable for any damages incurred by the general contractor. In other words, the subcontractor can be required to pay the general contractor the difference between their price and the next-lowest subcontract price received by the general contractor. In the case of *Bridgeport Pipe Engineering v. DeMatteo Construction Co.,* 159 Conn.242, 244 (1970), the subcontractor submitted a verbal bid by telephone to furnish labor and materials for plumbing, heating, and ventilating work for a housing project. The Connecticut Supreme Court ruled that the telephone bid was an oral offer, and the general contractor accepted the offer when it became the successful bidder on the housing project.

Although this Connecticut case involved a subcontractor supplying both labor and materials, several state courts have also ruled that received bids representing the sale of goods only constitute contracts. The acceptance of the contract is completed when the general contractor receives the contract from the client. Even if the subcontractor attempts to withdraw the bid before the general contractor is advised that they will be awarded the contract, promissory estoppel may still apply to prevent the subcontractor from withdrawing the bid.

In another court case, *H. W. Stanfield Construction Corp. v. Robert McMuller and Son, Inc.,* App.92 Cal.Rptr. 669 (1971), the court ruled that the subcontractor was liable for the bid submitted to the general contractor (GC), who was preparing a bid for the U.S. Navy. The GC had obtained prices from a number of painting contractors, and the low bid came from a company whose first bid was 50 percent below the next-highest price. After being advised about this low bid, the subcontractor resubmitted another price which H. W. Stanfield used in their bid. The general contractor told the painting contractor that they had used the bid, and after being advised by the U.S. Navy that a contract was forthcoming, the painting contractor would be receiving a contract for their portion of the work. The subcontractor refused to sign a contract when offered. The court held that the GC had relied on the promise of the subcontractor to do the work for the stipulated sum and would be damaged by refusal of the painting contractor to do that work. The decision was upheld by the California appellate court.

Disputes Regarding Contract Interpretation

Quite frequently there are ambiguities in the contract documents, and they are usually resolved by reasonable parties to the contract taking a reasonable approach. Sometimes reasonableness does not prevail, and someone starts to take a hard-line approach. There are no established patterns for contract document interpretation. What documents have priority over others? Do the plans or the specifications take precedence? Will the specifications take precedence over full-scale details? There will be a time when a contract clause will specifically set an order of precedence, and this will weigh heavily on the final outcome of the dispute.

The courts look at these questions individually. A specific statement will take precedence over a general statement. The courts will look at the purpose intended by a specification section of a certain drawing before making a decision. The point is that there is no hard-and-fast rule that applies to interpretation and which document has priority over another.

A common phrase which architects insert into the contract calls for the contractor to bring a discrepancy to the owner's attention before proceeding. If the contractors fail to do so, they will be whipped within an inch of their life and can proceed with the work only at their risk and expense. This type of confrontation is always frustrating. In most cases the contractors do not uncover a discrepancy until they are upon it; and when it is presented to the architect or owner, the response is that the contractors should have discovered the discrepancy at the time of bidding in accordance with the directive contained in the AIA General Conditions or the Supplementary Conditions. Since it was not presented at that time and in that fashion, the general contractor must do whatever is necessary to continue with the work. This is an unfair attitude with which some project managers are faced from time to time. Is there any answer to the predicament? We should think so.

Dealing with inadequate drawings

Often there is just enough time to adequately review the drawings and specifications before and during the hectic competitive bidding process. The contractor has to assume that the plans and specifications submitted by the owner or architect are reasonably complete for bidding purposes. If and when a contract is awarded, the general contractor will review the documents in more detail, and at that point, if there are any major discrepancies, rely on everyone's good faith to find a fair way to correct the errors.

In a case entitled *John McShain v. United States,* 412 F.2d 1218 (1969), the contractor said that the true condition of the drawings was not known at the time of bidding and that, after being awarded the contract for construction, they found that some of the drawings which were illegible at bid time were not replaced with legible ones. The addenda drawings, furthermore, did not correct many of the coordination errors in the bid documents. The general contractor sued to recover damages incurred by their company and their subcontractors because of the inadequate drawings. The U.S. Court of Claims said that although the plans furnished by the owner need not be perfect, they must be adequate for the purpose for which they were intended. The court went on to state that the contractor was under no legal or contractual obligation to inspect the drawings to determine their adequacy for construction prior to a contract award. The documents were to be used for estimating purposes only, and it had not been shown that McShain knew or should have known how defective the drawings actually were.

The owner and architect have a responsibility to present the general contractor with drawings and specifications which are adequate and reasonably accurate. The GC has a right to expect that. If there are considerable problems related to deficiencies in the documents, the GC has the right to expect compensation for any delays the substandard or deficient documents might have caused them. In the case of *J. D. Construction Co., Inc. v. United States,* 171 Ct.Cl.70 (1965), the court ruled that if faulty specifications prevent or delay completion of the contract, the contractor is entitled to recover delay damages from the defendant's breach of implied warranty. This breach cannot be cured by the simple expedient of extending the time and performance.

Contractor's guarantee as to design

When an architect specifies a certain component design and the installation results in poor performance, who is responsible? In a case brought before the courts in the state of Washington, an architect had modified a curtain wall design. The contract specifications contained the standard clause requiring the general contractor to notify the architect if any materials, methods of construction, or workmanship changes were needed to ensure compliance with the contract documents. The GC did not notify the architect of any changes they felt were necessary relating to this curtain wall design change.

Once the curtain wall was in place and the building was completed and signed off, a number of leaks started to occur in the curtain wall system. The GC refused to correct the leaks, and the owner sued. In this case, *Teufel v. Wienir*, 68 Wash.2d 31, 411 P.2d 151 (1966), the court concluded that the leaks were caused by design error. The owner had claimed that the specifications called for the curtain walls to be fabricated and installed by a manufacturer regularly engaged in the manufacture of the system and that the work was to be first-class and done in a manner so as not to allow any weather infiltration. The court's ruling was that the curtain wall was modified by the architect and was not suited to its use and the leaks were not caused by faulty materials or poor workmanship but were the result of a design defect.

Test Borings and the Question of Subsurface Conditions

Frequently the data contained in test boring logs will come into play in connection with a claim for extra work. Test borings accurately display the subsurface soil strata in the exact location where they are taken. If another test boring is taken nearby and shows the same soil composition as the first one, the areas between the two borings most likely have the same soil condition. Suppose, however, that in the course of excavating between the two borings, rock is discovered and must be blasted so that a subsequent item of work can be installed. Test borings showed no rock in that area, but work on the site revealed the existence of rock. Does the contractor have a legitimate claim for an extra? Don't rule out the possibility.

During the construction of a postal maintenance facility in Texas, a general contractor took the position that, on the basis of the test boring data made available to them, there was soft to medium limestone within the building area. There was an indication of hard limestone, but only outside the work area. When excavation was in progress, the contractor uncovered hard limestone within the construction area. As a result, the contractor had to substantially change their excavation procedures with a corresponding increase in excavation costs. The contractor expected to be paid for this extra work, claiming that additional compensation was warranted because the conditions encountered differed materially from those indicated in the contract, i.e., the test boring data. The government said that the extra costs were not justified because there were two visible rock outcroppings on the site.

In this case, McCann Co., Postal Service Board of Appeals (PSBCA) 152.76.2 BCA 12, 219 (Nov. 18, 1971), the PSBCA ruling was that neither the contractor nor the excavation subcontractor, nor the government, for that matter, had actual knowledge of the real subsurface conditions. The board further stated that a prebid inspection would not have revealed the problem which was encountered later. The board concluded that the contractor could be held responsible only for any knowledge gained from a reasonable visual site inspection and/or examination of the test boring data.

Don't be intimidated by restrictive contract language. The author had an experience relating to a claim for an extra involving rock that is noteworthy in two respects: (1) don't dismiss pursuing a claim because it appears that the contract language is so definitive that pursuit is futile and (2) if a situation appears to be truly unfair, it probably is.

Several years ago, the author's company entered into a contract to build two office buildings for one of the country's largest and most respected developers. The contract sum was approximately $30 million, a good-sized job, and the contract format was a guaranteed maximum price (GMP). In one section of the contract there was the following statement regarding subsurface conditions:

> Contractor represents that it has inspected the Project Site and has satisfied itself as to the condition thereof and that the Guaranteed Maximum Cost is just and reasonable compensation of all of the work including all foreseen and unforeseen risks, hazards and difficulties in connection therewith including any concealed conditions encountered in the performance of the work below the surface of the ground at variance with the conditions indicated by the Contract Documents or other documents furnished Contractor for his information except for, and only for, any hazardous or contaminated materials encountered by Contractor which shall be removed at the expense of the Owner.

This rather restrictive language was augmented by a section in the excavation portion of the specifications which stated:

> *Unclassified Excavation:* Excavation shall be unclassified and shall comprise and include the satisfactory removal and disposal of all materials encountered regardless of the nature of the materials and shall be understood to include rock, shale, earth, hardpan, fill, foundations, pavements, curbs, piping and debris.

Accompanying the plans and specifications were a series of test borings, an isometric of various rock locations, and a test boring log location plan (Figs. 10.1 to 10.3).

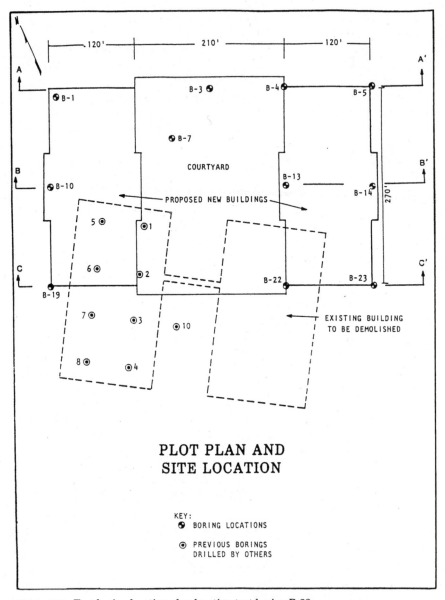

Figure 10.1 Test boring location plan locating test boring B-23.

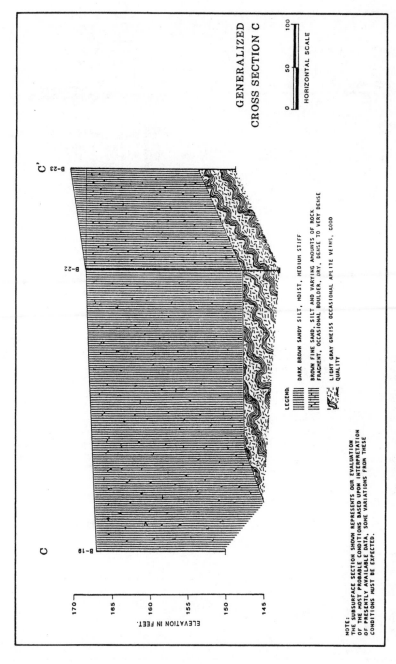

Figure 10.2 Isometric of rock elevations at test boring B-23.

GENERALIZED
CROSS SECTION C

HORIZONTAL SCALE
0   50   100

LEGEND:

||||| DARK BROWN SANDY SILT, MOIST, MEDIUM STIFF

||||| BROWN FINE SAND, SILT AND VARYING AMOUNTS OF ROCK
FRAGMENT, OCCASIONAL BOULDER, DRY, DENSE TO VERY DENSE

LIGHT GRAY GNEISS OCCASIONAL APLITE VEINS, GOOD
QUALITY

NOTE:
THE SUBSURFACE SECTION SHOWN REPRESENTS OUR EVALUATION
OF THE MOST PROBABLE CONDITIONS BASED UPON INTERPRETATION
OF PRESENTLY AVAILABLE DATA, SOME VARIATIONS FROM THESE
CONDITIONS MUST BE EXPECTED.

ELEVATION IN FEET.
170 165 160 155 150 145

C

C'

B-23

B-22

B-19

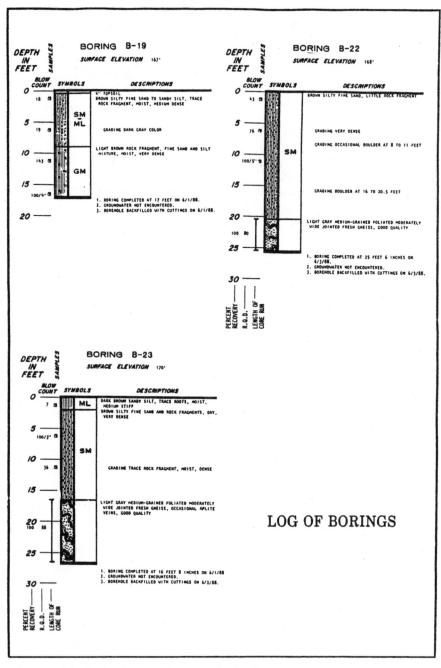

Figure 10.3 Test boring data relating to test boring B-23.

Excavation proceeded in the area of test boring B-23, and rock was discovered at elevation 162, 8 ft below the surface of the ground. Both the isometric and the test boring log clearly indicated the presence of rock at elevation 152. Continued excavation in areas represented by other test borings uncovered rock in areas at lower and higher elevations than those indicated by the borings. The architect and the owners were made aware of these conditions via visual inspections at the site and by letters written by the general contractor. In the spirit of harmony the general contractor continued to excavate and blast rock, and work proceeded at a rapid pace, but blasting and rock removal costs were escalating rapidly, finally totaling $288, 000. The architect and owner pointed to the contract and specification language stating that it was very clear that no matter what was encountered below ground, with the exception of hazardous materials, the contractor "owned" them. This didn't seem fair. The test borings seemed off the mark. A meeting with a top executive in the development company, a cowboy-boot-clad Texan, achieved nothing. He stated that this was their standard contract, and other general contractors in other parts of the country had, on occasion, run into the same problem and claims for rock removal were neither considered nor paid. After consultation with our lawyers, we were advised that unless the claim exceeded $500, 000, to pursue the matter via a lawsuit was not cost-effective! We were not going to give up. Something was wrong and unfair.

After weeks and weeks of in-house discussions, rereading the contract and specifications and reviewing the plans, not much headway was made, until the author made a template of the test boring location plan and began to overlay the site plan, shifting it to the east and west. Suddenly it became evident what had occurred. The geotechnical engineer had inadvertently shifted the entire test boring location plan approximately 50 ft to the west of where it should have been, and when this plan was shifted 50 ft to the east, all the test boring data matched the conditions that were actually encountered!

With this information in hand, another meeting was held with the owner and his geotechnical engineer, and armed with this information with veiled threats about a lawsuit alleging errors and omissions, the developer reluctantly agreed to pay the rock removal costs.

Change-Order Work Claims

The problem involved with change-order work has been discussed in other parts of the book, and the theories of quantum meruit and unjust enrichment have been explained in Chap. 8. A look at a few court decisions will shed additional light on the question of liability for payment for extra work not specifically authorized by written change orders. In a case known as *Universal Builders Inc. v. Moon Motor Lodge, Inc.*, 430 Pa.550, 244, A.2d 10 (1968), the owner's agent made several requests to the contractor involving extra work. The contract contained language related to change orders and required that all change orders be in writing and be executed by the owner or the architect. The contractor did some extra work without written change orders but with the promise of the owner's agent to pay for the added work. After the work was done, the owner refused to pay, invoking the contract clause that all change-order work must be in writing.

When the case was reviewed by the Pennsylvania Supreme Court, the ruling was that the owner's agent not only promised to pay for the extra work but also saw the contractor performing the extra work while visiting the site on several occasions. Rather than protest, the agent watched the extra work being incorporated into the job. The court interpreted this as an implied promise to pay for the extra work. The court also said that it would be unjust to let the owner accept the benefits of the extra work just because a written authorization did not exist.

In the case of the GC and a subcontractor, the GC required the subcontractor to submit proposals for all extra work before proceeding with the work. The subcontractor proceeded to do some work without complying with the GC's requirement for written authorization and had to sue to recover their time and material costs. The court ruled that there was clear evidence that the GC was aware that the subcontractor was doing the work without written authorization. As a result, the subcontractor was able to recover their costs [*Griffin v. Geneva Industries*, 228 N.W., 2d 880 (1975)].

Claims Due to Scheduling Problems

The AIA General Conditions article (Document A201) relating to contractor's schedules has changed over the years; the 1970 edition required the contractor to submit their schedule for the architect's *approval,*while the 1976 version required submission for the architect's *information*. The 1987 version of A201 merely states that the contractor shall prepare and submit a schedule promptly. These distinctions, while subtle, are important. Schedules are dynamic and change quite frequently, and with the submission being for the architect's information, the GC has more latitude and flexibility in modifying the schedule and documenting the reasons to substantiate any changes that may affect job progress or project completion without being held accountable for the initial schedule submitted to the architect.

The use of critical path method (CPM) scheduling means not only using CPM but also using a critical tool to represent the interrelations of all parts of the construction schedule. These CPM schedules now play an important part in substantiating claims for job delays. The general contractor has the responsibility to prepare a reasonable construction schedule and adhere to it. Part of that responsibility has to do with their relationship with their subcontractors. The subcontractors have a right to an orderly sequence of work scheduling, and they have a need to be able to work effectively. The GC who consistently maintains a smooth-running, rapid-paced construction job will find that subcontractors are eager to work in that environment and their pricing will be very competitive. The GC may find that, besides the economic reasons for administering a project properly and efficiently, legal problems can arise that are directly related to the published schedule. In the case of *Patchman Construction Co. v. Hi-Way Electric Co.*, 382 N.E.2d,111 (1978), the subcontractor argued that the GC was at fault in allowing job delays and therefore any damages incurred by the GC could not be apportioned to the subcontractor. In another case, *Freeman Contractors v. Central Surety and Insurance Corp.*, 205 F.2d 607, 8th Cir. (1953), the subcontractor, a painting company, sued, and was awarded damages because they stated that the GC did not schedule work in an orderly fashion so as to prevent conflicts with other subcontractors, which thereby delayed the completion of the plaintiff's painting work.

As far as CPM scheduling is concerned, the courts now recognize this type of scheduling not only as a reliable method of determining who is responsible for job delays, but also as a reliable basis for determining the impact of each event which caused the delay. This in turn can be used to determine who caused what delay and how the damages for those delays can be apportioned. As more and more subcontractors are holding GCs responsible for maintaining and adhering to proper scheduling techniques, the implementation of CPM takes on another dimension. In a case involving Natkin Co. and the George A. Fuller Company, the subcontractor alleged that, because the GC did not update the CPM schedule, disruptive delays were caused the subcontractor, who was suing to recover damages.

Computerized Evidence

The use of CPM as a method of pinpointing delays has been further enhanced by a change in the rules of evidence in the federal courts. In 1975, the federal courts adopted a new set of federal rules of evidence which filtered down to the state courts and has also been adapted to arbitration proceedings. Among the changes has been the recognition of the accuracy and reliability of computerized reports and summaries and the CPM schedule. Computer output is based on input quality; and as long as the records used for the input are reliable and accurate, the computer report is deemed reliable and accurate. The opposing party is given ample opportunity to test the validity of the computer-generated evidence. In what is called "fast-track litigation," the plaintiff might well be prepared but the defendant might not be. If a trial date is set 30 days after the date of an answer to a counterclaim, a great deal of documentation is required, and a defendant could be pressed to get ready for the trial. In one such case the defendant hired a construction consultant who, in turn, brought a number of analysts and several personal computers directly to the site of the disputed project. Approximately 100,000 documents were processed in less than 3 weeks. The computer-generated evidence obtained in this manner allowed the defendant to refute the plaintiff's charges and led to a settlement of the case before it came to trial.

In another computer-assisted case, the owner of a project instituted 25 apparently minor design changes. The contractor, who had had terrible cost overruns throughout the project, claimed that the 25 changes had significant impact on the other work. A computerized model that was developed showed how the 25 changes did in fact have a drastic effect on the project's system controls and mechanical processes. The analysis revealed that instituting the changes required between 200,000 and 300,000 other adjustments in the construction and balancing process. This type of analysis would once have been either too costly or too time-consuming to use, but with the aid of the personal computer, it is now neither.

Claims against Professionals

Architects and engineers, in recent years, have been subjected to an increase in lawsuits against them. The standard professional liability for malpractice insurance refers to "errors of commission" and "errors of omission," among other things. Now, developing a set of drawings and specifications for a major project is a very intricate and complex endeavor. Using the old phrase "Nobody is perfect," it is certainly understandable that the final construction documents might be lacking somewhat, and the GC routinely expects to have to add their expertise to the drawings to provide a completed project. With the drastically lowered cost of personal computers and computer-assisted-design (CAD) software, another element has been added to the equation. Construction details can be selected from an electronic brain and inserted into a building's design with the click of a mouse but without being guided by a hand experienced in how things fit together, the resultant drawings can have serious design deficiencies.

The courts have ruled that indeed the drawings do not have to be perfect, but they must be adequate for their intended purpose. Most of the problems that involve architects, engineers, and contractors seem to be due to the following shortfalls:

1. Drawings that are not coordinated among mechanical, electrical, fire protection, structural, and architectural trades

2. Conflicts between small and large details and between the written specifications and the graphic drawings

3. Failure to see if the boilerplate on the drawings or in the specifications actually applies to the project at hand

4. Lack of communication between design consultants so that a change made by one is not transmitted to the other to determine whether it has any effect on their design

5. Insufficient consultation with owners to afford them the opportunity to have a larger part in the decisions affecting their money

6. Insufficient time for proper review because the owner has requested an unrealistically short time frame for the production of the design documents—and being unwilling to advise the owner that proper review cannot be attained if the compressed time frame is enforced

Incidentally, this list was paraphrased from one prepared by a design professional who was expressing concern over the growing cost of malpractice insurance. The professional was making a point: problems are not being created by what the professionals *are* doing; they are being created by what is *not* being done. The courts have adopted the general principle that in a plan and specifications contract whereby the contractor is limited to any design change, the owner warrants that the design is proper and that when the contractors build the project in accordance with the plans and specifications, they cannot be held responsible if the results are not as the owner envisioned. When a dispute arises, the owner must look to their design consultants for relief. In other words, the contractors are bound to build according to the plans and specifications submitted by the owner and cannot be held accountable for the consequences of any defects in the plans and specifications.

The architect also can be sued by the contractors even though there is no contractual relationship between them. This is known as a *third-party claim,* and it has been used when an architect has failed to process shop drawings within a reasonable period of time. In *Peter Kiewit Sons Co. v. Iowa Utility Co.,* 355 f.Supp.376, 392, S.S.Iowa (1973), a claim was made to collect damages because the contractor suffered losses due to an unjustified delay in the architect's processing of shop drawings.

Acceleration: What It Is and How It Is Used

The legal term *acceleration* should be a part of every project manager's vocabulary. If an owner directs a general contractor to finish a project ahead of schedule or if the contractor's work has been delayed and the contractor is then ordered to complete the project in accordance with the original completion schedule, these instructions are known as a *demand for acceleration.*

There are two types of acceleration: actual and constructive. Actual acceleration occurs when the owner demands that the contractor complete the project ahead of the originally submitted completion schedule. Constructive acceleration occurs when the contractor is delayed by some action, normally an involved change order, or by an owner or architect's delay in reaching a decision on a question posed by the contractor. If the contractor then requests a job extension and is not granted one and the owner subsequently demands that the contractor complete the project according to the original contract schedule, a condition of constructive acceleration has been created. By claiming the condition of constructive acceleration, a contractor can attempt to get monetary relief because of the owner's actions. The legal elements of acceleration are as follows;

1. There is an excusable delay which entitles the contractor to a time extension.

2. The contractor submits a written request to the owner for a time extension.

3. The request for the time extension is refused, and the contractor proceeds with the work.

4. The owner issues an order to accelerate performance to complete the project within the original time period.

5. The contractor proceeds with the work at an accelerated pace and keeps track of the costs involved in the speedup effort.

6. The contractor then notifies the owner of the intent to file a claim to recover the costs incurred in this accelerated effort.

These situations will arise, and the project manager should be aware of the steps that can be taken to obtain reimbursement of costs caused by undue demands of the owner.

Mechanic's Lien

A mechanic's lien is a charge against the property that puts the owner of the property on notice that some of the labor and/or materials which have gone into their building have not been paid for. A mechanic's lien can be filed only against work in connection with a private contract; the filing of a mechanic's lien against unpaid goods and services on a public project is not allowed by law. The property on which the lien has been placed cannot be sold until the lien is somehow satisfied; it can either be paid or be bonded. The issuer of a bond will ultimately be responsible for satisfying the lien.

The normal expiration date of a lien may vary from state to state, and if the lien has not been paid or bonded by the expiration date, the issuer of the lien can file for foreclosure proceedings. The proceedings are started when the company attorney files a claim stating that a valid lien has been placed against the property and that a certain sum of money is due their client. Proof of the amount owed is necessary, as is proof that the lien was properly filed against the correct owner of the property, the correctly identified property was included, and the lien was filed in time. In theory, when foreclosure takes place, the property is sold and the lien holder gets paid from the proceeds from the sale. In practice, the sale of the property very rarely occurs and the lien is eventually satisfied.

The rules and regulations governing the filing of liens vary with the state, but generally a lien must be filed within 90 days of the last date on which work was performed on the job site. When the filing of a lien is contemplated, there are certain pitfalls to look out for and to avoid:

1. *Make certain the lien is filed within the filing limit time.* If the filing time is within 90 days after the last date that work was performed on the job, make certain that filing is done before the deadline. If it is not, the right to file a lien will be lost.

2. *Make certain the lien is filed against the right property.* Although this might seem rather simple, when urban property is involved, it can get complicated, particularly in subdivisions or projects composed of a number of different parcels. If the wrong property is described, the line will be invalid.

3. *Is the lien filed against the proper owner?* The proper owner can sometimes be found on the land records in the tax assessor's office, but quite often defining legal ownership is difficult. When a project involves a limited partnership, a joint venture between corporations, a syndication, or a shell corporation, it might be difficult to identify the proper owner of record.

A word about lien waivers submitted by subcontractors. On more than one occasion, a subcontractor will falsify a lien waiver. Although the subcontractor may sign the waiver indicating payment for all labor and materials placed in the building during the period covered by the waiver, either knowingly or unknowingly the information may not be true. Some subcontractors may not know whether their subcontractors, i.e., the insulator working for the plumber, have paid for all labor and materials for the period covered by the waiver and never bother to obtain lien waivers from these second- or third-tier contractors. So don't assume that with lien waivers in hand from subcontractors that the potential for filing a lien is nonexistent.

Arbitration and Mediation

Arbitration provides another method of settling construction disputes. It has the benefit of providing a panel of experts who are either associated with or familiar with the practices of the construction industry. Any contract which includes AIA Document A201, General Conditions, 1987 edition, will have provisions for arbitration. Article 4, Section 4.5 sets forth the procedures for commencing the arbitration process, although some clients will delete this provision from Document A201 or will include a "no arbitration" clause in the contract.

The arbitration process is started when an unresolved claim or dispute has been referred to the architect. The architect will render a decision on the matter that is final but subject to appeal. A demand for arbitration can then be initiated, but it cannot be made later than 30 days after receipt of the architect's written decision. Failure to demand arbitration within these time constraints may have the effect of rendering the architect's decision final and binding. At that point, litigation is the probable means to achieve a remedy.

When a demand for arbitration is received by the American Arbitration Association (AAA), the AAA sends a list of proposed, technically qualified arbitrators to each party to the action. Each party has 7 days to object to the selection of any of the arbitrators and to number the remaining names on the list in order of preference. If there can be no agreement on the first list, a second list may be requested.

After the arbitrators are chosen, the AAA establishes a mutually agreed-on time and place for a hearing. Sometimes a prehearing conference is scheduled to discuss procedural problems, witness lists, documents that are proposed to be submitted, any on-site inspections that may be necessary, and other matters that might arise in a complex case. Each party to the hearing can be represented by legal counsel, even though the proceedings are conducted in an atmosphere more businesslike than legal. The complaining party will present their side of the dispute first. Witnesses, letters, inspection reports, filed reports, and any other relevant information can be introduced to substantiate the validity of each party's claim. Expert witnesses can be called to testify, and the qualifications and experience of these expert witnesses can be brought to the attention of the arbitrators. The object of all this testimony is to convince the board that one's position in the dispute is the valid one. When all parties have had a chance to present their cases, the board will retire to render a decision. This decision must be handed down within 30 days and can be changed only if both parties agree to reopen the case.

As can be seen by the 30-day decision rule, one advantage of having a dispute arbitrated is the speed in arranging to have the dispute heard, and normally, in having the dispute presented, ruled on, and concluded quickly, often within 2 weeks from start to finish in simple cases. The rapidity of starting the process and proceeding quickly allows a hearing to take place while the facts are fresh in everyone's mind and while the documents are current and expert witnesses are more readily available. Another advantage of arbitration is that the board will be composed of people who are knowledgeable in construction practices and terminology and will be more prone to grasp the significance of the situation than a jury of laypersons.

The cost of arbitration, if not moderate, is often not staggering. The arbitrator will not receive compensation for the first day of service. Beyond that compensation will depend on the length of time the arbitrator's services will be required, and an appropriate daily rate will be established. All other expenses, including the arbitrator's travel and other expenses, expenses of witnesses, costs of documents requested by the arbitrator, and other such costs, are shared by the parties to the proceedings. The balance of the arbitration fee is based on the amount of the claim and/or the counterclaim as filed. The fees at the time of writing were as follows:

Amount of claim or counterclaim	Fee
Up to $10,000	$300
$10,000 to $25,000	3%
$25,000 to $50,000	$750, plus 2% of excess over $25,000
$50,000 to $100,000	$1250, plus 1% in excess over $50,000
$100,000 to $500,000	$1750, plus $1/2$% of excess over $100,000
$500,000 to $5 million	$3750, plus $1/4$% of excess over $500,000
$5 million to $50 million	$14,250, plus $1/10$% in excess over $5,000,000

A $300 filing fee is required when the claim is filed and there are postponement fees levied against the party or parties requesting the postponement.

Mediation outside the legal system

A more informal approach to settling disputes is also offered by the AAA and other for-profit dispute resolution organizations in the form of mediation. This method brings together parties to the dispute to discuss the matter in a more informal setting. The mediator, appointed by the AAA or designated by the for-profit organization, participates impartially with an eye to advising and consulting with the parties involved in the dispute. Although the mediators cannot impose a settlement, they may be able to guide the participants into a mutually acceptable settlement. The mediator can obtain expert advice, if needed, providing both parties to the dispute are in agreement and also agree on a basis for paying the expenses of these witnesses.

No stenographic records are kept of mediation proceedings, whereas in arbitration proceedings these records are provided if both parties request them. Mediation can be initiated by the interested parties by contacting the nearest regional AAA office or consulting the telephone Yellow Pages for these kinds of services.

Mediation within the legal system

Some states provide what is known as a *Master's Hearing,* which resembles the mediation process and is an attempt to seek resolution of disputes in an informal setting in the hope that resolution will assist in unclogging a congested court calendar. When a judge feels that a case stands a good chance of being settled through mediation, a board of lawyers, acting in a pro bono capacity, will be appointed by the court and will meet with each party to the dispute in an informal setting in the court house. These lawyers will listen to each side's argument separately. After weighing the facts presented by each aggrieved party, they will render their opinion as to the strength and validity of each party's case. They may also advise each party that if compromises could be considered, taking into the account the legal expenses that a court hearing could entail, it may be wise to seek a settlement. When the parties to a dispute are truly interested in settling the dispute and are willing to compromise, to a degree, this kind of extralegal hearing can be very effective.

11

Rehabilitation of Older Buildings

Rehabilitating or recycling older buildings can be a profitable and rewarding experience or a frustrating and painful one. This type of construction has its own idiosyncrasies, and the project manager embarking on the first such project should be aware of them. Often the drawings for the new work to be performed in these projects are prepared without the architect's having the benefit of a partial or complete set of the original building's plans. The building could have been erected years ago, and as it changed hands throughout the years drawings were either misplaced or destroyed. Even if the drawings are available, the contractor who built the original structure might have taken liberties with the plans and made substantial changes which were not reflected on any as-built drawings.

In the preparation of plans and specifications for the new use of the building, the architect, for reasons of monetary or time restrictions, might not be able to adequately define the existing structure and its components. Trying to envision the skeleton of some older buildings, without removing substantial portions of walls, ceilings, and floors and finishes is a very difficult, time-consuming, and costly job. There are two basic types of rehabilitations and various shades of the spectrum in between. At one end of the spectrum will be found the total or complete rehabilitation in which demolition work will remove all the interior finishes back to the structural system and will include the removal of all the existing plumbing, heating, sprinkler, and electrical systems as well. The other type of rehabilitation, at the opposite end of the scale, is the partial rehabilitation in which the finishes will be left intact, some mechanical and electrical components or systems will be left in place, and possibly, sound wood flooring, nonbearing partitions, and ceilings will remain with the idea that new finishes can be applied to them. In between total and partial rehabilitation, depending on the age, condition, and reuse of various components, any number of these parts or systems could be left in place to be reconditioned or refurbished. If a great portion of the existing structure is to be demolished back to the skeletal frame, the new drawings will have been produced with certain assumptions of what the exposed structure will reveal. If, after demolition has taken place, the structural system differed from the assumed construction, or differs dimensionally, the architectural, mechanical, and electrical drawings will have to be modified.

Preparing a Bid for the Rehabilitation Project

When a bid on a rehabilitation project is requested, the drawings should be reviewed very carefully in the office and a checklist of questions to be answered during a visit to the site should be prepared. Plan to spend some time at the site for a thorough inspection *before* starting the estimate. Among other things, the checklist can contain the following:

1. What is involved in removing existing finishes from walls, ceilings, and other structures? Will these finishes be easy or difficult to remove?

2. Can any existing utilities be used during construction for temporary light, heat, or power supply, or will all new temporary utilities have to be provided?

3. Determine whether that which is indicated to exist does in fact exist, and vice-versa, that which is not supposed to exist does not exist.

4. Do the bid documents correctly indicate the proper construction of the items to be removed; that is, do the drawings indicate that a steel stud and drywall partition is to be removed, when, in fact, the partition in question is plaster on wood lath on rough wood framing members?

5. Make note of the condition of a surface, subsurface, or area to be refinished or to be retained. Will it be possible to apply a new finish over the existing surface as is, or will it be possible to laminate gypsum board over the existing surface, if that is what the drawings indicate?

6. Do any of the items or materials to be removed have any appreciable salvage or scrap value?

7. Approximately how long will it take to demolish enough of the building components so that the new work can be started? (This kind of information will be needed to prepare a construction schedule, determine the length of the project, and estimate the general requirements portion of the estimate.)

8. Does there appear to be any hazardous materials in the building, asbestos, old transformers which could contain PCBs, or peculiar odors that could signal environmental problems? Although many contracts hold the contractor harmless from dealing with such materials, they may exist but were overlooked by other inspecting parties.

During this job-site inspection, be on the lookout for areas in the building where water might have been infiltrating. If the bid documents so state, part of the restoration work might involve watertight integrity of the building. If that is not the case and an inspection of the exterior walls reveals missing or loose mortar joints, caulking joints that have failed, cracks in the exterior wall system, or loose or missing flashings, make a note of these conditions. Also look inside carefully to see if there are interior water stains and rotted materials. Although these conditions might not be part of the bid package scope, if they exist, they will have to be dealt with in the near future. Installing new finishes where there has been water penetration for any length of time will certainly cause problems.

If in assembling a competitive bid the project manager or estimator assumes too many things not specifically noted on the bid documents, the assumptions, when converted to dollar costs, can make the resulting bid noncompetitive. On the other hand, if some of the assumptions are ignored, the related costs will not be incorporated in the bid and the total estimate might be artificially low. There is no easy way out of this dilemma, and quite often a flip of the coin will determine whether a questionable cost item is added to the estimate. Review the drawings very carefully, looking for obscure notes that may direct the contractor to include, exclude, leave as is, replace entirely, remove back to sound surfaces, and so forth.

Cutting and patching

One item in particular should be thoroughly investigated while visiting the site, and that is how much and what kind of cutting and patching will be needed. If all-new material and electrical systems are going to be installed and the building is multistoried, the cutting and patching will involve creating large chases for the new systems. The chases may require structural support and will have to be closed up once the systems are passed through them. Penetrations through thick stone or old concrete walls and foundations can be quite costly. Cutting through masonry partitions or walls so that new openings can be made for doors and windows will also be costly. If unsound finishes are disturbed when such penetrations are made, large chunks of lath and plaster can fall off the wall or ceiling that is being penetrated. If that happens, added costs will be incurred to restore these surfaces.

Look very carefully at the dollar value assigned to the portion of the estimate for cutting and patching. Bear in mind that, if the estimate is so conservative that not all the contingencies are covered, the competitors might not be so conservative in their approach to estimating the project.

Inconsistencies in or addenda to the bidding documents

If during a field inspection of the project prior to assembling the bid, there appear to be any major inconsistencies in the bid documents, it is best to discuss them with the architect in time for them to be clarified for bidding purposes. It then becomes very important that a letter of clarification or an addendum be prepared by the architect and distributed to all bidders in time for them to take note of its content. Of course, if something that will give your company a competitive edge is found while complying fully with the bidding documents, this information should be treated differently.

Prior to Actual Demolition or Construction

Assuming that a well-prepared competitive bid has been submitted and a contract is awarded, demolition or construction can proceed. Review the drawings carefully and read *all* the notes on the architectural, mechanical, and electrical drawings to both existing conditions and new work. Often there will be small notes on the drawings such as "If any item is shown on the existing drawings and does not appear on the new work drawings, it shall be removed or relocated as shown." This statement means that if some electrical work, for instance, is to remain, it must be identified so that it is not removed by the demolition crew. Sometimes fluorescent paint is used to spray all items scheduled for removal or demolition. If that is done, anything not marked with this bright paint is to remain. But make certain that the demolition crews know that anything painted is to be *removed*; sometimes there is confusion about whether painted areas are scheduled for demolition when on previous jobs, all work painted was to remain, or vice versa.

Before any demolition takes place, the building should be closely inspected so that any significant or suspicious cracks, either structural or aesthetic, which exist prior to demolition, can be documented. This inspection is best done in the presence of the architect, and if the walkthrough can be documented with photographs, so much the better. Particular attention should be paid to exterior wall surfaces that may have developed cracks or otherwise deteriorated from age, freeze-thaw cycles, or possibly minor structural failures over the years. Any significant areas that have cracked, spalled, or deteriorated should be identified and reported to the architect by letter so that there can be no misunderstanding later on as to when the cracks occurred. This process is known as *preconstruction survey.* An inspection of interior walls, ceilings, or floors which are to remain should also be included in the survey. Again, documentation by high-resolution black-and-white photographs is invaluable. Be sure to orient the photographs so that their exact location can be pinpointed at a later date, if necessary. When plaster walls and/or ceilings are to remain, tap the surfaces to determine whether the surfaces are sound. Any investigation revealing loose plaster should be reported to the architect, since the surface might loosen further or might fall off while demolition is taking place in adjacent areas. Before sending a letter to the architect, scan the drawings carefully to determine whether there are any instructions for situations like this. Sometimes a statement such as "When a portion of an existing surface is to be removed, but adjacent areas are not sound, these removals must extend to sound surfaces" will appear in obscure places on the drawings. Make certain that no such instruction exists before firing off a letter to the architect. When portions of exterior walls are to be demolished and the building is located in or near densely populated areas, water should be available to wet down the portions of the building that are being torn down. This will reduce the dust problem and keep complaints to a minimum.

Fire extinguishers should be available in areas where open-flame torches have to be used to cut any metals inside the building. Remember that fires can smolder for hours in walls behind areas that have been exposed to open flames; therefore, a fire watch should be established when such cutting takes place. It is a good idea to confine all torch cutting operations to morning hours so that the fire watch can extend during normal working hours, but if it becomes necessary to use cutting torches late in the day, have someone remain on the job after hours to ensure that a fire will not occur.

Safety hazards abound in rehabilitation work. Besides the obvious dangers from falling debris during demolition, there are many other areas in which accidents can happen. Floor openings created by demolition should either be securely covered with temporary plates, or barricaded. Air compressor hoses and electric power cables strung out through the demolition area can easily become tripping hazards. Other tripping hazards can be created by failure to cut off pipes, conduits, or other projections flush with the floor level when removals are taking place. Water used in conjunction with cutting tools, or dust control can create slippery conditions on the floor.

Cutting through active electric cables is always a danger because some panels may remain active to provide temporary lighting and power for tools. And not all lines are easily traceable back to their respective panels so that they can be deactivated. Always err on the side of safety. If unsure when an electric cable is alive or dead, assume that it is active until the electrician determines otherwise.

The tendency to allow debris to accumulate before removing it can also be a cause of accidents. Boards ripped off walls or floors have exposed nails in them, and the nails should be removed or bent over so that no one steps on them and is injured.

Prior to the start of demolition it is a good idea to assemble all workers and conduct a safety meeting to stress proper procedures and the hazards that should be avoided. At this safety meeting it should be stressed that hard hats, safety goggles, and ear protection, when necessary, must be worn by all personnel working in the building. The proper footwear is also important; thin-sole shoes, sneakers, or running shoes must not be permitted.

Problem Areas During Construction

In the early stages of the demolition process, the job will require a great deal of close attention. Questions concerning what stays and what is to be demolished will arise on a daily basis. There will be questions when conditions that differ from those specified in the contract documents present themselves. Immediate resolution is required to maintain job progress.

When partial electrical and/or mechanical systems are to be retained in the building and parts of the systems are to be removed, demolition can be accomplished in one of two ways. The mechanical or electrical subcontractor can disconnect the pipe conduit or piece of equipment so that the demolition contractor can complete the removal, or the electrical or mechanical subcontractors can perform the entire removal process themselves. Since demolition work is usually accomplished by using laborers, having higher-paid mechanics do only the disconnecting should be the less expensive approach.

Electric cables and conduits will probably be found where they are not supposed to be, and the electrical subcontractor should be readily available during the entire demolition process to deal with such unexpected problems. That may be true of the plumbing contractor also, when some existing water lines are to be kept active for fire and dust control.

The problem with electric circuits is not as simple as disconnecting all electric lines in a rehabilitated building. Electricity will be needed for power tools used in the demolition process and will be required for temporary lighting, and to disconnect all power would mean that another temporary service, independent of the existing one, would have to be installed in the building. On the other hand, if the removals are complicated and safety is the key factor, another separate electrical service might be the best answer.

Many rehabilitation project contract documents will show existing conditions or systems on a separate set of drawings usually titled "Existing conditions." The portions of the existing building that are to remain will generally be shown on the applicable "new" architectural, structural, mechanical, and electrical drawings. Each subcontractor should be responsible for monitoring the items pertaining to their trade, i.e., those items that are required to remain and those which are scheduled for demolition. The appropriate subcontractor can tag, paint, or otherwise identify these items in any way that is easily recognizable. To carry out this responsibility will probably require the subcontractor to have a mechanic on the job to assist the demolition crew in identifying which items are which. This provision should be negotiated into the appropriate subcontracts.

If a great deal of interior demolition must take place, stop and check dimensions once the demolition has proceeded to the point at which new work can begin to be set in place. Do the dimensions of the exposed areas agree with the dimensions on the contract drawings? Are they greater or smaller? If the mechanical and electrical drawings were based on dimensions that are no longer valid, all drawings referring to new work must be carefully reviewed, and if major discrepancies are uncovered, the architect must be notified immediately.

The author once had an experience which very vividly dramatizes this point. He was the project manager of a contract for recycling a late-1920s hotel into units for elderly housing. The old hotel was a cast-in-place concrete structure, reported the oldest of its kind in New England. The building was 14 stories high with four stepbacks in the structure and facade as the building progressed upward. The exterior walls were brick, and the interior surfaces of the composite wall were terra cotta block with a wood lath and plaster facing. The ceilings on the underside of the concrete slab decks were plaster. This was to be a total rehabilitation job, and all finishes were to be removed back to the concrete structure and the interior of the exterior brick walls. All slabs, columns, and beams were to have finishes removed. All existing mechanical and electric piping, conduits, and equipment were to be removed along with two huge coal-burning furnaces which were under 10 ft of water in the subbasement. The two old traction elevators were to be removed, and new elevators were to be fitted into the existing shafts. All windows were to be removed and replaced with insulated glazed aluminum double-hung window units.

Apparently a set of original structural drawings existed, but the new owners of the building decided not to purchase them (from a third party) because they felt the asking price was too high. Instead, the drawings prepared for the project were based on an assumed system of column, beam, and slab thicknesses, and the dimensions of these structural parts were determined by poking through plaster surfaces around selected beams and columns on several floors. Needless to say, many of the assumptions proved to be wrong after the actual structural components had been fully exposed.

Demolition progressed from the basement up with one crew, while another demolition crew worked from the penthouse down. The plan of attack was to get the basement areas and the subbasement pumped out, clean out all the old mechanical equipment, cut up and remove the big old boilers, remove the coal chutes, and in general, clean out all areas so that new equipment and piping layouts could begin as quickly as possible. In the meantime, demolition starting from the top down would allow the room layouts to begin and mechanical and electric riser location to be established. This, in turn, would permit the concrete floors to be core-drilled so that mechanical piping risers could be plumbed down on a floor-to-floor basis. When the demolition was complete, the mechanical risers could be installed upward from the new equipment layouts in the basement.

After the top three floors had been stripped back to the concrete structure, centerlines were established along the north-south and east-west building axis. From these centerlines, partitions could be established in accordance with the architectural drawings and then electric and mechanical riser locations could be verified, slabs cored, and lines plumbed down to the floor below to start the process all over again.

Suddenly it was discovered that dimensions were just not adding up, and all kinds of dimensional discrepancies came to light. A thorough investigation of the three uppermost floors began with respect to actual dimensions versus dimensions shown on the contract drawings. It appeared that, among other things, the structural columns and beams on the top three floors were smaller in section than those on the floors below. This seemed logical, since the upper floors were carrying less dead load than the lower floors. However, the architectural drawings did not reflect the dimensional differences, because the team from the architect's office did not probe these members when they made their initial, spotty, investigation. All columns and beams on the new drawings, with just a few exceptions, were shown as the same size. The actual dimensions of the columns and beams, when stripped of their plaster coatings, changed in size every other floor.

Also, some structural columns in the exterior walls were found to be wider and deeper than the drawings indicated. The mechanical drawings, which called for hot-water baseboard heat to be installed on the exterior walls, did not take in account the fact that the columns protruded into the rooms. The required square footage of the rooms had to be maintained in order to comply with HUD's Minimum Property Standards, and these dimensions were very tight to being with. It appeared that some of the structural columns might have to be notched at their bottoms to allow the copper hot-water baseboard pipe to be installed. When the structural engineer requested that the columns not be notched, a chase wall had to be created. That took valuable inches from the bedroom areas, which were already dangerously close to HUD minimum standards.

Columns in the exterior walls and columns to be incorporated into interior partitions varied sufficiently in size that they affected various room configurations. That, in turn, affected kitchen and bathroom configurations and dimensions, which affected mechanical and electric riser locations.

Except for demolition, progress on the job stopped while a systematic review was made of each room of each apartment by the project manager, architect, structural, mechanical, and electrical engineers, accompanied by the major subcontractors. Many apartments had to be redesigned, primarily because of incorrectly dimensioned columns and the uncovering of junior concrete beams which were not even shown on the contract drawings. Some of these newly discovered beams were found to be in the path of vertical chases emanating from floors below. Certain dimensions were critical and had to be maintained to comply with local building codes: widths of kitchens, bathroom fixture locations, and widths of public corridors. All other dimensions were determined and revised after the mandated ones were established.

Drawings were revised on the spot, and cost estimates for the changes were hurriedly assembled so that the architect and owner could review them and give their approval so that work could proceed. The entire procedure was both time-consuming and costly. Since there were liquidated damages-clauses in the construction contract, the documentation of all the delays had to be prepared and submitted promptly. The job finally got back on track, but a lot of crisis management was involved in getting it there. In this type of construction, time must be spent early on to check dimensions and wall thicknesses for such things as hollow metal door frames and window frames. If variances do occur and there are conflicting dimensions, the shop drawings for the items can be changed to show the actual width of wall versus (plotted against) the width shown on the contract drawings. This will ensure that the items will fit when they are delivered to the job site. In most cases no other dimensions will be affected other than depth of frame or frame throat size.

If and when conditions that are at variance with the contract documents or ones that differ substantially from those normally encountered are discovered, the architect should be notified immediately. The conversation should be followed by a written confirmation of the facts discussed. For example, the contract drawings may have indicated that a certain wall is to be removed and that the wall was assumed to be nonbearing. On investigation, the wall is determined to be a bearing wall that requires substantial structural modifications before it can be removed. The project manager, after alerting the architect to the problem, should request, in writing, that the structural engineer visit the site as soon as possible and issue a sketch containing the structural modification. Alternately, the architect might elect to keep the wall and make other changes to compensate for it.

If any corrective action or changes are required by field conditions which are at variance with contract documents, they should be reported as quickly as possible and always followed by written clarifications. Request for Clarification forms (RFCs), Request for Information forms (RFIs), and Field Information Memos (FIMs) are particularly handy to use in such situations.

Once instructions are received from the architect, and the nature of the corrective work is detailed, a cost proposal should be established and submitted so that a change order can be authorized promptly and not delay the start of the necessary work. If it looks as though a change order will be slow in coming, have the architect authorize the work to proceed, in writing, so that some type of formal authorization is obtained. And if it appears that the corrective work will have an effect on the contract completion time, the number of days delay should be included in both cost proposal and subsequent change order.

All parties concerned should work closely together in a rehabilitation project. The relationship that must be established with the architect, engineer, and owner is that of team effort. It should be clearly stated that the contractor is not embarking on a campaign to find discrepancies in the contract documents but is there to assist the architect, who never appears to have enough time or money to thoroughly investigate the conditions of the existing structure prior to the preparation of the new drawings. If there are extra-cost items of work which must be done, perhaps ways to change other items of work and effect trade-offs can be investigated. Unfortunately, this process may be difficult or impossible to effect when public work is involved, since the sponsoring government agency may insist on strict compliance with the contract documents and not allow any substitutions. Because of the nature of rehabilitation projects, and the problems that will inevitably arise, everyone must attack the problems as expeditiously, harmoniously, amicably, and economically as possible.

Normally a contingency will be incorporated into the estimate of total project costs; the bid documents might even stipulate its size. In any event, the owner should provide for some kind of contingency account, because it is a rare rehabilitation project that doesn't need additional funds to cover the cost of unforeseen problems. Depending on the nature of the project, the contingency could be from 5 to 10 percent of the total amount set aside for construction.

It is not uncommon for new doors, windows, or other openings to be cut through existing load-bearing walls. Structural members such as steel beams or lintels will probably have to be installed above new openings to support the dead or live loads above. Preparing the load-bearing wall so that portions of it can be removed involves a process known as *needling*. Needling provides support for the structure above the new opening until a permanent structural support can be set in place. To needle a 12" brick wall, as an example, a series of holes spaced approximately 2' or more on centers is cut through that portion of the wall that is to be removed for the new opening. The holes are cut about 2' above the elevation of the new lintel or beam to be installed. The purpose of these wall penetrations is to allow steel or wood beams to be inserted through the holes and shored up on each side of the wall. This will temporarily support the existing dead load of the wall above the area to be removed. Once the needling beams and shores are in place, the opening, along with any pockets required to receive bearing plates or leveling plates and the new lintel or beam, can be created. When bearing plates have been installed and grouted and the structural support member is in place, the new opening can be cut out to the required dimension. At that point, the shores and the needling beams are removed. The needling pockets can be filled in with masonry, mortar, or concrete if necessary. All this work must be done after consultation with and under the direction of the structural engineer. Often, the engineer will require a sketch of the method to be employed by the contractor, being careful not to dictate means and methods of construction to the builder, but for general information purposes. Other terms frequently used in connection with rehabilitation work are *panning* and *expanders,* terms that are basically interchangeable. They refer to new or replacement window installations. Many older buildings have steel sash windows in steel frames which are not energy-efficient and in most cases do not meet the efficiency requirements of local building codes. Some older buildings had wood-framed windows which were secured to the surrounding masonry with metal anchoring devices. When frames were installed in that manner, removal of the complete frame could damage the facade or other exterior surfaces of the wall, and patching and matching repairs to older brick facades is a difficult task. So when rotten wooden windows or steel windows are to be removed and they have been installed with these anchors, it is customary to remove the frames and cut off the anchors, leaving them in place.

If the existing window frames are structurally sound, there should be no good reason to go to the additional expense of removing them. Many architects will specify on the contract drawings that the frames be left in place if they are structurally sound. New windows can be installed in the openings created by the removal of the sashes only. To cover existing frames or to install windows in existing openings, frame expanders, or pannings, are used. These metal expanders are fabricated from metal of the same type and color as the windows and are fitted into place after the new windows have been installed, shimmed, and secured in place. The expanders lock into the new window jambs and head and return on the jamb and head sides back to the rough openings, thereby covering the frames left in place. New sills can be installed over existing ones. Any unevenness of the old openings can be compensated for by the use of these expanders, which can be trimmed to fit into slightly out-of-square rough openings. When the expanders are caulked on the outside and the spaces between the new frames and old ones are filled with insulation on the inside, a weathertight installation has been completed.

Prior to the installation of new drywall partitions in the rehabilitated buildings, a walk around the exterior of the building is in order. If the scope of the contract does not include any masonry repointing or other waterproofing measures, the exterior should be looked at to determine whether there are any areas which might have water-leakage potential. Any such leaks will damage not only the gypsum board but also any finishes to be applied to it and any new floorings that may be installed. If it appears that there could be water infiltration through some area, the architect should be so advised and asked for instructions on how to proceed.

If any appreciable demolition work is to be performed by using heavy equipment inside the building, the structural engineer should be consulted to determine whether any shoring will be required. If permission to proceed is granted, a letter from the engineer stating under what conditions certain types of equipment can be employed should be requested.

Job progress photographs have a special purpose in rehabilitation projects. They can reflect the condition of various parts of the structure prior to the application of new finishes or new wall openings in progress or completed. These photos must be clean and concise (see Figs. 11.1 and 11.2). When a photograph is used to show unusual or uneven surfaces, a method of measurement should be introduced into the photograph. In Fig. 11.3 a carpenter's ruler is used to show that one section of floor is one inch lower than its adjacent surface. Other forms of documentation take on added importance in these types of projects. With the proper attention to detail and cooperation from subcontractors and consultants, the project manager can gain invaluable experience while also getting a great

Figure 11.1 Progress photograph showing condition of wall surfaces after selected demolition has taken place.

Figure 11.2 Another progress photograph showing existing opening prior to closing it up.

Figure 11.3 Photograph with carpenter's rule to show uneven-ness of existing floor.

deal of satisfaction from keeping the wrecker's ball away from a beautiful building.

Encountering Hazardous Materials in the Rehabilitation Project

The asbestos problem

In many older buildings, asbestos was used to insulate plumbing and heating lines, boilers and boiler breechings, and other pieces of heating-related equipment. It was also used in acoustical plaster walls and ceilings and certain types of flooring materials. As late as 1981, one half of all asbestos consumption in the United States came from roofing felt, felt-backed sheet flooring and tiles, asbestos-cement pipe and fittings (known as *transite pipe* and *fittings*), and some types of clothing. A survey conducted by the Environmental Protection Agency (EPA) some years ago revealed that 733,000 buildings in this country contain this hazardous material. According to the EPA, buildings constructed in the 1960s are likely to have sprayed-on or troweled-on materials containing asbestos, usually as a fireproofing material. Older buildings are more likely to have asbestos in the pipe and boiler insulation.

Asbestos in building construction materials takes two forms: friable and nonfriable. Friable asbestos can be crumbled, pulverized, or turned into a powder-like substance by crushing it in the hand. Nonfriable asbestos consists of asbestos fibers and a bonding matrix; the fibers will not be disturbed unless the product is cut, sawed, or drilled. Examples of nonfriable asbestos are vinyl asbestos tile, which contains about 21% asbestos, roofing felts which contain anywhere from 10 to 15% asbestos, and siding shingles, which contain 12 to 14% asbestos.

The presence of asbestos in older buildings may not be always noted in the bidding documents; however, most contracts nowadays have language relieving the contractor of removal of any hazardous materials that may be found in the building or on the site unless they have been specifically instructed that these materials are present and are to be removed as part of the contractor's contractual scope of work. Article 10 of the AIA General Conditions document states that

> In the event the contractor encounters on the site materials reasonably believed to be asbestos or polychlorinated biphenyl (PCB) which has not been rendered harmless, the contractor shall immediately stop work in the area affected and report the condition to the Owner and Architect in writing. The work in the affected area shall not thereafter be resumed except by written agreement by the owner and Contractor if in fact the material is asbestos or polychlorinated biphenyl (PCB) and has not been rendered harmless.

Other materials may resemble asbestos when viewed by the naked eye. If asbestos is suspected, it can be confirmed only by removing a sample and having it inspected by either a government or private testing laboratory. The spear-like fibers of the material are identified only by inspection under an optical microscope. In fact, one study criticizes fiber count determined solely by optical microscope inspection, because the instrument picks up only fibers larger than 0.2 μm, whereas potentially dangerous fibers can be as small as 0.02 μm. The latter can be detected only by using an electron microscope.

Once it has been determined that asbestos is present, the material can be removed, encapsulated, or enclosed. Encapsulation can be accomplished by coating the asbestos with a bonding-type sealant that will penetrate and harden it. The asbestos can also be covered with a protective material which is placed over it and sealed over the seam and around the edges. Enclosing the asbestos might be considered if the material is localized. The procedure involves constructing an airtight enclosure around the surfaces that are coated with or contain asbestos. The enclosure should be constructed of an impact-resistant material, and signs are to be placed on the outside of the enclosure warning that asbestos is contained therein.

When removal of asbestos-bearing materials is to take place, it is best accomplished by hiring a firm that specializes in this work. Local and federal authorities require the filing and notification of various forms and regulations covering the removal of this material. The EPA regulates the removal and/or disposal of asbestos materials and the Department of Labor's OSHA regulations contain restrictions on worker exposure to this material, so both agencies will be involved when asbestos is to be removed.

Lead-based paint

Prior to World War II, lead was a common ingredient in exterior and interior paints adding luster, longevity, and durability to the product. In the mid-1970s, the federal government became concerned about the health hazards associated with the use of lead-based paints and mandated that the percentage of lead in paint must be reduced to 0.06%. With the advent of latex and alkyd-based paints, which were fast-drying and durable, the use of oil-based enamels containing lead found less and less acceptance on the market, and finally because of government regulations, production of this type of paint ceased. Cases of brain-damaged children who had eaten flaking lead-based paints have been well documented and are testimony to the dangers created by this material. Cumulative exposure to lead damages the brain, blood, nervous system, kidneys, bones, heart, and reproductive system and contributes to high blood pressure.

Because of its widespread use (it was estimated that at least 60 million homes had been painted with lead-based paint by 1975), older buildings being rehabilitated might well have been painted with this material. In some cases, doors and frames that had been painted with lead-based paints are to be removed from the building site and replaced with new ones. But if lead-based paint is to be removed from existing surfaces, certain dangers present themselves. Power sanding to remove lead-based paint will release a great deal of harmful dust and find its way into every nook and cranny even though the workers may be protected with a respirator and protective clothing; a hazard is created unless every speck of lead-bearing dust can be removed. Exposure monitoring is recommended for all jobs involving extensive removals of lead-based materials and medical evaluations; biological monitoring and physical examinations are also recommended. If lead-based paints are discovered in a rehabilitation project, the architect should be notified in writing and the material treated as hazardous material.

Polychlorinated biphenyls, total petroleum hydrocarbons, and volatile organic chemicals

Two common contaminants in soils under older buildings or on the site are polychlorinated biphenyls (PCBs)—an ingredient in old electrical transformers and total petroleum hydrocarbons (TPHs)—caused by leaking underground fuel tanks. Volatile organic chemicals (VOCs) can be present when various types of cleaning fluids or other chemicals had been used on-site and either dumped on the ground after use, or dumped in an underground waste line that leaked. All three can be classified as hazardous materials, and depending on concentrations in the soil, these contaminants can be very expensive to remove.

Although local regulations may vary, PCB concentrations of less than 25 parts per million (ppm) can generally be disposed of on-site. Concentrations above this level require off-site disposal at an approved facility. TPH soil contamination in the <5000-ppm range may sometimes be disposed of on-site, and concentrations of VOCs <50 ppm can occasionally be disposed of on-site. In all cases, local authorities must be contacted to determine acceptable ranges for on-site disposal, and the location of approved disposal facilities for materials that must be taken off site.

Leaking underground storage tanks

Leaking underground storage tanks that have not been removed from a rehabilitation site can present yet another hazard. There are about 1.5 million known underground storage tanks that are to be replaced in accordance with a federal law enacted in 1984, and there are probably several million more that, while not subject to federal or state law, are slowly disintegrating, leaking oil residue into the soil. Most owners of underground tanks have taken steps to avoid the severe penalties imposed on them when the law has been violated, but there are a number of abandoned tanks that have been covered over and forgotten about. If, during the course of excavation at a site, an abandoned tank is uncovered, care must be taken not to puncture it. The architect should be notified immediately and instructions for removal requested. If, however, a tank is uncovered and inadvertently punctured, the architect should be notified immediately and the appropriate EPA office notified within 24 hours of the occurrence as required by law. And, unless directed otherwise, the following steps should be taken as soon as possible:

1. Remove as much product remaining in the tank as possible to prevent any more contamination.

2. Take steps to prevent further migration of the leaked material into the soil.

3. Monitor the area for fire and safety hazards.

4. Within 20 days after a leak has been reported, the property owner must file a detailed report summarizing the action that was taken to contain and remove the contaminants.

5. Within 45 days after this first report, another such report is required, updating the first one.

Depending on the severity of the leak, the nature of the product, and the geotechnical characteristics of the surrounding area, a series of soil monitoring wells may be required to track the underground migration of contaminants.

Environmental Audits

Open fields surrounding many major cities have been used as dumping grounds for everything from waste oil to plating chemical residues and other hazardous materials. When such areas are being considered as construction sites, any dangerous materials dumped years ago and unearthed during excavation can pose a severe health threat to everyone working there. The Superfund Amendment and Reauthorization Act, more commonly referred to as SARA, and the Comprehensive Environmental Response Compensation and Liability Act (CERCLA) place the responsibility for hazardous waste cleanup on the owner of the property; however, CERCLA can assign this responsibility to a contractor who had previously worked the land. The government takes the position that a contractor may have had some part in the "chain of custody" of the toxic land. Nowadays, banks and other lending institutions often require a site assessment prior to finalizing a construction loan, and a contractor considering working on a suspect site should request a copy of any such site assessment. Environmental audit consultants specializing in these types of investigations can be hired to determine whether previous landowners have dumped toxic wastes on the property or allowed others to do so. If contaminants are suspected, on-site soil samplings will be taken to determine the nature and extent of contamination.

Protection of Archaeological and Paleontological Remains and Materials

Contractors have to be alert to the possibility of the unearthing of archaeological and paleontological (fossils) materials that may be of significance in the recording of historic or prehistoric events. If there is reason to believe that any of these materials are unearthed while excavating on a site, either old or new, the contractor may be required, by law, to cease work immediately on discovery. Generally the contractor will be instructed to notify the architect or engineer and await further instruction. The contractor should make every effort to preserve the find until further direction is given and may, in fact, have to reschedule or redirect the work if the find is of historic importance.

12

Design-Build

Under a design-build contract, the general contractor provides the design services and also carries out the construction activities. Some design-build companies can provide all these services with in-house staff; others engage the services of architects and engineers and provide only the construction functions within their organizations. There are also firms which will act as clearinghouses or brokers and are essentially catalysts for bringing all the participants together. They have no staff capability for either design or construction. This chapter is devoted to the design-build contractor who utilizes outside consultants for the design phase but does have, and depends very heavily on, its ability to provide a full line of construction services and activities—in other words, a general contractor with design-build capability.

Usually the design-build company will be heavily sales-oriented and have a well-planned marketing program consisting of a sales force and a director of sales using a full range of marketing tools such as an active advertising commitment and professionally produced sales brochures. Whereas the general contractor engaged in conventional bid work is concerned with getting on bidders' lists, the design-build contractor is actively marketing their services. The advantages of design-build, as presented to the business community, are as follows:

1. A prospective client can have contact with only one source for design, cost estimating, budgeting, and construction expertise—the entire building program. On occasion, the design-build firm can even arrange for project financing.

2. A more rapid cycle involving design, budgeting, and construction time can be achieved through the control exhibited by the design-build contractor.

The Conventional Design-Construct Cycle

When prospective clients choose the conventional method of initiating a building program, they usually start with a visit to an architectural firm to discuss their program, design parameters, and related costs. As the discussion progresses, and a formal agreement is reached between client and designer, the architect will most likely engage the services of other consultants such as landscape architects and structural, mechanical, and electrical engineers. Depending on the architect's access to a construction cost data base, the project costs may not be firmly established until a general contractor has been selected, through either the competitive bid or negotiated process.

There are private estimating service companies who can provide cost estimates to the architect at various stages of the design, but it has been the author's experience that they do not produce an estimate as accurate as one prepared by a general contractor with a top-notch estimating department.

If the estimated cost, using the above scenario, appears to exceed the client's budget during the design development stage, possibly the design can be altered somewhat to bring the project back into budget. But when an estimate is not obtained until final plans and specifications have been produced and the project has been competitively bid, valuable time and money have been lost in the process. Any redesign is likely to be paid for by the client, and the time required to redraw and rebid could be considerable.

Comparison with the Design-Build Cycle

During times of rapid price escalation, the process described above can work to the client's disadvantage. Back in the 1970s there was a period of time when inflation in the construction industry was running at about 1 percent per month and a project budgeted in January, for example, could conceivably cost 10 percent more if construction did not commence until October. Even when price escalation is not a factor, when time means money, the design-build cycle can be very cost-effective. A first-rate design-build company can short-circuit the entire process and provide phased design with corresponding cost estimates and even guarantee them within a certain plus-or-minus factor. Utilizing this process, contracts can be awarded on a "fast track" basis, i.e., the structural systems, both foundations and super-structure can be awarded when these drawings have been completed. Contracts can be based on a limited number of design documents, and construction can start while the design is being completed. This ability to fast-track, with all its obvious advantages, is one of the selling points of the design-build scheme.

Achieving Design-Build Capability

The design-build concept can be applied to any number of types of construction projects, and quite possibly some general contractors have been involved in design-build work without knowing that they have been. General contractors who have negotiated contracts to build housing for the elderly under various Department HUD programs have probably developed a design-build capability. When an owner, either a not-for-profit or a for-profit sponsor, is searching for a general contractor to build one of these kinds of housing projects, the contractor who has successfully completed several of them is at a distinct advantage. Since a historical data base of construction costs is such an important part of the design-build company's repertoire, past projects of a similar nature are extremely helpful. In the case of HUD elderly housing projects, the client or owner has several goals:

1. Design must comply with HUD's minimum-property standards (MPS) and possibly the state housing authority in addition to other lender requirements, and, of course, local building codes.

2. The cash flow requirements must be met. The annual mortgage amortization must have a distinct relation to the project's projected income. Since the mortgage amortization is determined by construction costs, the budgetary requirement for the project is very important.

The general contractor with prior experience in building these kinds of government-subsidized housing projects will be able to guide the owner's design team toward the most cost-effective design of structural, mechanical, and electrical systems based, in part, on past experience. The contractor will have definite ideas as to what design will fit into the budget and what design will not. The contractor can also suggest various product vendors whose quality levels are commensurate with the project's budget requirements.

Developing a design-build capability

The general contractor who wishes to develop a design-build capability must have a few things in place before embarking on a campaign to attract clients. The contractor must have a data base of historical costs which will make them conversant with a specific type or specific types of project construction. Obviously, contractors who want to develop a design-build capability in hotel, motel, or restaurant construction will have a very difficult time doing so if they have never built such a structure before.

Conversely, the general contractor who has been building two or three office buildings per year for the past few years, and who has maintained a good record of associated costs, will have a much easier time operating in the arena of the design-build contractor.

Along with a competent staff and a strong data base of experience in a particular segment of the construction industry, the general contractor has to let it be known that they have the necessary skills and wish to be considered as a candidate for design-build proposals. Hence the need for a marketing capability. The marketing effort can be just as important as the contractor's ability to deliver the product, because if no one is aware of that capability, its value is greatly restricted. Some contractors develop a sales force for this purpose, and others will augment a small sales force with attractive brochures mailed periodically to a select list of potential clients. Some contractors develop relations with local industrial and commercial real estate firms in the hope of reaching prospective clients who have contacted these realtors in search of undeveloped land. In some areas, the local electric utility company maintains a real estate development department and has its finger on the pulse of possible newcomers to the area. Contractors may wish to develop a relationship with these departments to uncover new prospects.

Whichever approach is taken, the prospective design-build company should have a definite marketing program included in its future plans.

Building a design team

The selection of a design team—architects and engineers—should be under consideration before a prospective client is sought. The members of the design team ought to have experience in the type of construction that is being contemplated. These design professionals should also have a data base of costs associated with the various systems they will be designing, and the advantages and disadvantages of each system. A mechanical engineer, for example, should have cost information about various types of heating and cooling systems and the costs of major pieces of equipment, distribution networks, availability of the equipment, and knowledge of its performance and maintenance characteristics. This ability to equate design with cost is a valuable asset to be sought out in selecting design consultants.

Although the general contractor will be the team captain or project manager in a design-build program, the architect should be designated as the focal point for the design team. The design-build project manager should direct all other design disciplines to interact with the architect, who will have overall responsibility for coordinating the work of all the designers, making certain that everything fits.

Building a team of design-build subcontractors

A strong design-build team will include a nucleus of key subcontractors, primarily structural, mechanical, electrical, and automated controls systems because these trades represent the major cost components of a project. Second, site contractors and finish trade subcontractors are also valuable.

Subcontractors involved in the day-to-day cost structures of their respective trades are a most valuable part of the design team. Their input will augment the historical costs used in the assembling of estimates at various points in the development of the design. They can also furnish information about the performance and reliability of key pieces of equipment. When these subcontractors work with the design consultants, fairly accurate systems costs can be developed with a minimum amount of design work. By drawing on their individual data bases, the plumbing, HVAC, sprinkler, electrical, and Division 17 subcontractors can contribute current, valid systems cost information to the design team.

Subcontractor involvement and relations in the design-build mode can take several forms that might be slightly different from past subcontractor relations. A subcontractor team should be assembled in the early stages of a project, and their involvement may warrant some commitment from the design-build contractor to negotiate a final contract price with them when the plans and specifications have been completed. The team members will probably be the structural, mechanical, and electrical subcontractors; but because of the particular nature of a specific project, other subcontractors might be needed early on. For example, an excavating subcontractor as part of a design-build team might be very helpful in zeroing in on final finish-grade elevations on a site where major cuts and fills are required. An excavating subcontractor with access to computer-assisted design (CAD) can plot many variations of finish-grade contours and establish the costs for each scheme. Before subcontractors are invited to participate in the development of a project, the project manager must establish certain ground rules:

1. If the project goes ahead, will these subcontractors be awarded contracts for their particular phases of work via a negotiation process?

2. If the project is aborted along the way, will the subcontractors expect to be compensated for their involvement to date, and if that is their expectation, who will pay them, and on what basis?

3. If the project goes to contract, but along the way, the owner requires that competitive bids be obtained for each trade, will these subcontrac-

tors be agreeable to that arrangement? This scenario could arise when in the beginning stages of a project, the owner elects to use a lump sum contract form, but later changes it to a GMP contract where a portion of the savings will revert to the owner, and therefore competitive bids for each trade may be required.

Not all design-build projects will require concentrated subcontractor participation, but when it is needed, the project manager must keep the various subcontractors apprised of any potential problems and get their acceptance or refusal to participate beyond a certain point. A team cannot be built or a relationship developed if the relationship is not beneficial to all parties in the long run. Relations with the design team subcontractors should follow this rule.

Design Fees

It will be the responsibility of the design-build contractors to negotiate design fees with the various consultants. Separate fees may be negotiated with the structural, mechanical, and electrical engineers, or those fees may be incorporated into one fee for the architect, who will provide all the design work and issue contracts to whichever consultants are required. The fee structure will vary from job to job depending on the complexity of the design work, the size of the project, the services to be provided, and the relations established between the contractor and the designers. A standard fee arrangement includes all site, structural, mechanical, and electrical design, as well as architectural work, and is based on the overall construction budget. For instance, on a project ranging from $5 to $10 million, the total design fees may be between 7 and 10 percent. Ever since the American Institute of Architects abandoned their "blue book" fee structure, design fees are negotiable.

The Cost of Controlling a Site

Sometimes a prospective client already has a site selected for the project or either owns one or has one under option to purchase. Other clients may come to the design-build company with site selection criteria, and the company that is able to satisfy those needs along with a strong design-build proposal will ultimately be awarded the contract. Many design-build companies have found it advantageous to maintain very active lines of communication with the real estate community to have a better feel for what land parcels are available and the cost of acreage in various parts of their operating area.

When site selection is part of the proposal package, this does present another dilemma. The design-builder must not only locate one or more potential sites but also be able to obtain the site if their proposal is accepted. The contractor will first attempt to reserve any potential site or sites on a no-cost option basis, but probably will not be too successful except in a very depressed market. Furthermore, no matter how rapidly a prospective client says they will decide on a design-build contractor, the time is invariably much longer. In the meantime, the site being offered by the design-builder must be kept off the market until the selection has been made.

The design-builder might have to pay for keeping a specific site off the market by obtaining an option on the land. If the client intends to select a design-build firm within 30 days, the land should be put under option for 30 days, plus a specifically designated renewal period—hopefully at no additional cost, but more realistically at the same cost as the initial option. If the design-builder is not selected as the successful candidate after paying option money to control a certain parcel of land, there are two choices: chalk the cost of the option up to the cost of doing business or try to find another client for the land under option.

Unique Problems Associated with Design-Build Work

Besides the cost of securing options on land that may or may not result in a contract, there are other unique problems associated with the design-build process. Communication skill—the ability to ask the proper questions and listen to the proper answers when trying to define the client's design criteria—is a very important aspect of the program. The entire process is, after all, selling a client on the concept that a project incorporating all or most of their requirements can be delivered within the constraints of a budget. In order to deliver on that promise, the design-builder must ask all of the pertinent questions to elicit the necessary information from the client. A term that will be heard many times is "You should have known," as in "You should have known that we were planning to install a kitchen in the employees' lounge in the near future, so you should have provided the necessary rough-in provisions" or "You should have known that the president would have wanted a wet bar in one of the closets and rosewood veneer on the walls instead of vinyl wall fabric because that's what was in the present office." Since the design-builder is responsible for proper design and construction, all these "you should have knowns," when known, will be expected to be included in the contract sum with no increase in the contract amount. Defining the program, in detail, when the design consultants have been brought on board, becomes a key factor in establishing creditability as a design-build contractor.

As design and development costs are established, "wish lists" can also be created so that if the final design comes in under budget, some of these extra items can be added into the project. Possibly the best way to illustrate and explain the design-build process is to go through a typical, hypothetical proposal from the sales-marketing contact to the construction contract preparation.

Although some design-build proposals will proceed directly toward a contract design and scope, many will proceed in stages. A client may wish to develop preliminary design and budget costs at a minimum expenditure of funds for any number of reasons: to obtain a board of directors' approval before making a final commitment to proceed, to obtain a more positive response from lending institutions, or to assist in marketing a building with a more definable pro forma and design criterion.

A design-build proposal can take a preliminary step toward a potential contract signing by what could be known as a budget proposal, which would incorporate very elementary design work and cost estimates with considerable latitude.

The Budget Proposal

A budget proposal, as a preliminary step toward a complete design-build proposal and contract, will include the following documents in order to establish a scope commensurate with the budget:

1. A rudimentary site plan locating the building and including driveway access from the main street, parking facilities, and some indication of landscaping

2. A floor plan, or typical floor plan for a multistoried building, showing work areas, toilet facilities, mechanical rooms, elevators, stairwells, and special areas peculiar to the specific project

3. An elevation showing exterior wall treatment, window areas, entrances, and enough design work to give the client a feel for the way the building will look

4. A section through a typical exterior wall to show exterior and interior wall construction

5. A project parameter description including outline specifications

6. A project estimate for the various components of construction and the mechanical and electrical systems

7. A project construction schedule which will include the design phase along with the construction phase

8. Qualifications; if exclusions or allowance items are included in the preliminary cost estimate, they should be so designated

Once the design-builder has reached this state of design development, and on the basis of their past experience, they should be able to "guarantee" the budget included in their proposal within tolerances of 10 percent plus or minus. In order for a proposal such as this to be prepared, there will have to be some expenditure for preliminary design work. For that and a few other reasons, a letter of authorization should be obtained from the client prior to beginning the budget proposal work. The letter of authorization will commit the client to reimburse the design-builder for the cost of any preliminary design work if the project is abandoned at a later date. The cost of the initial design work will be reasonable; a client who is reluctant to authorize the small expenditure required probably does not have a very firm commitment to the project. That is another reason for requesting a letter of authorization—to weed out the inquisitive from the truly interested.

The start of a design-build proposal

Now that some of the design-build ground rules have been explained, let's get back to that hypothetical proposal and follow a project from start to contract. The salesman for Construction Consultants, a design-build company, has convinced client Thomas Rodgers of Western Industries, that their company should be selected to develop a design-build proposal for a 32,000-ft^2 speculative office building to be built on Rodgers' 4.5-acre suburban site located on Route 66 and Treadwell Street in Woodbridge, Connecticut. Construction Consultants' president, Sidney M. Levy, will be submitting a request for a letter of authorization whereby Western Industries will agree to commit $5000 for preliminary design work so that a budget cost proposal can be formulated. In the event that the project does not proceed beyond the budget proposal stage, no additional monies will be requested by Construction Consultants and the design documents produced to that point will belong to the client. If the project proceeds to a higher level of design work, and finally to contract, the initial design fees will be incorporated in the final design costs.

Once the initial letter of authorization has been executed by the client, a design team can be assembled and the preliminary drawings can be started on the basis of the client's needs and the initial cost parameters mutually agreed on. A typical letter of authorization is shown in Fig. 12.1. The object of this budget proposal is to convert design and budget data to some form of documentation so that there is consensual agreement between client and design-builder that the building program has been properly interpreted to date. The goal is to obtain acceptance of the initial design and corresponding cost information so that the design-builder can obtain authorization to proceed to the next level of design and cost refinement.

Submission of a budget proposal

Once all the preliminary design work has been received from the design-builder's design consultants and has been developed along the path of cost parameters given to each consultant, a presentation must be made to the clients to convey all the information to them. The manner in which the information is transmitted is very important. A slipshod, amateurish presentation is bound to convey a similar impression of competence. Some care should be taken in the preparation of the proposal so that it has a professional look about it. The proposal could incorporate photographs of similar projects, a brief description of the design-build company history, biographical information on key personnel who will be working with the client, and a list of successfully completed design-build projects. Along with this sales-oriented material, the contents of a budget proposal for the Western Industries project is shown in the following pages, although not all the documents included in the Table of Contents are illustrated in this sample presentation.

The Next Step in the Process

After the budget proposal has been accepted, the next step in the design-build process is to obtain an authorization to proceed with more detailed design drawings, which in turn will allow a more definite construction budget to be assembled. When the budget proposal was submitted, it contained design criteria and a projected building cost of $2,065,000 plus or minus 10 percent, representing costs ranging from $1,858,500 to $2,271,500. With more detailed drawings, the cost of the project can be determined more exactly and the guaranteed price will not need to contain a plus or minus factor.

A project of the size and nature of the Western Office Building, even though it is not complex, may still require a complete site plan, including a site utility drawing for review by local authorities and utility companies. As far as architectural drawings are concerned, a floor plan with a finish schedule, exterior elevations, and a typical wall section will be needed. A structural drawing containing a typical bay framing plan will also be required. Mechanical and electrical drawings are not essential inasmuch as the systems they will contain are really not needed in order to establish

CONSTRUCTION CONSULTANTS

22 PROSPECT COURT   WOODBRIDGE, CONNECTICUT 06525
(203) 397-3598

INITIAL LETTER OF AUTHORIZATION TO SUBMIT A BUDGET PROPOSAL

March 1, 1993

Mr. Thomas Rodgers
President
Western Industries
555 Longacre Road
Bethmoor, Connecticut 06555

Dear Mr. Rodgers:

We appreciated the time you spent with Jim Benajamin and myself on February 28, 1993, and we wish to thank you for selecting our company to develop a design-build proposal to construct a 32,000 square foot office building in Woodbridge, Connecticut.

This letter, when executed by both parties, will be authorization for our company to proceed with preliminary design so that a budget for the project may be established. The cost of this initial design work will not exceed $5,000.00. If the project advances to contract, this payment will be applied against the total design fees.

We look forward to the beginning of a successful relationship with your company, and will proceed with the design work as soon as you have executed this agreement.

With best regards,

Sidney M. Levy

_____
For Western Industries
Mr. Thomas Rodgers its President

Figure 12.1 A typical budget proposal initial letter of authorization.

A BUDGET PROPOSAL FOR
WESTERN INDUSTRIES INCORPORATED

TABLE of CONTENTS

THE PROJECT PARAMETERS FOR
THE WESTERN OFFICE BUILDING

BUDGET PROPOSAL

1. THE SITE

The project will be located on land owned by Western Industries and located on the corner of Route 66 and Treadwell Street in Woodbridge, Connecticut. The total area of the site is 4.5 acres, and it is anticipated that 2.45 acres will be disturbed. Parking for 120 cars is planned.

2. THE BUILDING

The building will be 32,000 ft^2 on one level, subdivided for a two-tenant occupancy— 16,000 ft^2 for each tenant.

   A. *Structure:* Structural-steel columns and beams with bar joists and metal roof deck. Bay sizes to be 24' by 36'.

   B. *Exterior Wall Construction:* Non-load-bearing. Brick veneer on exterior gypsum sheathing and steel stud framing. Windows to be nonoperative. $1^{1}/_{2}$" insulating glass in anodized aluminum frames. Total height of building to be 16' 4". Ceiling height to be 10' 4".

   C. *Floor Slab:* Concrete 4" thick, 3000 lb/in^2, with wire-mesh reinforcement.

   D. *Roofing:* Single-ply EPDM type with insulating value of R-32.

   E. *Finishes:* Ceilings to be 2'×2' acoustical lay-in except in utility rooms. Walls to be $^{5}/_{8}$" Fire Code Sheetrock on $3^{1}/_{2}$" steel studs. Walls taped, prime-painted, and two finish coats applied.
   Floors: In office area, carpeted. (See Allowance section.)
   Toilet areas: Acoustical tile ceilings, ceramic tile floors, and walls to wainscot height, painted above.
   Mechanical and Utility Rooms: Painted concrete floors, painted gypsum board walls, ceilings as required.

   F. *Electrical System:* One 600-A panel for each 16,000-ft^2 area, plus a third house panel. Lighting to be 2' × 2' recessed troffers to provide 80 foot-candles in office areas. Emergency lighting, exit lighting to meet codes. Telephone conduit from street to electric closet only. Exterior and site lighting as required.

   G. *Mechanical:* HVAC. Two gas-fired hot-water boilers and perimeter hot-water baseboard heat. Air-conditioning via two rooftop units. Ductwork and diffusers for open office space only. Plumbing. Toilet facilities for 150 people, including handicapped. Roof drains (internal) as required. Four electric water coolers. Sprinkler system. Sprinkler throughout to meet NFPA requirements for light hazard occupancy.

THE PROGRAM SCHEDULE
FOR WESTERN OFFICE BUILDING

Initial Letter of Authorization	March 1, 1993
Submission of Budget Proposal	March 15, 1993
Acceptance of Budget Proposal	March 25, 1993
Letter of Authorization for Preparation of Contract Proposal	March 28, 1993
Submission of Contract Proposal	April 28, 1993
Acceptance of Contract Proposal	May 15, 1993
Contract Signing	May 18, 1993
Structural Steel Ordered	May 20, 1993
Application for Building Permit	May 25, 1993
Owner Review and Approval of Final Plans and Specifications	June 1, 1993
Sitework Start	June 5, 1993
Foundation Work Start	June 25, 1993
Structural Steel Erection Start	August 1, 1993
Building Enclosed	November 15, 1993
Building Complete	February 1, 1994

THE COST BREAKDOWN—BUDGET PROPOSAL—
WESTERN OFFICE BUILDING

1. Sitework, site utilities, paving, landscaping (see Allowance) $200,000
2. Building Envelope
   Foundations, structural steel, exterior walls, roof, windows,
   fascia, soffits $900,000
3. Interior Finishes
   Floor finishes, wall construction—interior, wall finishes,
   doors and hardware, ceilings, tile work $225,000
4. Mechanical and Electrical Systems
   Plumbing fixtures, roof drains, HVAC, switchgear, light
   fixtures, controls, sprinkler system $600,000

Total construction cost	$1,925,000
Design Fees	140,000
Total Project Cost	$2,065,000

LIST OF ALLOWANCES/EXCLUSIONS—
BUDGET PROPOSAL—WESTERN OFFICE BUILDING

List of Allowances

1. Landscaping, seeding, and sod $20,000
2. Carpet: 3000 yd^2 @ $20.00   60,000

(Continued)

3. Signage: exterior and interior   4,500
4. Finish hardware   3,500
5. Brick allowance for materials only,
   $200 per 1000 bricks   ----
6. Utility company charges, all   3,000

All the above allowances are included in the Cost Breakdown.

LIST OF EXCLUSIONS

1. Window treatment—blinds and drapes
2. Interior partitions other than those shown on floor plan
3. Security system
4. Internal telephone conduit and wiring
5. Tenant improvements
6. Rock excavation and other unforeseen subsurface conditions
7. Land costs

closer tolerance costs. Quite possibly, additional authorization for design development of $35,000 to $50,000 should produce enough drawings that, in combination with the design-builder's cost data base, will permit the assembling of a very close tolerance estimate.

The Contract Proposal

When the authorization for further design development is obtained from the client, a contract proposal can be formulated.

Contents of the contract proposal

The contract proposal contains the following elements:

1. A covering letter

2. Table of contents

3. A project description, which will be more detailed than the project parameter description contained in the budget proposal

4. A list of drawings and possibly reduced-size drawings to be incorporated directly into the contract proposal

5. The project schedule

6. The project cost breakdown

7. A list of allowances, alternates, and exclusions

8. Information about the design-build company, photographs of similar projects, biographical information about the company's key people, and possibly a list of the personnel directly involved in the project and the roles they will play

The sample contract proposal shown on the following pages includes

1. The covering letter

2. The table of contents

3. The project description

4. The project schedule (in narrative form, not bar-chart format)

5. A list of drawings (this sample does not include any drawings, but they would be included in an actual proposal)

6. The cost breakdown

7. The list of allowances and exclusions

The other items to be assembled, such as the reduced working drawings, list of previous projects and clients, photographs, company biographies, and other marketing-related items will not be illustrated. The covering letter is reproduced in Fig. 12.2.

Sitework, site improvements, and site utilities

Items in this cost category have been predicated on estimates for rough grading of the 4.5-acre site owned by Western Industries on Route 66 and Treadwell Street, Woodbridge, Connecticut and includes the following:

1. *Clearing.*   Clearing of approximately 2.45 acres, removal of all trees and stumps off-site.

2. *Topsoil excavation.*   Stripping and storing all topsoil within the disturbed area, and respreading prior to seeding, sodding, and landscaping.

3. *Mass excavation.*   All cutting, filling, and compacting of earthwork required to obtain the finish-grade contours shown on the site plan. Any off-site material required is included in this cost category.

4. *Bituminous paving and curbs.*   Preparation of the subbase, grading, compaction of process base material, and a two-course application of bituminous concrete paving consisting of a 2" binder course and a

CONSTRUCTION CONSULTANTS
22 PROSPECT COURT   WOODBRIDGE, CONNECTICUT 06525
(203) 397-3598

THE COVER LETTER ACCOMPANYING THE CONTRACT PROPOSAL

April 24, 1993

Mr. Thomas Rodgers
President
Western Industries
555 Longacre Road
Bethmoor, Connecticut 06555

Dear Mr. Rodgers:

We enclose our Contract Proposal pertaining to the construction of a new 32,000 square foot office building to be located on your property in Woodbridge, Connecticut.

This proposal incorporates all of the building requirements you have conveyed to our office and, with your approval, the next step is to proceed at once to the completion of the construction drawings. Incorporated into our proposal is a schedule showing the major steps and corresponding dates necessary to complete your new facility by February 1, 1993.

It is our intention, if you accept the terms and conditions of this proposal, to prepare a formal contract to be executed on or about May 18, 1993. If you do not feel that this is practical, we recommend that you authorize us to continue to complete the drawings for construction at a cost not to exceed the design fees stipulated in Section 3 of our Proposal.

We very much appreciate the opportunity you have given us to work with your company and look forward to the start of construction in the near future.

With best regards,

Sidney M. Levy
President

Figure 12.2   Typical format for contract proposal covering letter.

THE CONTRACT PROPOSAL

TABLE OF CONTENTS

THE PROJECT DESCRIPTION—THE WESTERN INDUSTRIES OFFICE BUILDING

CONTRACT PROPOSAL

The following building description will elaborate on the components of construction for the 32,000-ft^2 office building contemplated to be built for Western Industries.

In an attempt to define the scope of work included in each cost category of the Cost Breakdown in Section 6 of this proposal, this description will contain sufficient detail of the components. Specific types of materials as well as the quality and manner of workmanship will be more adequately defined in the Construction Specifications when they are prepared, completed, and submitted for review and approval.

Included in the Cost Breakdown in Section 6 are the General Conditions related to the entire project. These General Conditions costs relate to the temporary facilities needed during construction, the energy consumption during construction, costs related to the job superintendent, the field office, payroll taxes, insurance, and permits required for construction.

Note. If project management costs, or other significant costs, are generally included in this category by your company, they should be so noted in this description of General Conditions.

$1\frac{1}{2}$" finish course. Bituminous curbing to be provided on both sides of the entrance driveway and around the perimeter of the parking lot. Line striping, handicapped parking space designations, and traffic lanes also to be provided.

5. *Topsoil replacement.* If the amount of topsoil stripped and stockpiled is insufficient to do the job, off-site materials will be supplied as required at no extra cost to the contract.

6. *Fine grading and seeding.* All areas to be seeded will be fine-graded, limed, fertilized as required, and then seeded. The lawn will be maintained by the contractor through two mowings only.

7. *Planting.* An allowance of $20,000 has been provided for the purchase and planting of all landscape materials.

8. *Water and site service.* Underground installation of domestic and fire service requirements will be provided to meet local authority and underwriter approvals. Costs include tap-in charges and other related fees.

9. *Sanitary sewer system.* A line from the existing city sewer in Route 66 will be brought into the site and connected to the sanitary line emanating from the building. Any manholes required are included. Connection fees are also included.

10. *Storm drainage.* A network of drainage pipe and catch basins accepting surface water from the paved areas is included. Roof drains are tied into the drainage system, which is connected to the existing system in Route 66. All fees relating to the work are included.

11. *Gas service.* An underground main will be installed by the local gas company to a meter which the company will install on a concrete pad provided by the contractor. This gas service will be connected to the building lines.

12. *Electrical and telephone service.* Underground electrical service will be provided to a pad-mounted transformer at the rear of the building. Underground telephone empty conduit only will be installed from the street to the telephone closet inside the building.

13. *Concrete walks, stairs, and miscellaneous pads.* Concrete walks will be provided in locations shown on the drawings. Concrete ramps, stairs, and curb cuts to meet existing ADA requirements will be provided as shown. Any concrete pads for gas and electrical transformers will also be provided. All such concrete will be 4000-lb/in^2 concrete.

Concrete work. Footings to be designed for 2 tons/ft^2 bearing capacity. Foundation walls to be reinforced concrete. Footings and walls to be 3000-lb/in^2 concrete. Slab on grade to be 4" concrete, 3000 lb/in^2 with welded wire-mesh reinforcing.

Masonry. The exterior wall section of the building will be constructed of an architectural face brick veneer attached to a steel stud framing backup. This steel stud framework will have a face of exterior-grade gypsum sheathing. Galvanized cavity wall masonry ties will secure the brick veneer to the steel stud framework. Sufficient insulation will be placed in this wall assembly to meet or exceed all state and local energy conservation codes.

Windows, glass, and glazing. Glass at all exterior elevations to be Low-E 1^1/$_2$" insulating type and set into anodized aluminum frames. Interior glass panels at vestibules shall be clear tempered glass. Toilet room mirrors are included.

Fascia and exterior soffit construction. A continuous 6' 0"-wide overhang will be constructed around the entire building. The fascia and soffit of the overhang will be faced with "V" groove cedar boards and stained with a transparent stain.

Roofing. The roofing membrane shall be a single-ply EPDM material. Related sheet-metal work and flashings to be 0.040 aluminum, mill finish. Roofing insulation to meet or exceed all local and state energy conservation codes will be installed. The entire roof assembly will have an unconditional 10-year labor and materials warranty.

Interior partitions, doors, and hardware.

1. Interior partitions to be 25-gauge steel stud partitions extended to the underside of the deck; sheetrock to be ^{5}/$_8$" Fire Code

2. Doors to all interior spaces except mechanical and utility rooms to be solid-core, oak veneer, stain grade, hung in hollow metal frames; doors and frames to utility and mechanical rooms to be hollow metal.

3. Finish hardware is included (see Allowance list)

Finishes. Carpeting to be installed throughout the office area (see Allowance list). Toilet rooms to have 1" × 1" mosaic tile floors and 4" × 4" ceramic tile walls to wainscot height. Ceramic tile in standard colors only. Utility rooms to have painted concrete floors. Acoustical ceilings throughout office area to be 2' × 2' grid lay-in type. Armstrong Second Look will be the standard of quality.

Painting. All gypsum wallboard surfaces to be prime-coated and given two finish coats of eggshell alkyd enamel. All metal door frames to have two finish coats of eggshell enamel. Interior wood doors to be stained and sealed.

Plumbing. Roof drainage to be via interior drains connected to the site storm system. Storm sewer pipe under the slab to be cast-iron, extra-heavy-weight. Plumbing fixtures to include 10 wall-mounted water closets, 2 wall mounted urinals, 12 lavatories, 2 slop sinks, and an electric water heater in each toilet room; one interior floor drain in each toilet room and one in the mechanical room. There will be two outdoor, frost-proof sill cocks. All water closets and urinals to have flush valves. Fixture layout and design to comply with ADA. All overhead hot- and cold-water piping to be insulated.

HVAC. There will be one cast-iron boiler for each half of the building. From each boiler, water will be circulated to hot-water baseboard radiation around the perimeter of the building. A unit heater above the ceiling will provide heat to interior spaces during the morning warm-up cycle. Air conditioning will be provided by one gas-fire rooftop unit for each half of the building. Distribution ductwork with variable-air-volume controls will be installed for an open-office environment. Exhaust fans will be provided for toilet exhaust.

Fire protection. A complete underground fire protection system is included in the site utilities cost breakdown. Interior sprinkler installation is based on light hazard occupancy and open office configuration. Sprinkler heads to be of the chrome-plated, concealed type.

Electrical. The incoming electrical service will terminate at a pad-mounted transformer located in the rear of the building. The secondary service will terminate at one 600-A panel for each half of the building. There will be a house panel for exterior and miscellaneous lighting loads. The house panel will be 225 A. All panels are to be 277 V. Lighting in the office will be by 2' × 2' two-tube fluorescent fixtures providing a lighting level of 80 foot-candles. Utility and mechanical rooms will have fluorescent fixtures to provide 30-foot-candle illumination. Exit and emergency lights will be provided to meet code requirements. Power receptacles will be provided on exterior walls, 8 ft on centers, and two will be provided on each interior sheetrocked column. Exterior parking lot illumination will be provided by 20-foot-high site lights utilizing high-pressure sodium lamps.

	List of Design Drawings	
L-1	Site Layout	May 15, 1993
L-2	Site Grading and Drainage	May 15, 1993
L-3	Site Planting	May 15, 1993
A-1	Floor Plan	May 18, 1993
A-2	Building Elevations	May 18, 1993
A-3	Schedules and Details	May 18, 1993
A-4	Wall Sections	May 18, 1993
SU-1	Site Utilities	May 20, 1993
S-1	Foundation Plan	May 12, 1993
S-2	Roof Framing Plan	May 12, 1993

THE PROGRAM SCHEDULE FOR WESTERN OFFICE BUILDING

Submission of the Contract Proposal	April 25, 1993
Review and Acceptance of the Proposal	May 15, 1993
Authorization to Proceed with Design	May 15, 1993
Contract Signing	May 18, 1993
Order Structural Steel	May 20, 1993
Application for Building Permit	May 25, 1993
Review and Approval of Final Drawings	June 1, 1993
Sitework Commencement	June 5, 1993
Foundation Work Start	June 25, 1993
Structural Steel Erection Start	August 1, 1993
Building Envelope Enclosed	November 15, 1993
Building Completion and Turnover	February 1, 1994

THE COST BREAKDOWN—CONTRACT PROPOSAL— WESTERN OFFICE BUILDING

1. Sitework and site utilities, paving, seeding, and landscaping — $204,000
2. Building Envelope
   Foundations, footings, floor slabs, structural and miscellaneous metals, exterior wall system, windows, fascia, soffit construction — $944,000
3. Finishes
   Tile, toilet partitions, acoustical ceilings, carpet, hardware, interior partitions, painting — $208,000

4. Plumbing, HVAC, electrical, and sprinkler systems	$625,000
5. Design fees	$140,000
Total Project Cost	$2,121,000

Note to design-builder.   The List of Allowances and the List of Exclusions should be prepared and inserted at this point.

The obvious difference between the budget proposal and this contract proposal is the project cost. The budget proposal yielded a project cost of $2,065,000 plus or minus 10 percent. It was based on very sketchy drawings and the design-builder's data base of historical costs. As the drawings were developed further and the mechanical and electrical engineers firmed up their design, which was budgeted by the mechanical and electrical subcontractors, a more refined project cost of $2,121,000 was obtained. As indicated in the contract proposal, this represents an increase of $56,000 from the budget proposal. The client should be rather happy with this slight increase in project cost that occurred as the design progressed from its early stages.

The design-build work is still far from being over. On acceptance of the contract proposal, a formal AIA or other acceptable form of contract can be prepared. Either a lump-sum or a guaranteed-maximum-price (GMP) contract can be formulated. The contract will incorporate the contract proposal as a basis for scope definition and project cost. The contract will also contain a clause which states that the final contract drawings, when prepared, will be reviewed and approved by the client and will then become a part of the contract. Up to this date, probably no more than three or four site drawings, along with two or three architectural and a couple of structural drawings, will have been prepared and reviewed by the client. However, when the completed set of drawings has been prepared, they should be carefully reviewed with the client to ensure that all program requirements have been met. It is a good idea to have the client initial each page of the drawings to provide verification that they have been reviewed.

The construction process will start on contract signing; and since structural steel is scheduled to be ordered in a few days, the structural steel drawings must be rushed to completion. The structural-steel supplier will submit a "cutting list" to the mill as their first involvement and will await a "rolling schedule," an indication from the steel mill as to when each structural shape is scheduled to be produced. This buys the design-builder a few days or possibly a week before the steel drawings must be turned over to the fabricator so that shop drawing preparation can begin.

The Project Manager's Role

All other consultants will be requested to complete their designs so that final prices can be obtained by the design-builder. The project manager assigned to the project should set regular meeting dates with the consultants to ensure that drawing preparation is proceeding as scheduled. Another very important reason for regular meetings is to review what is being incorporated into the design drawings. Remember, at this time, that there is an actual signed contract for a specific sum of money. One of the project manager's most critical tasks is to make certain that the drawings and specifications being developed are consistent with the scope of work and the budgets established for each component of construction contained in the contract cost proposal. Unexpected things have a way of creeping into the design development and must be kept under control.

In design-build work, the cost of drawing reproduction can be considerable. Progress drawings created by the architect will be sent to the structural, mechanical, and electrical engineers for informational and coordination purposes. Conversely, mechanical and electrical drawings will be transmitted to the architect for review and comment. If subcontractors have been asked to become involved in the design-build development and budget cycle, they will also need progress drawings. The project manager's responsibility in the design-build process takes on another critical aspect at this juncture. Being aware of the client's requirements and expectations and also of the restraints and constraints imposed by the construction budget, the project manager has to ensure that both obligations are being met. As each building component is developed on the drawings and in the specifications, a careful review of corresponding costs is necessary. Hopefully, there will be a balance of over-budget items and under-budget items that together will maintain the integrity of the budget.

The completed design development represented on the drawings will be reviewed by the client and approved prior to formal issuance of the drawings. When the project manager is satisfied that the drawings meet the client's requirements and are within the confines of the construction budget, the drawings are reviewed by the client, who will initial each drawing to indicate acceptance of the contents. It is, however, not enough to merely have the client look at each drawing and initial it. To avoid possible misunderstandings at a later date, each drawing should be explained by the project manager. Starting with the site drawings, the locations of walks, stairs, grade changes, walls, and site utilities should be reviewed and clarified. Parking configurations, areas to be seeded or sodded, and the basic landscape plan can also be explained. The structural drawings will probably be of little concern to the client, who will assume that their design is adequate.

Time should be spent reviewing the architectural drawings in some detail and pointing out the various finishes on walls, floors, and ceilings. The client probably is not adept at interpreting drawings and may sign off on a drawing without really knowing what it contains. For example, the client may be surprised to learn that the wall tile in the toilet rooms does not extend to the ceiling because no one explained what the term *wainscot height* means.

Now is the time to work out any misunderstandings over what is or what is not included in the drawings. If there are disparities between the quality and types of finishes included in the drawings and what was anticipated or perceived to be included by the client, there is probably still some time to make some tradeoffs. There is an old maxim which many builders have yet to accept, "The customer is always right." If this saying is implemented with moderation, the final stages of development and clarification can produce a satisfied client and a successful contract.

13

Safety in Construction

Rapid readers will complete this chapter in about 10 minutes, during which time, statistically speaking, two fellow workers in the construction industry will die as a result of an industrial accident and 170 others will have sustained an accident resulting in a disabling job-incurred injury. Extrapolating on the number of job-related deaths and injuries reported in previous years, approximately 3000 construction workers will be fatally injured in 1993, and more than 0.5 million more will suffer some form of on-the-job injury. What better reason to enforce an already established safety program, or immediately lay plans to initiate one? The soaring cost of Workman's Compensation insurance and commercial liability insurance is another reason why all contractors should look to a well-balanced, consistently enforced safety program as part of their normal business operations. And finally, the increased fines established by OSHA, effective November 1990, make it imperative that a general contractor police each and every job site in order to avoid, what in some cases could be, a financially crippling fine.

The Occupational Safety and Health Act (OSHA)

In 1970, the U.S. Congress passed the Williams-Steiger Occupational Safety and Health Act, referred to now as simply *OSHA*. The rules and regulations set up by OSHA are regulated and enforced by the U.S. Department of Labor, Occupational Safety and Health Administration Division. Over the past two decades many states have also enacted industrial safety legislation that parallels many of the safety regulations contained in the 1970 Act. In 1990, OSHA announced the establishment of a separate Construction and Engineering Division, and in November of that year President George Bush signed the Omnibus Budget Reconciliation Act, which included, among other provisions, substantially increased monetary penalties for OSHA violations. These increased fines, which took effect on March 21, 1991, were meant to be a further attempt to reduce construction deaths and injuries.

Civil penalty violation	Penalty assessed before March 21, 1991	Penalty assessed after March 21, 1991
Serious or other-than serious	$1,000 maximum	$7,000 maximum
Posting requirement	$1,000 maximum	$7,000 maximum
Failure to abate violation	$1,000/day maximum	$7,000/day maximum
Willful	(No such category)	$70,000 maximum

The Construction Safety Program

A basic safety program consists of the following components:

1. Organization of the program
2. Administration of the program
   a. As it relates to the company's employees
   b. As it relates to subcontractors employed at the job site
3. Training and safety meetings
4. Emergency-situation procedures
5. Accident reporting requirements
6. Job safety standards
7. Fire prevention policies

Organization of a safety program

The first step in organizing a safety program is to obtain the commitment from top management to the program and the selection of a safety director or administrator to be the focal point for all safety-related matters. The safety director's first priority will be to develop the safety program, and this can be done in concert with consultants from the company's insurance carrier. Construction trade organizations such as the Associated General Contractors of America (AGC) and the Associated Builders and Contractors (ABC) can provide a great deal of information pertaining to safety programs.

Not only do rules and regulations have to be established, but a procedure for administering the program has to be put in place. The flow of safety procedures should be from the safety director to the general field superintendent to the job superintendent to the various crew foremen and then to the field workers. The project manager's role will be as a staff member who will see to it that the safety regulations are being implemented and complied with during job-site visits.

Along with the safety regulations and reporting procedures, there should be a process whereby accident reports are reviewed to determine the cause of the accident and ways in which future occurrences can be prevented. There must be a specific disciplinary process which will be put in force if accidents occur because of blatant disregard for established safety rules. The disciplinary action can be in the form of a verbal warning, backed up with a written confirmation, or a written notice, copies of both to be placed in the employee's personnel file. After a certain number of warnings, or in the case of a serious breach of safety, further action will be taken, up to and including discharge. With regard to subcontractors, the rules and regulations might have to be modified somewhat. All subcontractors should be requested to submit their safety programs for approval prior to working on the site. The subcontractor should be requested to designate a safety representative so that all safety-related instructions can be directed to this person.

Creating a set of safety rules and regulations

The company safety rules should be distributed to all employees and a set posted in each field office. Included in the rules and regulations must be the procedure for reporting violations and the corresponding disciplinary action to be taken. Disgruntled employees have been known to institute lawsuits on the basis of what they perceive as wrongful discharge, and if an employee is dismissed for repeated safety violations without being aware that rules have been violated, the company may end up with a legal battle. Before posting the new set of safety rules, copies should be distributed to all workers and to each subcontractor safety designee, and this should be followed by a job-site meeting to explain the new rules and regulations and field any questions. Some companies request that all attendees sign a copy of the safety rules indicating that the rules have been explained to them, they understand the rules, and agree to abide by them. Copies of this agreement will be placed in the employee's personnel file.

A typical set of safety rules and regulations should encompass, as a minimum, the following topics:

1. A poster containing a list of emergency telephone numbers to be determined and filled in prior to the commencement of work on the site: ambulance, paramedics, emergency service numbers, nearest

hospital with emergency room facilities to include address and directions, fire department and police department or 911 service if available

2. Personal protective equipment and policies:

Hard hats—worn at all times on entering the site, except when a specific directive is issued by the job superintendent (such as working in a fully occupied building performing nonhazardous work, i.e., touch-up painting, floor tile repairs, etc.

Goggles, safety glasses or face shields—mandatory when drilling, burning, cutting, grinding, sawing, jack hammering

Ear plugs and respirators when prescribed by the job superintendent

Gloves when handling rough lumber or materials that can splinter, metal with burrs or sharp edges or when other conditions warrant their use

Shirts worn *at all times.* The wearing of 100% synthetic materials by anyone engaged in burning, welding, or using open flames will be strictly prohibited. (If this kind of clothing catches fire, it will continue to smolder until removed from the victim. Wool or cotton will self extinguish when ignited.)

Shoes—safety toe shoes are preferable. Sneakers or running shoes will not be permitted. Shoe laces must be tied *at all times.*

Radios—if permitted at all, are to be kept on low volume. No walkman-type radio or tape player with ear plugs will be permitted on the job.

Raingear and protective footgear will be worn when inclement weather warrants.

3. Safety check of tools and equipment:

Tools that do not operate properly will not be used.

Electric tools with frayed cords must either be repaired or not operated at all.

Cutting tools such as chisels, hatchets, or hammers with mushroom heads cannot be used since they are the cause of injuries from flying metal chips when these mushroom heads shatter.

Cables, chains, hoists, lifting equipment will be checked daily for visual defects.

4. Electrical safety check:

Ground-fault protection to be in operation at all times.

Safety guards on electrical equipment cannot be removed or blocked open.

When checking or repairing any piece of electrical equipment, it must always be *unplugged* first.

Extension cords should not be placed on the floor without planks on each side to prevent a tripping hazard. A preferable location would be to suspend them at least 7 ft overhead.

5. Power-actuated tools:

Power-actuated tools should not be operated by anyone who has not been qualified in their use.

Tools to be inspected daily before use, and prior to being put away at the end of the day. Defective tools are to be taken out of use. Loaded tools must never be left unattended.

Workers in areas adjacent to where these tools are to be used shall be notified as to exact location of their use.

6. A hazardous material checklist should include:

Gasoline and other flammable materials, stored in factory-sealed containers or approved safety containers.

Oxygen cylinders stored at least 25 ft away from other types of cylinder gas and secured properly.

In storage, all cylinder gases should have safety caps installed.

When transporting cylinder gases, they are to be properly secured in special carriers designed for that purpose.

All gas cylinders are to be kept away from open flames and welding operations.

When using acid-based cleaners or other corrosive liquids, their containers are to be secured with proper closures.

7. Ladders and scaffolding:

All ladders to be inspected daily and prior to use.

Field-made ladders are to be constructed of sound lumber only. Broken cleats or rungs on existing ladders are to be replaced before use, or taken out of service. Wood ladders are not to be painted, as this causes them to become slippery.

Ladders must have a firm footing and are to be secured to the structure so they extend 3 ft above a landing.

Pipe scaffolding is to be properly cross-braced and tied back to the structure. Scaffolding planks are to be sound and of the proper width, length, and thickness.

Scaffolding "Release" forms should be signed by any subcontractor using the general contractor's scaffolding.

8. Floor and perimeter openings:

   All open stairwells are to have temporary railings until permanent ones have been installed.

   Perimeter railings and cables and toeboards are to be installed on all elevated floors before workers are allowed on those floors.

   All floor openings are to be covered completely or barricaded to prevent anyone from falling through them. If a worker removes any temporary protection in order to install or perform work, it will be replaced immediately when that work has been completed.

9. Fire protection:

   Every effort is to be made to extend a water main into a new site as quickly as possible in case it is needed for emergency purposes.

   Every worker operating welding equipment, cutting torches, or soldering with open flame must post a fire extinguisher in the immediate area before these operations can begin. No open fire will be permitted on the job site at any time. Temporary heating equipment must be installed only with the approval of the superintendent. No heaters with open flames can be in operation without an attendant on the site or in the building.

10. Disciplinary action for safety violators—causes for suspension:

    Anyone violating OSHA regulations or company safety rules and regulations

    Any worker reporting for work intoxicated

    Any worker found using alcoholic beverages or controlled substances on the site

    Horseplay

    Fighting or provoking a fight

    Failure to report an accident in which the worker was involved

Note. The word *suspension* is used rather than dismissal. If an employee is wrongfully discharged for a safety violation, the potential for a lawsuit is created. It is wiser to suspend an employee either caught in the act or accused of a serious violation until an investigation can be conducted and produce enough evidence to support or refute the accusation. There have been cases where someone appeared to be intoxicated when actually they were having a reaction to a prescription drug. When a set of company rules has been prepared and distributed to workers at the first job-site meeting, the project manager should have everyone attending this meeting sign a form acknowledging that they have received the program, it had been explained to them, they understand the rules and regulations, and agree to abide by them. Such a statement can be added to the last page of the safety program as follows:

Date: _____ Project: _____

I, _____(Name)_____ state that I have received and read the Safety Rules and Regulations presented to me on this date and that I understand and agree to abide by them,

_____   _____
(Employee's signature)   (Superintendent's signature)

Administration of the safety program

The safety director or coordinator has the responsibility to delegate authority for the administration of the safety program, which will include the following:

1. Designate the job superintendent as the person responsible for the day-to-day enforcement of the safety program at the job site.

2. Appoint the project manager or designee as the individual who will conduct the initial job orientation safety meeting and also conduct monthly job safety meetings thereafter.

3. Require that the safety director be notified immediately of all accidents of a serious nature and/or job-site safety violations so that the appropriate action can be taken.

4. Personally investigate accidents of a serious nature and, when the facts are developed, report findings to all concerned parties.

5. Establish procedures to deal with repeated offenders or accident-prone individuals.

6. Provide all subcontractors employed on the project with safety program information and obtain their written agreement to abide by all these rules and regulations.

Preparing a company safety manual

The basic safety manual should initially be a draft instead of a finished product. In that way, it can be distributed to the field for review and comment on clarity and whether all points have been covered adequately. The manual can be discussed at a company training session, at which time suggestions can be solicited from the people attending the meeting. If certain provisions of the manual are unclear and confusing, now is the time to make revisions. When all the comments and suggestions have been reviewed, a final copy can be printed and distributed to all company personnel.

Emergency procedures

Incorporated in the safety manual should be a section dealing with emergency procedures. When a superintendent is assigned to a new job, emergency procedures for that particular job are to be established within the first 72 hours. The nearest hospital with emergency room facilities is to be located. The address and phone number of the hospital are to be posted and clear directions to the hospital included. A call to the emergency room alerting their personnel to any unusual hazards that may be encountered during construction will also be helpful. Local fire and police department locations should be posted along with their telephone numbers, if the community does not have a 911 system in operation. It is a good idea to conduct a dry run to the local hospital so that in the case of an emergency, the quickest route will have been established.

Personnel training

Safety procedures require skills that must be learned, and it is unfair to assign responsibility for safety practices and enforcement to a job superintendent who has little or no training in safety techniques. Few people would wholeheartedly participate in a program if they did not fully understand how to handle the responsibility that comes with the authority.

Training can be accomplished in several ways. Safety seminars can be held at each job site, or all participants in the administration of the program can congregate in one location for instruction. Insurance underwriters are usually most anxious to conduct, or at least participate in, these sessions. All superintendents should be encouraged to enroll in Red Cross first-aid courses and coronary pulmonary resuscitation (CPR) courses.

Safety meetings

In order for a safety program to be effective, people have to be constantly reminded of good safety practices, and they have to be aware of job and company accident records. One approach to heightening that awareness is to conduct regular safety meetings at the site. These meetings, known as "toolbox meetings," can be conducted by either the job superintendent or the project manager. They should be held on company time and not after hours. It will be necessary to obtain the permission of all subcontractors to include their workers in these meetings. At the initial meeting, the purpose and objective of the safety program should be announced, the program explained, and the ground rules for safety practices set forth. An agenda should be prepared beforehand and used for all subsequent meetings and include the following points:

1. The previous meeting will be reviewed to briefly summarize what was discussed.

2. Any accidents or injuries which occurred after the last meeting will be reviewed.

3. The job superintendent's findings during random inspections made since the last meeting will be reported.

4. Comments, suggestions, and criticisms, as they relate to safety, will be solicited form all attendees.

5. If at all possible, written minutes of the meetings will be prepared and distributed.

It is worthwhile to discuss one specific safety procedure or safety problem at each toolbox meeting. The meetings should be made as interesting as possible so that they will not be looked on as a chore. If outside consultants or safety experts can be brought in from time to time, that will be helpful. Contests with prizes can also help to keep safety in the forefront of everyone's mind. The main idea is to try to keep the meetings from becoming boring.

Housekeeping and safety

Good housekeeping is essential if safety programs are to succeed. Conversely, if a job is littered with materials and debris is strewn all over the place, it will surely be an accident just waiting to happen. Most subcontract agreements contain provisions for subcontractors to clean their own debris and either remove it from the site or deposit it in a dumpster provided by the general contractor. These contractual provisions must be rigidly enforced. If a subcontractor, after having been given a reasonable period of time to clean up his debris, fails to do so, the job superintendent, after consulting with the project manager, should clean the area in question as quickly as possible and prepare a backcharge for the subcontractor's foreman to sign.

Housekeeping also involves the proper storage areas for materials not only on the site but also within the building. Materials of the general contractor and subcontractors must be stored so that proper access to the various portions of the building can be maintained. Areas where workers congregate for coffee breaks, or where lunches are eaten, should be provided with trash barrels so that bags, cups, and the like can be disposed of easily. These areas must be policed on a regular basis and barrels emptied.

Whenever oil, grease, or other liquids are accidentally spilled, they must be cleaned up promptly so that a tripping or slipping hazard is avoided or, in the case of a flammable liquid, a fire hazard is eliminated.

Temporary lighting within a building under construction is a very important element of safety. Electrical subcontract agreements usually contain provisions for the installation and maintenance of temporary lighting. Not only do temporary lights have to be installed, but they should be sufficient in number and intensity to provide acceptable levels of lighting in all work areas and access ways to these works areas. If there is reluctance on the part of the electrical subcontractor to provide adequate temporary lighting, prompt action is required to correct the situation before an accident occurs.

Fire protection

Fire prevention and fire protection go hand in hand with safety procedures, but they introduce some other and rather specific criteria. As in the safety program, when a job superintendent is working in an unfamiliar area, the nearest local fire department should be located and the emergency telephone number posted in the field office. When working in a rural area, there may not be a local fire department but one that serves several areas.

The question of fire prevention relates to three specific job-site areas:

1. The actual structure under construction

2. The site and areas adjacent to the structure

3. Construction office and storage trailers and shanties

Precautions required inside the building. The following are potential fire hazards in buildings under construction:

1. Electrical fires caused by defective extension cords or defective electrical tools and/or equipment

2. Trash fires caused by cigarettes, cigars, or open flames coming in contact with paper products or other readily combustible materials

3. Combustible construction materials catching fire because of their proximity to welding or sweat-soldering operations

4. Spontaneous combustion caused by improperly stored waste materials

5. The use of temporary heaters with open flames that are either out of adjustment, improperly connected, or too close to combustible materials.

To prevent fires from occurring, the following fire prevention regulations should be incorporated into the company safety manuals and reviewed at the first job-site safety meeting:

1. All temporary electric power and lights must be installed in strict accordance with existing local codes.

2. All electrical extension cords and electrical tools must comply with OSHA standards. (Even if this statement had been included in the safety manual under another section, it is worth repeating in the fire prevention portion of the manual.)

3. Fire extinguishers shall be placed throughout the building as required. Anyone caught tampering with or removing fire extinguishers from the building may be subject to immediate suspension.

4. Fifty-five-gallon steel drums, filled with water and equipped with two 5-gallon plastic pails, may be required inside the building if the job superintendent deems it necessary.

5. Any subcontractor using welding equipment or any other equipment with an open flame must have a 20-lb ABC-type fire extinguisher in

the immediate area. A fire watch must be continued for at least one hour after the operation has been completed.

6. All fuel and flammable liquids must be stored in Underwriters Laboratories (UL)-rated containers.

7. Readily combustible packing materials such as paper, cardboard, and wood must be removed from the building by the end of the workday and placed in designated trash containers.

8. Temporary heat involving open flames must be turned off at the end of the normal work day unless supervision is provided after regular working hours.

9. Open fires in drums will not be permitted within the building.

10. Pressurized gas cylinders must be provided with safety caps. Cylinders are to be stored and secured in a vertical position.

11. Oxygen and acetylene cylinders shall be secured in their carriers with a fire extinguisher attached.

Precautions to be followed on the site. The following guidelines ought to be observed to eliminate or reduce the potential for fires on the construction site:

1. No materials can be stored within 10 ft of an active fire hydrant.

2. Open fires in drums will not be permitted on the site.

3. Fire lanes are to be designated and kept free of all obstructions.

4. Periodic policing of the site is to be performed to clean up and dispose of combustible litter.

Precautions related to trailers and shanties. When there are numerous field offices, storage trailers, and shanties on a job site, each structure can present a fire hazard that affects not only one trailer but the entire trailer and storage area. A section relating to job office and material trailers and shanties should be included in the fire prevention section of the safety manual. Some of the specific regulations to be included are listed below:

1. Open fires will not be permitted within any job trailer, field office, or shanty.

2. Oily rags are to be stored in UL-approved containers only.

3. Trailer and shanty spacing shall be such that if a fire does occur, a fire hose can be played around all sides of every trailer or other structures.

4. Each trailer or shanty must be equipped with at least one 20-lb ABC-type fire extinguisher.

5. All trailers or shanties must be policed on a regular basis to prevent combustible materials from accumulating.

As when other safety regulations and procedures are in effect, the fire prevention regulations should be periodically reviewed at job-site safety meetings. Violations must be pointed out promptly and the violators given a reasonable time to take corrective action.

Compliance with OSHA Regulations

Along with the employer's desire to provide a safe place of employment, the federal government is also concerned about these issues. There are federal laws relating to the creation of a safe working environment that must be complied with. Compliance with OSHA is mandatory, and its provisions should be thoroughly understood by each project manager and job superintendent. They are summarized in the following chapter.

Chapter

14

OSHA Safety and Health Standards

The complete volume of OSHA publications is a rather cumbersome assortment of government manuals covering the industry as a whole, but only certain booklets pertain specifically to the construction industry. A telephone call to the local U.S. Department of Labor will provide the caller with information about booklets available on all aspects of OSHA regulations, including HazCom—Hazard Communication Standard and CFR 1926, a relatively new regulation dealing with trenching and excavation. One of the handiest booklets available from OSHA is *OSHA 2202*, a pocket-sized compilation of construction industry safety and health guidelines.

The Most Common OSHA Violations

Although most project managers are familiar with OSHA rules and regulations, a list of the most frequently reported violations will refresh memories. These violations are listed according to order of frequency as of 1990 when 70,859 construction-related violations were issued by OSHA (number of violations given in parentheses):

1. Hazard Communication violations—all (22,639)

2. Electrical violations: (9482)

   (*a*) Lack of ground-fault interruption (GFI) and grounding devices on all electrical equipment in service, (*b*) Frayed electrical cables on power tools, (c) Exposed wires on temporary lighting lines and lamps in these lines not protected against breakage, (d) Extension cords strung on the floor in such a manner as to constitute a tripping hazard, (e) Covers on active panels missing, (f) Covers missing on active junction boxes used for temporary power and boxes themselves not firmly secured to the structure

3. Ladders constructed of faulty materials, scaffolding improperly installed and secured (7536)

4. OSHA job-site record keeping not in place, including lack of posting of required documents and up-to-date record of accidents (5936)

5. Lack of perimeter protection on upper floors; lack of proper guarding of floor openings, slab penetrations; lack of guardrails and kickplates around stair openings; lack of fill in steel pan stairs that can create a tripping hazard; improperly installed netting when structural steel erection is in progress (5201)

6. Improperly dug, shored, or braced trench excavation (3378)

7. Workers without proper personal protection, i.e., hard hats, goggles, ear protection (2589)

8. Violations relating to cranes, derricks, and hoisting equipment (2172)

OSHA Regulations Condensed

Hazard Communication Standard—OSHA's HazCom Program

In March 1989, OSHA published a new set of regulations to alert workers to the potential dangers associated with exposure to various chemicals and hazardous materials that may be encountered on the job site. This program became known as *HazCom*, and while originally written for employees in manufacturing industries, was extended to workers in the construction industry.

The HazCom program has five parts:

1. Employers are required to establish a companywide program to prepare and disseminate information about hazardous products in use on the job site.

2. A Material Safety Data Sheet (MSDS) file is to be established and maintained.

3. An inventory of chemicals in use on the job site is to be established and maintained.

4. Hazardous materials must have the proper labels on their containers.

5. An employee training program is to be created.

The written program. Every contractor is to prepare a written program setting forth the procedures to be followed in order to comply with HazCom. One person in the organization is to be appointed administrator of the program and is responsible for, among other things, advising the job superintendent whenever a hazardous material or product has been ordered and will be shipped to the job site for the first time. The proper MSDS for that product is to be at the site prior to, or concurrent with, the arrival of the product. A copy of the company's HazCom program is to be kept on each job site.

The Material Safety Data Sheet file (MSDS). When hazardous products or materials are purchased, the vendor of these products or materials is to send a copy of the corresponding MSDS sheet to the construction company's office, from which point it will be distributed to the job site. These sheets contain instructions for the proper handling and use of the product and how it must be stored. The MSDS sheets include maximum allowance exposure rates, and first-aid and emergency instructions in case the product or material is ingested, or comes in contact with the skin or eyes.

The job superintendent should be thoroughly familiar with the data contained in the MSDS sheets and instruct fellow workers in the safe usage of the product. Copies of all MSDS sheets are to be filed at the job site.

The chemical inventory list. A list of all hazardous chemicals on a particular construction project is to be prepared and maintained at the job site. When a hazardous chemical first appears on the job site, the program administrator is to add it to that list. If a product arrives at the site and the superintendent is uncertain as to whether it is hazardous, the program administrator is to be contacted for clarification.

Container labeling. HazCom stipulates that vendors affix labels to all hazardous-material containers. The label is to contain the identity of the hazardous chemical, that part of the body that may be affected by exposure to the chemical and how the body will be affected, e.g., inhaling of fumes that may cause irritation to the lungs, exposure to skin that could cause redness and mild or severe rash, or other such warnings.

The name and address of the product manufacturer must also appear on the label. If a portion of the product is transferred to another container, that container must have a label affixed to it with the same information as the original container's label. If containers of suspected hazardous materials show up on the job site without this kind of label, the program administrator must be promptly notified so the product can be correctly identified and labeled.

Employee training. A company training program has to be set up to acquaint employees with all aspects of the program and alert them to the dangers inherent in the use of certain products. Employees must become familiar with the physical and health hazards associated with the products used on the job site and are to be informed if protective measures are to be taken when using these chemicals or hazardous materials. Job-site safety talks are suggested so that this familiarization process can take place. Actual product labels and MSDS sheets can be passed around and explained at that time.

OSHA Regulation CFR 1926 (Subpart P)

In 1990, OSHA enacted Regulation CFR 1926 (Subpart P), dealing with shoring procedures for trenching and excavation. This regulation establishes the position of "competent person," CP for short, as the on-site individual responsible for ensuring that excavated areas are made safe for tradesmen to work in.

A significant number of on-site injuries and fatalities occur each year because trenches are dug or shored improperly, and CFR 1926 was created to reduce these dangers. This regulation requires that a "competent person" identify and predict dangerous excavation situations and have the authority to take the corrective action necessary to prevent workers from entering into excavated areas deemed unsafe.

These on-site supervisors now have the responsibility of determining when an excavation is safe enough to work in and, because these supervisors can now be prosecuted in some states if they could have prevented an accident from happening, this responsibility and authority cannot be taken lightly.

The CP must be able to classify soil according to the classifications contained in Subpart P of the regulation and depending on soil classifications, determine whether shoring is required and how it is to be installed.

CFR 126 soil classifications and corresponding excavating requirements are as follows:

Stable rock—requires no specific slope angle, and trenches with 90° walls are acceptable.

Type A soil (most desirable type)—can be sloped on an angle of $3/4$ to 1, or 53°, as long as there is no groundwater present and no source of excessive vibration nearby.

Type B soil (average material)—can be sloped on a one-to-one slope or at a 45° angle.

Type C soil (the least desirable)—must be open cut to a slope of $1^{1}/_{2}$ to 1 or on a 34° slope.

OSHA includes the tests necessary to establish soil types, and this can be done by a soils testing laboratory to determine compressive or shear strength, or by a simpler test performed on site. The "thumb print," on-site test, as set forth by OSHA, requires the CP to pick up a handful of the soil under investigation and press the thumb into it. If under slight pressure the CP's thumb penetrates the sample, it is probably Type C material. If the thumb pressure causes slight indentation in the soil sample, it is probably Type A soil. And if the thumb pressure begins to penetrate the indentation made in the sample, it can more than likely be classified as Type B. This method appears to be a way to preliminarily determine soil types, and if there is a question as to proper classification, a laboratory analysis would be the preferred method, taking into account the liability issues involved.

A superintendent or project manager should do the following when an OSHA inspector arrives on the site:

1. Ask the inspector for proper identification, if it has not been offered.

2. Inquire whether this is a routine inspection or if the visit was to investigate a complaint received by OSHA, or whether the visit is to investigate a previously reported accident.

3. Call the home office and notify them that an OSHA inspector is on the site in case they wish to have someone from management present. Advise the home office of the type of investigation to be conducted. If management wishes to be present, ask the inspector to wait for a reasonable period of time. If the inspector won't wait, the inspection should proceed with the job superintendent present.

4. The inspector will start the investigation by asking to review OSHA Form 200—Log and Summary of Occupational Injuries and Illnesses and OSHA Form 101—Supplementary Record of Occupational Injuries and Illnesses Survey. The inspector will also request to see OSHA Form 2005—Summary of Occupational Injuries and Illnesses Survey. The law requires that all of these forms be posted in a prominent place in the field office.

5. An OSHA inspector may request a meeting with the foreman from each subcontractor working on the site so as to conduct a preinspection interview meeting prior to a job walk-through. If this is the case, the project superintendent should assemble these foremen as quickly as possible.

6. When the inspector walks through the site the superintendent, or project manager, should accompany the inspector, carefully noting any deficiencies or items requiring corrective action. The inspector may take photographs and, if so, the nature of what was photographed and why they were taken should be noted.

7. If a violation is observed by the inspector and prompt corrective action is suggested, the superintendent should direct someone to take care of the matter immediately. Any violation that poses a life-threatening condition must be taken care of as quickly as possible.

8. If there are questions about the nature or validity of any violation, the inspector should be asked to explain more fully. The questioning should not be argumentative, but the exact nature of any violation must be clearly understood and the specific OSHA regulation cited should be noted. Detailed notes must be made at the time of the walk-through in case a formal protest is lodged if the company disagrees with the inspector's ruling.

9. An inspector has no legal right to shut down a job without a court order, so if that threat is made, ask to see the court order.

10. When the inspection has been completed, a worksheet similar to the one shown in Fig. 14.1 should be completed and forwarded to the office. Often the formal OSHA inspection results may not arrive for 30 to 45 days, so it is important to document all critical points to refresh one's memory when the official report is received at the office.

OSHA Standard Digest—Booklet 2002. The U.S. Department of Labor publishes a pocket-sized digest of OSHA Safety and Health Standards, identified as *OSHA 2202.* The latest reprint is 1990 and copies of this handy booklet can be obtained from the local U.S. Department of Labor office, or by writing to the Superintendent of Documents, U.S.

CONTRACTOR'S JOBSITE OSHA
INSPECTION WORKSHEET   Page 1 of 2

Name
Employer_____

Address_____

Job Location_____

Type of Construction
Building_____   Heavy_____   Highway____   Other____

Name of Compliance Officer(s)
_____   State C.O._____   Federal C.O._____

_____   State C.O._____   Federal C.O._____

Persons attending (give name and affiliation)

_____

_____

_____

(For notes on walk-around inspection see reverse side)

Closing conference was held   Yes___   No___

Persons attending (give name and affiliation)

_____

_____

_____

Closing conference summary:

_____

_____

_____

           Submitted by_____

           Title_____

           Date_____

Figure 14.1 (a) Contractor's OSHA inspection worksheet, page 1.

CONTRACTOR'S JOBSITE OSHA INSPECTION WORKSHEET

Employer_____

Job Site_____

Address_____

City_____

Date_____

Compliance Officer(s)_____   _____

On the basis of the walk-around inspection the C.O. noted the following violation:

Location	Apparent violation(s) noted	Comments

Signed_____

Title_____

Figure 14.1   (b) Contractor's OSHA inspection worksheet, page 2.

Government Printing Office, Washington, DC 20402. The preface in the booklet states that it does not contain all the construction industry safety and health standards, but it does contain those standards most frequently overlooked. The author has paraphrased some of the text in this booklet in order to cover the material in a more rapid fashion.

1. Abrasive grinding

   a. All abrasive wheel bench and stand grinders shall be provided with safety guards which cover the spindle ends and nut and flange projections and are strong enough to withstand the effects of a bursting wheel.

   b. An adjustable work rest of rigid construction shall be used on floor- and bench-mounted grinders with the work rest adjusted to a clearance not to exceed $1/8$ in between rest and surface of the wheel.

   c. All abrasive wheels shall be closely inspected and ring-tested before mounting to ensure that they are free from defects.

2. Access to medical and exposure records

   a. Each employer shall permit employees, their designated representative and OSHA direct access to employer-maintained exposure and medical records. The standard limits access only to those employees who are, have been (including former employees), or will be exposed to toxic substances or harmful physical agents.

   b. Each employer must preserve and maintain accurate medical and exposure records for each employee. Exposure records and data analyses based on them are to be kept for 30 years. Medical records are to be kept for at least the duration of employment plus 30 years. Records of employees who have worked for less than one year need not be retained after employment, but the employer must provide these records to the employee on termination. First-aid records of one-time treatment need not be retained for any specified period.

3. Accident recordkeeping and reporting requirements

   a. Each employer shall maintain OSHA Form 200 and list all recordable injuries and illnesses (resulting in a fatality, hospitalization, lost workdays, medical treatment, job transfer or termination, or loss of consciousness) for that establishment and enter each recordable event no later than 6 workdays after receiving the information. When this log and summary records are maintained at a place other than the establishment, a copy of the log shall be available at the establishment which reflects separately the injury and illness experience of that establishment complete and current to a date within 45 calendar days.

b. In addition to the log of occupational injuries and illnesses, each employer shall have available for inspection at each establishment within 6 workdays after notification of a recordable case, a supplementary record (OSHA Form 101) for each occupational injury or illness for that establishment.

c. Each employer shall post an annual summary of occupational injuries and illness for that establishment (OSHA Form 200). The summary shall be posted by February 1st of each year and shall remain in place until March 1st of that same year.

d. The log and summary, the supplementary records, and the annual summary shall be retained in each establishment for 5 years following the end of the year to which they relate.

e. Within 48 hours after its occurrence, an employment accident which is fatal to one or more employees shall be reported by the employer, either orally or in writing, to the nearest OSHA Area Director.

4. Air tools

a. Pneumatic power tools shall be secured to the hose or whip in a positive manner to prevent accidental disconnection.

b. Safety clips or retainers shall be securely installed and maintained on pneumatic impact tools to prevent attachments from being accidentally expelled.

c. The manufacturer's safe operating pressure for all fittings shall not be exceeded.

d. All hoses exceeding $1/2$ in inside diameter shall have a safety device at the source of supply or branch line to reduce pressure in case of hose failure.

5. Asbestos

a. The employer shall ensure that no employee is exposed to an airborne concentration of asbestos in excess of 0.2 fiber per cubic centimeter of air as an eight (8)-hour time-weighted average (TWA) and the excursion limit of 1.0 fiber per cubic centimeter of air (1 fiber/cm^3) as averaged over a sampling period of thirty (30) minutes.

    b. Wherever feasible, the employer shall establish negative pressure enclosures before commencing removal, demolition, and renovation operations.

    c. Each employer who has a workplace or work operations covered by this standard shall perform monitoring to determine accurately the airborne concentration of asbestos to which employees may be exposed.

    d. Respirators must be used (1) while feasible engineering and work practices are being installed or implemented; (2) during maintenance and repair activities where engineering and work practice controls are not feasible; (3) if feasible engineering and work practice controls are insufficient to reduce employee exposure; and (4) in emergencies.

    e. The employer shall provide and require the use of protective clothing such as coveralls or similar whole-body clothing, head coverings, gloves, and foot coverings for any employee exposed to airborne concentrations of asbestos that exceed the TWA and/or excursion limit.

    f. The employer shall institute a medical surveillance program for all employees engaged in work involving levels of asbestos, at or above the action level and/or excursion level for 30 or more days per year, or who are required by the standard to wear negative-pressure respirators.

6. Belt sanding machines

    a. Belt sanding machines shall be provided with guards at each nip point where the sanding belt runs onto a pulley.

    b. The unused run of the sanding belt shall be guarded to prevent accidental contact.

7. Chains (see Wire ropes, chains, hooks, etc.)

8. Compressed air, use of

    a. Compressed air used for cleaning purposes shall not exceed 30 psi (lb/in^2), and then only with effective chip guarding and personal protective clothing.

    b. This requirement does not apply to concrete form, mill scale, and similar cleaning operations.

9. Compressed gas cylinders

    a. Valve protection caps shall be in place when compressed gas cylinders are transported, moved, or stored.

b. Cylinder valves shall be closed when work is finished and when cylinders are empty or are moved.

c. Compressed gas cylinders shall be secured in an upright position at all times, except if necessary for short periods of time when cylinders are actually being hoisted or carried.

d. Cylinders shall be kept at safe distance or shielded from welding or cutting operations. Cylinders shall be placed where they cannot become part of an electric circuit.

e. Oxygen and fuel gas regulators shall be in proper working order while in use.

f. For additional details not covered in this subpart, applicable technical portions of American National Standards Institute Z-49.1-1967, Safety in Welding and Cutting, shall apply.

10. Concrete and masonry construction

a. No construction loads shall be placed on a concrete structure or portion of a concrete structure unless the employer determines, based on information received from a person who is qualified in structural design, that the structure or portion of the structure is capable of supporting the loads.

b. All protruding reinforcing steel onto and into which employees could fall shall be guarded to eliminate the hazard of impalement.

c. No employee shall be permitted to work under concrete buckets while buckets are being elevated or lowered into position.

d. To the extent practical, elevated concrete buckets shall be routed so that no employee, or the fewest number of employees, is (are) exposed to the hazards associated with falling concrete buckets.

e. Formwork shall be designed, fabricated, erected, supported, braced, and maintained so that it will be capable of supporting without failure all vertical and lateral loads that may reasonably be anticipated to be applied to the formwork.

f. Forms and shores (except those used for slabs-on-grade and slip forms) shall not be removed until the employer determines that the concrete has gained sufficient strength to support its weight and superimposed loads. Such determination shall be based on compliance with one of the following:

(1) The plans and specifications stipulate conditions for removal of forms and shores, and such conditions have been followed, or

(2) The concrete has been properly tested with an appropriate American Society for Testing Materials (ASTM) standard test

method designed to indicate the concrete compressive strength, and the test results indicate that the concrete has gained sufficient strength to support its weight and superimposed loads.

g. A limited-access zone shall be established whenever a masonry wall is being constructed. The limited-access zone shall conform to the following:

  (1) The limited-access zone shall be established prior to the start of construction of the wall.

  (2) The limited-access zone shall be equal to the height of the wall to be constructed plus 4 ft, and shall run the entire length of the wall.

  (3) The limited-access zone shall be established on the side of the wall which will be unscaffolded.

  (4) The limited-access zone shall be restricted to entry by employees actively engaged in constructing the wall. No other employees shall be permitted to enter the zone.

  (5) The limited-access zone shall remain in place until the wall is adequately supported to prevent overturning and to prevent collapse unless the height of the wall is over 8 ft, in which case the limited-access zone shall remain in place until the requirements of paragraph (b) of this section have been met.

h. All masonry walls over 8 ft in height shall be adequately braced to prevent overturning and to prevent collapse unless the wall is adequately supported so that it will not overturn or collapse. The bracing shall remain in place until permanent supporting elements of the structure are in place.

11. Cranes and derricks

  a. The employer shall comply with the manufacturer's specifications and limitations where available.

  b. Rated load capacities, recommended operating speeds, and special hazard warnings or instructions shall be conspicuously posted on all equipment. Instructions or warnings shall be visible from the operator's station.

  c. Equipment shall be inspected by a competent person before each use and during use, and all deficiencies corrected before further use.

  d. Accessible areas within the swing radius of the rear of the rotating superstructure shall be properly barricaded to prevent employees from being struck or crushed by the crane.

    e. Except where electrical distribution and transmission lines have to be deenergized and visibly grounded at the point of work, or where insulating barriers not a part of or an attachment to the equipment or machinery have been erected to prevent physical contact with the lines, no part of a crane or its load shall be operated within 10 ft of a line rated 50 kV or below; 10 ft plus or minus 0.4 in for each kilovolt (1 kV) over 50 kV for lines rated over 50 kV, or twice the length of the line insulator, but never less than 10 ft.

    f. An annual inspection of the hoisting machinery shall be made by a competent person or by a government or private agency recognized by the U.S. Department of Labor. Records shall be kept of the dates and results of each inspection.

    g. All crawler, truck, or locomotive cranes in use shall meet the requirements as prescribed in the ANSI B30.5-1968, Safety Code for Crawler, Locomotive and Truck Cranes.

    h. The use of a crane or derrick to hoist employees or a personnel platform is prohibited, except when the erection, use, and dismantling of conventional means of reaching the worksite, such as a personnel hoist, ladder, stairway, aerial lift, elevating work platform, or scaffold, would be more hazardous, or is not possible because of structural design or worksite conditions.

12. Disposal chutes

    a. Whenever materials are dropped more than 20 ft to any exterior point of a building, an enclosed chute shall be used.

    b. When debris is dropped through holes in the floor without the use of chutes, the areas where the material is dropped shall be enclosed with barricades not less than 42 in high and not less than 6 ft back from the projected edges of the opening above. Warning signs of the hazard of falling material shall be posted at each level.

13. Drinking water

    a. An adequate supply of potable water shall be provided in all places of employment.

    b. Portable drinking water containers shall be capable of being tightly closed and be equipped with a tap.

    c. The common drinking cup is prohibited.

14. Electrical installations

    a. Electrical installations made in accordance with the 1984 National Electrical Code are considered to be in compliance with

OSHA's electrical standards for construction, except for the following additional requirements:

(1) Employers must provide either ground-fault circuit interrupters (GFCIs) or an assured equipment grounding conductor program to protect employees from ground-fault hazards at construction sites. The two options are detailed below:

   (a) All 120-V, single-phase, 15- to 20-A receptacles that are not part of the permanent wiring must be protected by GFCIs. Receptacles on smaller generators are exempt under certain conditions, or

   (b) An assured equipment grounding program covering extension cords, receptacles, and cord-and-plug-connected equipment must be implemented. The program must include the following:

   (i) A written description of the program

   (ii) At least one competent person to implement the program

   (iii) Daily visual inspections of extension cords and cord-and-plug-connected equipment for defects.

   (iv) Continuity tests of the equipment grounding conductors of receptacles, extension cords, and cord-and-plug-connected equipment. These tests must generally be made every 3 months.

b. Lamps for general illumination must be protected from breakage, and metal shell sockets must be grounded.

c. Temporary lights must not be suspended by their cords, unless they are so designed.

d. Portable lighting used in wet or conductive locations, such as tanks or boilers, must be operated at no more than 12 V or must be protected by GFCIs.

e. Extension cords must be of the three-wire type. Extension cords and flexible cords used with temporary and portable lights must be designed for hard and extra-hard usage (e.g., types S, ST, or SO).

15. Electrical work practices

a. Employers must not allow employees to work near live parts of electric circuits, unless the employees are protected by one of the following means:

   (1) Deenergizing and grounding the parts

   (2) Guarding the part by insulation

(3) Any other effective means

b. In work areas where the exact location of underground electrical power lines is unknown, employees using jack hammers, bars, or other hand tools that may contact the lines must be protected by insulating gloves.

c. Barriers or other means of guarding must be used to ensure that work space for electrical equipment will not be used as a passageway during periods when energized parts of equipment are exposed.

d. Worn or frayed electrical cords or cables must not be used. Extension cords must not be fastened with staples, hung from nails, or suspended by wire.

e. Equipment and circuits that are deenergized must be rendered inoperative and must have tags attached at all points where the equipment or circuits could be energized.

16. Excavating and trenching

a. Before opening any excavation, efforts shall be made, including utility company contact to determine if there are underground utilities installations in the area, and they shall be located and supported during the excavation operation.

b. The walls and faces of trenches 5 ft or more deep and all excavations in which employees are exposed to danger from moving ground or cave-in shall be guarded by a shoring system, sloping of the ground, or some other equivalent means.

c. In excavations which employees may be required to enter, excavated or other materials shall be effectively stored and retained at least 2 ft from the edge of the excavation.

d. Daily inspections of excavation shall be made by a competent person. If evidence of possible cave-ins or slides is apparent, all work in the excavation shall cease until the necessary precautions have been taken to safeguard the employees.

e. Trenches 4 ft deep or more shall have an adequate means of exit such as ladders or steps, located so as to require no more than 25 ft of lateral travel.

17. Explosives and blasting

a. Only authorized and qualified persons shall be permitted to handle and use explosives.

b. Explosive material shall be stored in approved facilities as required by provisions of the Internal Revenue Service regulations published in 27 CFR 181, *Commerce in Explosives*.

c. Smoking and open flames shall not be permitted within 50 ft of explosives and detonator storage magazines.

d. Procedures that permit safe and efficient loading shall be established before loading is started.

18. Eye and face protection
   a. Eye and face protection shall be provided when machines or operations present potential eye or face injury.

   b. Eye and face protective equipment shall meet the requirements of ANSI Z87.1-1968, *Practice for Occupational and Educational Eye and Face Protection.*

   c. Employees involved in welding operations shall be furnished with filter lenses or plates of at least the proper shade number.

   d. Employees exposed to laser beams shall be furnished suitable laser safety goggles which will protect for the specific wavelength of the laser and be optical density (O.D.) adequate for the energy involved.

19. Fire protection
   a. A fire fighting program is to be followed throughout all phases of the construction and demolition work involved. It shall provide for effective fire fighting equipment to be available without delay, and designed to effectively meet all fire hazards as they occur.

   b. Fire fighting equipment shall be conspicuously located and readily accessible at all times, shall be periodically inspected, and be maintained in operating condition.

   c. Carbon tetrachloride and other toxic vaporizing liquid fire extinguishers are prohibited.

   d. If the building includes the installation of automatic sprinkler protection, the installation shall closely follow the construction and be placed in service, as soon as applicable laws permit, following completion of each story.

   e. A fire extinguisher, rated not less than 2A, shall be provided for each 3000 ft² of the protected building area, or major fraction thereof. Travel distance from any point of the protected area to the nearest fire extinguisher shall not exceed 100 ft.

   f. One or more fire extinguishers, rated not less than 2A, shall be provided on each floor. In multistory buildings, at least one fire extinguisher shall be located adjacent to stairway.

   g. The employer shall establish an alarm system at the worksite so that employees and the local fire department can be alerted for an emergency.

20. Flagmen

    a. When signs, signals, and barricades do not provide necessary protection on or adjacent to a highway or street, flagmen or other appropriate traffic controls shall be provided.

    b. Flagmen shall be provided with and shall wear a red or orange warning garment while flagging; warning garments worn at night shall be of reflectorized material.

21. Flammable and combustible liquids

    a. Only approved containers and portable tanks shall be used for storage and handling of flammable and combustible liquids.

    b. No more than 25 gallons of flammable or combustible liquids shall be stored in a room outside of an approved storage cabinet. No more than 60 gallons of flammable or 120 gallons of combustible liquids shall be stored in any one storage cabinet. No more than three storage cabinets may be located in a single storage area.

    c. Inside storage rooms for flammable and combustible liquids shall be of fire-resistive construction, have self closing fire doors at all openings, 4-in sills or depressed floors, a ventilation system that provides at least six air changes within the room per hour, and electrical wiring and equipment approved for Class 1, Division 1 locations.

    d. Storage in containers outside buildings shall not exceed 1000 gallons in any one pile or area. The storage area shall be graded to divert possible spills away from building or other exposures, or shall be surrounded by a curb or dike. Storage areas shall be located at least 20 ft from any building and shall be free from weeds, debris, and other combustible materials not necessary to the storage.

    e. Flammable liquids shall be kept in closed containers when not in use.

    f. Conspicuous and legible signs prohibiting smoking shall be posted in service and refueling areas.

22. Floor openings, open sides, hatchways, etc.

    a. Floor openings shall be guarded by a standard railing and toeboards or cover. In general, the railing shall be provided on all exposed sides, except at entrances to stairways.

    b. Every open-sided floor or platform, 6 ft or more above adjacent floor or ground level, shall be guarded by a standard railing, or the equivalent, on all open sides except where there is entrance to a ramp, stairway, or fixed ladder.

c. Runways 4 ft or more high shall have standard railings on all open sides, except runways 18 in or more wide used exclusively for special purposes may have the railing on one side omitted where operating conditions necessitate.

d. Ladderway floor openings or platforms shall be guarded by standard railings with standard toeboards on all exposed sides, except at entrance to opening, with the passage through the railing either provided with a swinging gate or offset so that a person cannot walk directly into the opening.

e. Temporary floor openings shall have standard railings.

f. Floor holes into which persons can accidentally walk shall be guarded by either a standard railing with standard toeboard on all exposed sides, or a standard floor hole cover. While the cover is not in place, the floor hole shall be protected by a standard railing.

23. Gases, vapors, fumes, dust, and mists

a. Exposure to toxic gases, vapors, fumes, dusts, and mists at a concentration above those specified in the *Threshold Limit Values of Airborne Contaminants for 1970* of the ACGIH, shall be avoided.

b. Administrative or engineering controls must be implemented whenever feasible to comply with threshold limit values.

c. When engineering and administrative controls are not feasible to achieve full compliance, protective equipment or other protective measures shall be used to keep the exposure of employees to air contamination within the limits prescribed. Any equipment and technical measures used for this purpose must first be approved for each particular use by a competent industrial hygienist or other technically qualified person.

24. General-duty clause.

Hazardous conditions or practices not covered in an OSHA standard may be covered under Section 5(a)(1) of the Occupational Safety and Health Act of 1970, which states: "Each employer shall furnish to each of his employees employment and a place of employment which are free from recognized hazards that are causing or likely to cause death or serious physical harm to his employees."

25. General Requirements

   a. The employer shall initiate and maintain such programs as may be necessary to provide for frequent and regular inspections of the job site, materials, and equipment.

   b. The employer shall instruct each employee in the recognition and avoidance of unsafe conditions and in the regulations applicable to his work environment to control or eliminate any hazards or other exposure to illness or injury.

   c. The use of any machinery, tool, material, or equipment which is not in compliance with any applicable requirement of Part 1926 is prohibited.

26. Hand tools

   a. Employers shall not issue or permit the use of unsafe hand tools.

   b. Wrenches shall not be used when jaws are sprung to the point that slippage occurs. Impact tolls shall be kept free of mushroomed heads. The wooden handles of tools shall be kept free of splinters or cracks and shall be kept tight in the tool.

   c. Electric-power-operated tools shall either be double-insulated, be properly grounded, or used with ground-fault circuit interrupters.

27. Hazard communication

   a. The purpose of this standard is to ensure that the hazards of all chemicals produced or imported are evaluated, and that information concerning their hazards is transmitted to employers and employees. This transmittal of information is to be accomplished by means of comprehensive hazard communication programs, which are to include container labeling and other forms of warning, materials safety data sheets, and employee training.

   b. Employers shall develop, implement, and maintain at the workplace, a written hazard communication program for their workplaces. Employers must inform their employees of the availability of the program, including the required list(s) of hazardous chemicals, and material safety data sheets required.

   c. The employer shall ensure that each container of hazardous chemical in the workplace is labeled, tagged, or marked with the identity of the hazardous chemical(s) container therein; and must show hazard warnings appropriate for employee protection.

   d. Chemical manufacturers and importers shall obtain or develop a material safety data sheet for each hazardous chemical they produce or import. Employers shall have a material safety data sheet for each hazardous chemical which they use.

e. Employers shall provide employees with information and training on hazardous chemicals in their work area at the time of their initial assignment, and whenever a new hazard is introduced into their work area. Employers shall also provide employees with information on any operations in their work area where hazardous chemicals are present; and the location and availability of the written hazard communication program, including the required list(s) of hazardous chemicals, and material safety data sheets required by the standard.

28. Head protection

a. Head protective equipment (helmets) shall be worn in areas where there is a possible danger of head injuries from impact, flying or falling objects, or electrical shock and burns.
b. Helmets for protection against impact and penetration of falling and flying objects shall meet the requirements of ANSI Z89.1-1969.
c. Helmets for protection against electrical shock and burns shall meet the requirements of ANSI Z89.2-1971.

29. Hearing protection

a. Feasible engineering or administrative controls shall be utilized to protect employees against sound levels in excess of those shown in Table D-2.
b. When engineering or administrative controls fail to reduce sound levels within the limits of Table D-2, ear protective devices shall be provided and used.
c. Exposure to impulsive or impact noise should not exceed 140-dB peak sound pressure level.
d. In all cases where the sound levels exceed the values shown in Table D-2 of the *Safety and Health Standards,* a continuing, effective hearing conservation program shall be administered.
e. Table D-2, Permissible Noise Exposures

Duration per day hours	Sound level dB slow response
8	90
6	92
4	95
3	97
2	100
$1^{1}/_{2}$	102
1	105
$^{1}/_{2}$	110
$\leq^{1}/_{4}$	115

f. Plain cotton is not an acceptable protective device.

30. Heating devices, temporary

   a. Fresh air shall be supplied in sufficient quantities to maintain the health and safety of workers.

   b. Solid fuel salamanders are prohibited in buildings and on scaffolds.

31. Hoists, material and personnel

   a. The employer shall comply with the manufacturer's specifications and limitations.

   b. Rated load capacities, recommended operating speeds, and special hazard warnings or instructions shall be posted on cars and platforms.

   c. Hoistway entrances of material hoists shall be protected by substantial full-width gates or bars.

   d. Hoistway doors or gates of personnel hoist shall be not less than 6 ft 6 in high, and be protected with mechanical locks which cannot be operated from the landing side and are accessible only to persons on the car.

   e. Overhead protective coverings shall be provided on the top of the hoist cage or platform.

   f. All material hoists shall conform to the requirements of ANSI A10.5-1969, Safety Requirements for Material Hoists.

32. Hooks (see Wire ropes, chains, hooks, etc.)

33. Housekeeping

   a. Form and scrap lumber with protruding nails and all other debris, shall be kept clear from all work areas.

   b. Combustible scrap and debris shall be removed at regular intervals.

   c. Containers shall be provided for collection and separation of all refuse. Covers shall be provided on containers used for flammable or harmful substances.

   d. Wastes shall be disposed of at frequent intervals.

34. Illumination

   a. Construction area ramps, runways, corridors, offices, shops, and storage areas shall be lighted to not less than the minimum illumination intensities listed in Table D-3 while any work is in progress.

b. Table D-3, Minimum Illumination Intensities

Illumination foot-candles	Area or operation
5	General construction area lighting
3	General construction areas, concrete placement, excavation, waste areas, accessways, active storage areas, loading platforms, refueling field maintenance areas
5	Indoor warehouses, corridors, hallways, exitways
5	Tunnels, shafts, general underground work (exception: minimum of 10 foot-candles is required at tunnel and shaft heading during drilling, mucking, scaling; Bureau of Mines approved cap lights shall be acceptable for use in the tunnel heading)
10	General construction plant and shops (e.g., batch plants, screening, plants, mechanical and electrical equipment rooms, carpenter shops, rigging lofts and active storerooms, barracks or living quarters, locker or dressing rooms, mess halls, indoor toilets, and workrooms
30	First-aid stations, infirmaries, and offices

35. Jointers

a. Each hand-fed planer and jointer with a horizontal head shall be equipped with a cylindrical cutting head. The opening in the table shall be kept as small as possible.

b. Each hand-fed jointer with a horizontal cutting head shall have an automatic guard which will cover the section of the head on the working side of the fence or cage.

c. A jointer guard shall automatically adjust itself to cover the unused portion of the head, and shall remain in contact with the material at all times.

d. Each hand-fed jointer with horizontal cutting head shall have a guard which will cover the section of the head back of the cage or fence.

36. Ladders

a. The use of ladders with broken or missing rungs or steps, broken or split side rails, or with other faulty or defective construction is prohibited. When ladders with such defects are discovered, they shall immediately be withdrawn from service.

b. Portable ladders shall be placed on a substantial base at a 4-1 pitch, have clear access at top and bottom, extend a minimum of 36 in above the landing, or where not practical, be provided with grab rails and be secured against movement while in use.

c. Portable metal ladders shall not be used for electrical work or where they may contact electrical conductors.

d. Job-made ladders shall be constructed for their intended use. Cleats shall be inset into $1/2$-in side rails, or filler blocks shall be used. Cleats shall be uniformly spaced, 12 in, top-to-top.

e. Except where either permanent or temporary stairways or suitable ramps or runways are provided, ladders shall be used to give safe access to all elevations.

37. Lasers

a. Only qualified and trained employees shall be assigned to install, adjust, and operate laser equipment.

b. Employees shall wear proper eye protection where there is a potential exposure to laser light greater than 0.005 W (5 mW).

c. Beam shutters or caps shall be utilized, or the laser turned off, when laser transmission is not actually required. When the laser is left unattended for a substantial period of time, such as during lunch hour, overnight, or at change of shifts, the laser shall be turned off.

d. Employees shall not be exposed to light intensities above: direct staring—1 mW/cm²; incidental observing—1 mW/cm²; diffused reflected light—2.5 W/cm². Employees shall not be exposed to microwave power intensities in excess of 10 mW/cm².

38. Liquefied petroleum gas (LPG)

a. Each system shall have containers, valves, connectors, manifold valve assemblies, and regulators of an approved type.

b. All cylinders shall meet DOT (Department of Transportation) Specifications.

c. Every container and vaporizer shall be provided with one or more approved safety relief valves or devices.

d. Containers shall be placed upright on firm foundations or otherwise firmly secured.

e. Portable heaters shall be equipped with an approved automatic device to shut off the flow of gas in the event of flame failure.

f. Storage of LPG within buildings is prohibited.

g. Storage locations shall have at least one approved portable fire extinguisher, rated not less than 20B–C.

39. Medical services and first aid

    a. The employer shall ensure the availability of medical personnel for advice and consultation on matters of occupational health.

    b. When a medical facility is not reasonably accessible for the treatment of injured employees, a person trained to render first aid shall be available at the work site.

    c. First aid supplies approved by the consulting physician shall be readily available.

    d. The telephone number of the physician, hospital, or ambulance service shall be conspicuously posted.

40. Motor vehicles and mechanized equipment

    a. All vehicles in use shall be checked at the beginning of each shift to ensure that all parts, equipment, and accessories that affect safe operation are in proper operating condition and free from defects. All defects shall be corrected before the vehicles are placed in service.

    b. No employer shall use any motor vehicle, earthmoving or compacting equipment having an obstructed view to the rear unless:

        (1) The vehicle has a reverse signal alarm, distinguishable from the surrounding noise level, or

        (2) The vehicle is backed up only when an observer signals that it is safe to do so.

    c. Heavy machinery, equipment, or parts thereof which are suspended or held aloft shall be substantially blocked to prevent falling or shifting before employees are permitted to work under or between them.

41. Noise (see Hearing protection)

42. Personal protective equipment

    a. The employer is responsible for requiring the wearing of appropriate personal protective equipment in all operations where there is exposure to hazardous conditions or where the need is indicated for using such equipment to reduce the hazard to employees.

    b. Lifelines, safety belts, and lanyard shall be used only for employee safeguarding.

    c. Employees working over or near water, where the danger of drowning exists, shall be provided with U.S. Coast Guard–approved life jackets or buoyant work vests.

43. Power-actuated tools

    a. Only trained employees shall be allowed to operate power-actuated tools.

    b. All power-actuated tools shall be tested daily before use, and all defects discovered before or during use shall be corrected.

    c. Tools shall not be loaded until immediately before use. Loaded tools shall not be left unattended.

44. Power transmission and distribution

    a. Existing conditions shall be determined before starting work, by an inspection or a test.

    b. Electrical equipment and lines shall be considered energized until determined otherwise by testing or until grounding.

    c. Operating voltage of equipment and lines shall be determined before working on or near energized parts.

    d. Rubber protective equipment shall comply with the provisions of ANSI J6 series, and shall be visually inspected before use.

45. Power transmission, mechanical

    a. Belts, gears, shafts, pulleys, sprockets, spindles, drums, flywheels, chains, or other reciprocating, rotating, or moving parts of equipment shall be guarded if such parts are exposed to contact by employees or otherwise constitute a hazard.

    b. Guarding shall meet the requirements of ANSI B15.1-1953 (R 1958), Safety Code for Mechanical Power Transmission Apparatus.

46. Radiation, ionizing

    a. Pertinent provisions of the Atomic Energy Commission's Standards for Protection Against Radiation (10 CFR Part 20), relating to protection against occupational radiation exposure, shall apply.

    b. Persons using radioactive materials or X rays shall be specially trained, or licensed if required.

47. Railings

    a. A standard railing shall consist of top rail, intermediate rail, toeboard, and posts, and have a vertical height of approximately 42 in from upper surface of top rail to the floor, platform, etc.

b. The top rail of a railing shall be smooth-surfaced, with a strength to withstand at least 200 lb. The intermediate rail shall be approximately halfway between the top rail and the floor.

c. A stair railing shall be of construction similar to a standard railing, but the vertical height shall not be more than 34 in nor less than 30 in from upper surface of top rail to surface of tread in line with face of riser at forward edge of tread.

48. Respiratory protection

a. In emergencies, or when feasible engineering or administrative controls are not effective in controlling toxic substances, appropriate respiratory protective equipment shall be provided by the employer and shall be used.

b. Respiratory protective devices shall be approved by the Mine Safety and Health Administration–National Institute for Occupational Safety and Health or acceptable to the U.S. Department of Labor for the specific containment to which the employee is exposed.

c. Respiratory protective devices shall be appropriate for the hazardous material involved and the extent and nature of the work requirements and conditions.

d. Employees required to use respiratory protective equipment devices shall be thoroughly trained in their use.

e. Respiratory equipment shall be inspected regularly and maintained in good condition.

49. Rollover protective structures.

Rollover protective structures (ROPs) applies to the following types of materials handling equipment: to all rubber-tired, self-propelled scrapers, rubber-tired front-end loaders, rubber-tired dozers, wheel-type agricultural and industrial tractors, crawler tractors, crawler-type loaders, and motor graders, with or without attachments that are used in construction work. This requirement does not apply to sideboom pipe-laying tractors.

50. Safety nets

a. Safety nets shall be provided when workplaces are more than 25 ft above the surface where the use of ladders, scaffolds, catch platforms, temporary floors, safety lines, or safety belts is impractical.

b. Where nets are required, operations shall not be undertaken until the net is in place and has been tested.

51. Saws, band

   a. All portions of band saw blades shall be enclosed or guarded, except for the working portion of the blade between the bottom of the guide rolls and the table.
   b. Band saw wheels shall be fully encased.

52. Saws, portable circular

   a. Portable, power-driven circular saws shall be equipped with guards above and below the base plate or shoe. The lower guard shall cover the saw to the depth of the teeth, except for the minimum arc required to allow proper retraction and contact with the work, and shall automatically return to the covering position when the blade is removed from the work.
   b. (see General-duty clause)

53. Saws, radial

   a. Radial saws shall have an upper guard which completely encloses the upper half of the saw blade. The sides of the lower exposed portion of the blade shall be guarded by a device that will automatically adjust to the thickness of and remain in contact with the material being cut.
   b. Radial saws used for ripping shall have nonkickback fingers or dogs.
   c. Radial saws shall be installed so that the cutting head will return to the starting position when released by the operator.

54. Saws, swing or sliding cutoff

   a. All swing or sliding cutoff saws shall be provided with a hood that will completely enclose the upper half of the saw.
   b. Limit stops shall be provided to prevent swing- or sliding-type cutoff saws from extending beyond the front or back edges of the table.
   c. Each swing or sliding cutoff saw shall be provided with an effective device to return the saw automatically to the back of the table when released at any point of its travel.
   d. Inverted sawing of sliding cutoff saws shall be provided with a hood that will cover the part of the saw that protrudes above the top of the table or material being cut.

55. Saws, table

a. Circular table saws shall have a hood over the portion of the saw above the table, so mounted that the hood will automatically adjust itself to the thickness of and remain in contact with the material being cut.

b. Circular table saws shall have a spreader aligned with the blade, spaced no more than ¹/₂ in behind the largest blade mounted in the saw. This provision does not apply when grooving, dadoing, or rabbeting.

c. Circular table saws used for ripping shall have nonkickback fingers or dogs.

d. Feed rolls and blades of self-feed circular saws shall be protected by a hood or guard to prevent the hands of the operator from coming in contact with the inrunning rolls at any time.

56. Scaffolds (general)

a. Scaffolds shall be erected on sound, rigid footing, capable of carrying the maximum intended load without settling or displacement.

b. Scaffolds and their components shall be capable of supporting, without failure, at least four times the maximum intended load.

c. Guardrails and toeboards shall be installed on all open sides and ends of platforms more than 10 ft above the ground or floor, except needle-beam scaffolds and floats. Scaffolds 4 to 10 ft in height, having a minimum dimension in either direction of less than 45 in, shall have standard guardrails installed on open sides and ends of the platform.

d. There shall be a screen with maximum ¹/₂-in openings between the toeboard and the guardrail, where the persons are required to work or pass under the scaffold.

e. All planking shall be Scaffold Grade or equivalent as recognized by approved grading rules for the species of wood used. The maximum permissible spans for planks 2×10 in or wider are shown in the following table:

	Full-thickness undressed lumber			Nominal thickness	
Working load, lb/ft²	25	50	75	25	50
Permissible span, ft	10	8	6	8	6

The maximum permissible span for $1^{1}/_{4} \times 9$-in or wider plank of full thickness is 4 ft, with medium loading of 50 lb/ft² *f.* Scaffold planking shall be overlapped a minimum of 12 in or secured from movement.

g. Scaffold planks shall extend over their end supports not less than 6 in nor more than 12 in.

h. All scaffolding and accessories shall have any defective parts immediately replaced or repaired.

i. An access ladder or equivalent safe access shall be provided.

57. Scaffolds (mobile)

a. Platforms shall be tightly planked for the full width of the scaffold except for necessary entrance opening. Platforms shall be secured in place.

b. Guardrails made of lumber, not less than 2 × 4 in (or other materials providing equivalent protection), approximately 42 in high, with a midrail, of 1 × 6-in lumber (or other material providing equivalent protection) and toeboards, shall be installed at all open sides and ends of all scaffolds more than 10 ft above the ground or floor. Toeboards shall have a minimum of 4 in in height. Where persons are required to work or pass under the scaffolds, wire mesh shall be installed between the toeboard and the guardrail, extending along the entire opening, consisting of 18-gauge (American wire gauge No. 18), U.S. Standard wire $^1/_2$-in mesh, or the equivalent.

58. Scaffolds (swinging). On suspension scaffolds designed for a working load of 500 lb, no more than two people shall be permitted to work at one time. On suspension scaffolds with a working load of 750 lb, no more than three people shall be permitted to work at one time. Each employee shall be protected by an approved safety line belt attached to a lifeline. The lifeline shall be securely attached to substantial members of the structure (not scaffold), or to securely rigged lines, which will safely suspend the employee in case of a fall. In order to keep the lifeline continuously attached, with a minimum of slack, to a fixed structure, the attachment point of the lifeline shall be appropriately changed as the work progresses.

59. Scaffolds (tubular welded frame)

a. Scaffolds shall be properly braced by cross bracing or diagonal braces, or both, for securing vertical members together laterally, and the cross braces shall be of such length as will automatically square and align vertical members so that the erected scaffolds are always plumb, square, and rigid. All brace connections shall be made secure.

b. (See Saws, swing or sliding, b)

60. Stairs

a. Every flight of stairs having four or more risers shall be equipped with standard stair railings or standard handrails as specified below.

b. On stairways less than 44 in wide having one side open, at least one stair railing on the open side.

c. On stairways less than 44 in wide having both sides open, one stair railing on each side.

d. On stairways more than 44 in wide but less than 88 in wide, one handrail on each enclosed side and one stair railing on each open side.

e. On all structures 210 ft or over in height, stairways, ladders, or ramps shall be provided.

f. Rise height and tread width shall be uniform throughout any flight of stairs.

g. Hollow pan-type stairs shall be filled to the level of the hosing with solid material.

61. Steel erection

a. Permanent floors shall be installed so there are no more than eight stories between the erection floor and the uppermost permanent floor, except when structure integrity is maintained by the design.

b. During skeleton steel erection, a tightly planed temporary floor shall be maintained within two stories or 30 ft, whichever is less, below and directly under that portion of each tier of beams on which any work is being performed.

c. During skeleton steel erection, where the requirements of the preceding paragraph cannot be met, and where scaffolds are not used, safety nets shall be installed and maintained wherever the potential fall distance exceeds two stories or 25 ft.

d. A safety railing of 1/2-in wire rope or equivalent shall be installed around the perimeter of all temporarily floored buildings, approximately 42 in high, during structural-steel assembly.

e. When placing structural members, the load shall not be released from the hoisting line until the member is secured by at least two bolts, or the equivalent, at each connection, drawn up wrench tight.

62. Storage

   a. All material stored in tiers shall be secured to prevent sliding, falling, or collapse.
   b. Aisles and passageways shall be kept clear and in good repair.
   c. Storage of materials shall not obstruct exits.
   d. Material shall be stored with due regard to their fire characteristics.
   e. Weeds and grass in outside storage areas shall be kept under control.

63. Tire cages.   A safety tire rack, cage, or equivalent protection shall be provided and used when inflating, mounting, or dismounting tires installed on split rims equipped with locking rings or similar devices.

64. Toeboards (floor and wall openings and stairways)

   a. Railings protecting floor openings, platforms, scaffolds, etc., shall be equipped with toeboards wherever, beneath the open side, persons can pass, there is moving machinery, or there is equipment with which falling material could cause a hazard.
   b. A standard toeboard shall be at least 4 in in height, and may be of any substantial material either solid or open, with openings not to exceed 1 in in greatest dimensions.

65. Toilets

   a. Toilets shall be provided according to the following: 20 or fewer persons—one facility; 20 or more persons—one toilet seat and one urinal per 40 persons; 200 or more persons—one toilet seat and one urinal per 50 workers.
   b. This requirement does not apply to mobile crews having transportation readily available to nearby toilet facilities.

66. Underground construction

   a. The employer shall provide and maintain safe means of access to and egress from all workstations.
   b. The employer shall control access to all openings to prevent unauthorized entry underground. Unused chutes, passageways, or other openings shall be tightly covered, bulkheaded, or fenced

off, and shall be posted with signs indicating "keep out" or similar language. Completed or unused sections of the underground facility shall be barricaded.

c. Unless underground facilities are sufficiently completed, the employer shall maintain a check-in/check-out procedure that will ensure that above-ground designated personnel can determine and accurately count the number of persons underground in the event of an emergency.

d. All employees shall be instructed to recognize and avoid hazards associated with underground construction activities.

e. Hazardous classifications and potentially gassy operations are to be defined and noted.

f. The employer shall assign a competent person to perform all air monitoring to determine proper ventilation and quantitative measurements of potentially hazardous gases.

g. Fresh air shall be supplied to all underground work areas in sufficient quantities to prevent dangerous or harmful accumulation of dust, fumes, mist, vapors, or gases.

67. Wall openings

a. Wall openings, from which there is a drop of more than 4 ft, and the bottom of the opening is less than 3 ft above the working surface, shall be guarded.

b. When the height and placement of the opening in relation to the working surface are such that a standard rail or intermediate rail will effectively reduce the danger of falling, one or both shall be provided.

c. The bottom of a wall opening, which is less than 4 in above the working surface, shall be protected by a standard toeboard or an enclosing screen.

68. Washing facilities

a. The employer shall provide adequate washing facilities for employees engaged in operations involving harmful substances.

b. Washing facilities shall be in near vicinity to the work site and shall be equipped as to enable employees to remove all harmful substances.

69. Welding, cutting, and heating

a. Employers shall instruct employees in the safe use of welding equipment.

b. Proper precautions (isolating welding and cutting, removing fire hazards from the vicinity, providing a fire watch, etc.) for fire prevention shall be taken in areas where welding or other "hot work" is being done. No welding, cutting, or heating shall be done where the application of flammable paints, or the presence of other flammable compounds, or heavy dust concentration creates a fire hazard.

c. Arc welding and cutting operations shall be shielded by noncombustible or flameproof shields to protect employees from direct arc rays.

d. When electrode holders are to be left unattended, the electrode shall be removed and the holder shall be placed or protected so that they cannot make electrical contact with employees or conducting objects.

e. All arc welding and cutting tables shall be completely insulated and be capable of handling the maximum current requirements for the job. There shall be no repairs or splices within 10 ft of the electrode holder, except where splices are insulated equal to the insulation of the cable. Defective cables shall be repaired or replaced.

f. Fuel gas and oxygen hose shall be easily distinguishable and shall not be interchangeable. Hoses shall be inspected at the beginning of each shift and shall be repaired or replaced if defective.

g. General mechanical or local exhaust ventilation or airline respirators shall be provided, as required, when welding, cutting, or heating:

(1) Zinc-, lead-, cadmium-, mercury-, or beryllium-bearing, -based, or -coated materials in enclosed spaces

(2) Stainless steel with inert-gas equipment

(3) In confined spaces

(4) Where an unusual condition can cause an unsafe accumulation of contaminants

h. Proper eye protective equipment to prevent exposure of personnel shall be provided.

70. Wire ropes, chains, ropes, etc.

a. Wire ropes, chains, ropes, and other rigging equipment shall be inspected prior to use and as necessary during use to assure their safety. Defective gear shall be removed from service.

b. Job or shop hooks and links, or makeshift fasteners, formed from bolts, rods, etc., or other such attachments shall not be used.

  c. When U-bolts are used for eye splices, the U-bolt shall be applied so that the "U" section is in contact with the dead end of the rope.

  d. When U-bolt wire rope clips are used to form eyes, the following table, showing number and spacing of U-bolt wire rope clips, shall be used.

Improved plow steel, rope diameter, in	Number of clips		Max. spacing, in
	Drop forged	Other mat'l.	
$1/2$	3	4	3
$5/8$	3	4	$3^3/4$
$3/4$	4	5	$4^1/2$
$7/8$	4	5	$5^1/4$
1	5	6	6
$1^1/8$	6	6	$6^3/4$
$1^1/4$	6	7	$7^1/2$
$1^3/8$	7	7	$8^1/4$
$1^1/2$	7	8	9

71. Woodworking machinery

  a. All fixed power-driven woodworking tools shall be provided with a disconnect switch that can be either locked or tagged if in the off position.

  b. All woodworking tools and machinery shall meet applicable requirements of ANSI 01.1-1961, Safety Code for Woodworking Machinery.

Industry Association and Trade Group Listings

There are many excellent construction-related organizations and trade groups that serve as focal points for their related interests. These organizations can be important sources of information, and they are willing to assist in disseminating the information they possess, often at no cost.

Industry Organizations

The American Institute of
 Architects
1735 New York Ave.
Washington, DC 20006
Telephone: (202) 626-7300

American Institute of Constructors
9887 N. Gandy, Suite 104
St. Petersburg, FL 33702
Telephone: (813) 578-0317

American National Standards
 Institute
11 W. 42nd St.
New York, NY 10036
Telephone: (212) 642-4900

American Public Works Association
1313 E. 60th St.
Chicago, IL 60637
Telephone: (312) 667-2200

American Road and Transportation
 Builders Association
501 School St., SW, 8th Floor
Washington, DC 20024
Telephone: (202) 488-2722

American Society for Testing and
 Materials (ASTM)
1916 Race St.
Philadelphia, PA 19103
Telephone: (215) 299-5400

American Society of Civil Engineers
345 E. 47th St.
New York, NY 10017
Telephone: (212) 705-7496

American Society of Home
 Inspectors
1735 N. Lynn St., Suite 950
Arlington, VA 22209
Telephone: (800) 296-2744

American Subcontractors
 Association, Inc.
1004 Duke St.
Alexandria, VA 22314
Telephone: (703) 684-3450

Associated Builders and
 Contractors, Inc.
729 15th St., N.W.
Washington, DC 20005
Telephone: (202) 637-8800

Associated General Contractors of
America
1957 E St., NW
Washington, DC 20006
Telephone: (202) 393-2040

Building Officials and Code
Administrators International, Inc.
4051 W. Flossmoor Rd.
Country Club Hills, IL 60478
Telephone: (708) 799-2300

Building Research Board
2101 Constitution Ave., NW, Room
HA274
Washington, DC 20418
Telephone: (202) 334-3376

Construction Management
Association of America (CMAA)
1893 Preston White Dr., Suite 130
Reston, VA 22091
Telephone: (703) 391-1200

The Construction Specifications
Institute, Inc.
601 Madison St.
Alexandria, VA 22314
Telephone: (703) 684-0300

National Society of Professional
Engineers
1420 King St.
Alexandria, VA 22314
Telephone: (703) 684-2800

Scaffolding, Shoring and Forming
Institute, Inc.
1300 Sumner Ave.
Cleveland, OH 44115
Telephone: (216) 241-7333

Trade Organizations and Associations

Site work

Association of Engineering Firms
Practicing in the Geosciences

8811 Colesville Rd. Silver Spring,
MD 20907
Telephone: (301) 565-2733

Concrete and concrete reinforcement

American Concrete Institute (ACI)
P.O. Box 19150, 22400 W. Seven
Mile Rd.
Detroit, MI 48219-0150
Telephone: (313) 532-2600

Portland Cement Association
5420 Old Orchard Road
Skokie, IL 60077
Telephone: (708) 966-6200

Wire Reinforcement Institute
1101 Connecticut Ave., NW, Suite
700
Washington, DC 20036-4303
Telephone: (202) 429-4303

Concrete Reinforcing Steel Institute
933 North Plum Grove Rd.
Schaumberg, IL 60173
Telephone: (708) 517-1200

National Precast Concrete
Association
825 E. 64th St.
Indianapolis, IN 46220
Telephone: (317) 253-0486

Precast/Prestressed Concrete
Institute
175 W. Jackson Blvd., Suite 1859
Chicago, IL 60604
Telephone: (312) 786-0300

Tilt-Up Concrete Association
2431 W. Cummings Wood Lane
Hendersonville, NC 28739
Telephone: (704) 891-9578

Masonry

International Masonry Institute
823 15th St., NW

Washington, DC 20005
Telephone: (202) 783-3908

Masonry Institute of America
2550 Beverly Blvd.
Los Angeles, CA 90057
Telephone: (213) 388-0472

Brick Institute of America
11490 Commerce Park Dr.
Reston, VA 22091
Telephone: (703) 620-0010

Building Stone Institute
P.O. Box 5047
White Plains, NY 10602-5047
Telephone: (914) 232-5725

Cast Stone Institute
Pavilions at Greentree, Suite 408,
Highway 70
Marlton, NJ 08053
Telephone: (609) 858-0271

Indiana Limestone Institute of
America
Stone City Bank Building, Suite 400
Bedford, IN 47421
Telephone: (812) 275-4426

Italian Marble Center, Italian Trade
Commission
499 Park Ave.
New York, NY 10022
Telephone: (212) 980-1500

Marble Institute of America
33505 State St.
Farmington, MI 48335
Telephone: (313) 476-5558

Metals

Aluminum Association
900 19th Street, NW, Suite 300
Washington, DC 20006
Telephone: (202) 862-5100

American Institute of Steel
Construction
1 E. Wacker Dr., Suite 3100

Chicago, IL 60601-2001
Telephone: (312) 670-2400

American Iron and Steel Institute
1133 15th St., NW
Washington, DC 20005
Telephone: (202) 452-7100

Copper Development Association
Greenwich Office Park 2
Greenwich, CT 06836
Telephone (203) 625-8210

Metal Lath/Steel Framing
Association
600 S. Federal St., Suite 400
Chicago, IL 60606
Telephone: (312) 922-6222

National Association of
Architectural Metal Manufacturers
600 S. Federal St., Suite 400
Chicago, IL 60606
Telephone: (312) 922-6222

Steel Structures Painting Council
4400 5th Ave.
Pittsburgh, PA 15213-2683
Telephone: (412) 268-3327

Steel Joist Institute
1205 48th Ave., N, Suite A
Myrtle Beach, SC 29577
Telephone: (803) 449-0487

Steel Deck Institute
P.O. Box 9506
Canton, OH 44711
Telephone: (216) 493-7866

Wood and plastics

Southern Forest Products
Association
P.O. Box 52468
New Orleans, LA 70152
Telephone: (504) 443-4464

Western Wood Products Association
Yeon Building, 522 SW 5th Ave.
Portland, OR 97204
Telephone: (503) 224-3930

American Institute of Timber
Construction
11818 SE Mill Plain Blvd., Suite 415
Vancouver, WA 98684-5092
Telephone: (206) 254-9132

American Plywood Association
P.O. Box 11700
Tacoma, WA 98411
Telephone: (206) 565-6600

Architectural Woodwork Institute
2310 S. Walter Reed Dr., P.O. Box
1550
Centerville, VA 22020
Telephone: (703) 222-1100

National Particleboard Association
18928 Premiere Ct.
Gaithersburg, MD 20879
Telephone: (301) 670-0604

American Wood Preservers Bureau
P.O. Box 5283
Springfield, VA 22150
Telephone: (703) 339-6660

Cultured Marble Institute
435 N. Michigan Ave., Suite 1717
Chicago, IL 60611
Telephone: (312) 644-0828

Decorative Laminate Products
Association
600 S. Federal St., Suite 400
Chicago, IL 60605
Telephone: (312) 922-6222

Mineral Insulation Manufacturers
Association
1420 King St., Suite 410
Alexandria, VA 22314
Telephone: (703) 684-0084

Perlite Institute
88 New Dorp Plaza
Staten Island, NY 10306-2294
Telephone: (718) 351-5723

Polyisocyanurate Insulation
Manufacturers Association
1001 Pennsylvania Ave., NW
Washington, DC 20004
Telephone: (202) 624-2709

Exterior Insulation Manufacturers
Association
2759 State Rd. 580, Suite 112
Clearwater, FL 34621
Telephone: (813) 231-6477

Asphalt Roofing Manufacturers
Association
6288 Montrose Rd.
Rockville, MD 20852
Telephone: (301) 231-9050

Cedar Shake and Shingle Bureau
515 116th Ave., NE, Suite 275
Bellevue, WA 98004
Telephone: (206) 453-1323

Single Ply Roofing Institute
104 Wilmot Rd., Suite 201
Deerfield, IL 60015
Telephone: (708) 940-8800

Thermal and moisture protection

Institute of Roofing and
Waterproofing Consultants
4242 Kirchoff Rd.
Rolling Meadows, IL 60008
Telephone: (708) 991-9292

Sealant, Waterproofing and
Restoration Institute
3101 Broadway, Suite 585
Kansas City, MO 64111
Telephone: (816) 561-8230

Doors and windows

American Architectural
Manufacturers Association
1540 E. Dundee Rd., Suite 310
Palatine, IL 60067
Telephone: (708) 202-1350

National Wood Window and Door
Association
1400 E. Touhy Ave.

Des Plaines, IL 60018
Telephone: (708) 299-5200

Vinyl Window and Door Institute
355 Lexington Ave.
New York, NY 10017
Telephone: (212) 351-5400

Steel Window Institute
1230 Keith Bldg., 1621 Euclid St.
Cleveland, OH 44115
Telephone: (216) 241-7333

Door and Hardware Institute
7711 Old Springhouse Rd.
McLean, VA 22102
Telephone: (703) 556-3990

Steel Door Institute
30200 Detroit Rd.
Cleveland, OH 44145
Telephone: (216) 899-0010

National Glass Association
8200 Greensboro Dr., Suite 302
McLean, VA 22012
Telephone: (703) 442-4890

Finishes

International Institute of Lath and
  Plaster
820 Transfer Rd.
St. Paul, MN 55111
Telephone: (612) 645-0208

Gypsum Association
810 1st St., NE, Suite 510
Washington, DC 20002
Telephone: (202) 289-5440

Ceramic Tile Institute
700 North Virgil Ave.
Los Angeles, CA 90029
Telephone: (213) 660-1911

Tile Council of America
P.O. Box 326
Princeton, NJ 08542
Telephone: (609) 921-7050

National Terrazzo and Mosaic
  Association
3166 Des Plaines Ave., Suite 132
Des Plaines, IL 60018
Telephone: (708) 635-7744

Acoustical Society of America
500 Sunnyside Blvd.
Woodbury, NY 11797
Telephone: (516) 349-7800

Ceilings and Interior Systems
  Construction Association
104 Wilmot Rd., Suite 201
Deerfield, IL 60015
Telephone: (708) 940-8800

National Wood Flooring Association
11046 Manchester Rd.
St. Louis, MO 63122
Telephone: (800) 422-4556

Resilient Floor Covering Institute
966 Hungerford Dr., Suite 12B
Rockville, MD 20850
Telephone: (301) 340-8580

National Plant and Coatings
  Association
1500 Rhode Island Ave., NW
Washington, DC 20005
Telephone: (202) 462-6272

Wallcovering Manufacturers
  Association and Wallcovering
  Information Bureau
355 Lexington, Ave.
New York, NY 10017
Telephone: (212) 661-4261

Mechanical

Plumbing Manufacturers Institute
800 Roosevelt Rd., Bldg. C, Suite 20
Glen Ellyn, IL 60137
Telephone: (708) 858-9172

Air Diffusion Council
111 E. Wacker Dr., Suite 200
Chicago, IL 60601
Telephone: (312) 616-0800

American Society of Heating,
Refrigerating and Air Conditioning
Engineers (ASHRAE)
1791 Tullie Circle, NE
Atlanta, GA 30329
Telephone: (404) 636-8400

Cooling Tower Institute
P.O. Box 73373
Houston, TX 77272
Telephone: (713) 583-4087

Air Movement and Control
Association
30 W. University Dr.
Arlington Heights, IL 60004
Telephone: (703) 394-0150

Institute of Heating and Air
Conditioning Industries (IHACI)
606 N. Larchmont Blvd., Suite 4A
Los Angeles, CA 90004
Telephone: (213) 467-1158

Electrical

Lighting Research Center,
Rennselaer Polytechnic Institute
Green Bldg., No. 115
Troy, NY 12180-3590
Telephone: (518) 276-8716

Edison Electric Institute
701 Pennsylvania Ave., NW
Washington, DC 20004
Telephone: (202) 508-5000

National Electrical Contractors
Association
7315 Wisconsin Ave.
Bethesda, MD 20814
Telephone: (301) 657-3110

Index

About the Author

Sidney M. Levy is Senior Vice President, Construction
Division, of a Fairfield County, Connecticut, general contrac-
tor and developer. He is the author of McGraw-Hill's
Japan's Big Six: Inside Japan's Construction Industry, as
well as *Construction Superintendent's Handbook* and
Japanese Construction: An American Perspective.